UN-RESTRICTED WARFARE

TRANSLATED FROM THE ORIGINAL
PEOPLE'S LIBERATION ARMY DOCUMENTS

UN-
RESTRICTED
WARFARE

BY COL. QIAO LIANG AND
COL. WANG XIANGSUI

ECHO POINT BOOKS & MEDIA, LLC

Published by Echo Point Books & Media
Brattleboro, Vermont
www.EchoPointBooks.com

Bibliographical Note
This book is presented in summary translation. Originally published in
1999 by China's People's Liberation Army, Beijing.

Unrestricted Warfare
ISBN (Paperback): 978-1-62654-305-8
ISBN (Hardcover): 978-1-62654-306-5

Cover design by Rachel Boothby Gualco,
Echo Point Books & Media

Editorial and proofreading assistance by Ian Straus,
Echo Point Books & Media

Printed and bound in the United States of America

Contents

Translator's Note

Please note:

The following selections are taken from *Unrestricted Warfare*, a book published in China in February 1999 which proposes tactics for developing countries, in particular China, to compensate for their military inferiority vis-à-vis the United States during a high-tech war. The selections include the table of contents, preface, afterword, and biographical information about the authors printed on the cover. The book was written by two PLA senior colonels from the younger generation of Chinese military officers and was published by the PLA Literature and Arts Publishing House in Beijing, suggesting that its release was endorsed by at least some elements of the PLA leadership. This impression was reinforced by an interview with Qiao and laudatory review of the book carried by the party youth league's official daily, *Zhongguo Qingnian Bao*, on 28 June.

Published prior to the bombing of China's embassy in Belgrade, the book has recently drawn the attention of both the Chinese and Western press for its advocacy of a multitude of means, both military and particularly non-military, to strike at the United States during times of conflict. Hacking into websites, targeting financial institutions, using the media, and conducting terrorism and urban warfare are among the methods proposed. In the *Zhongguo Qingnian Bao* interview, Qiao was quoted as stating that "the first rule of unrestricted warfare is that there are no rules, with nothing forbidden." Elaborating on this idea, he asserted that strong countries would not use the same approach against weak countries because "strong countries make the rules while rising ones break them and exploit loopholes. . . . The United States breaks [UN rules] and makes new ones when these rules don't suit [its purposes], but it has to observe its own rules or the whole world will not trust it." (see FBIS translation of the interview, OW2807114599)

Preface

Everyone who has lived through the last decade of the 20th century will have profound sense of the changes in the world. We don't believe that there is anyone who would claim that there has been any decade in history in which the changes have been greater than those of this decade. Naturally, the causes behind the enormous changes are too numerous to mention, but there are only a few reasons that people bring up repeatedly. One of those is the Gulf War.

One war changed the world. Linking such a conclusion to a war which occurred one time in a limited area and which only lasted 42 days seems like something of an exaggeration. However, that is indeed what the facts are, and there is no need to enumerate one by one all the new words that began to appear after 17 January 1991. It is only necessary to cite the former Soviet Union, Bosnia-Herzegovina, Kosovo, cloning, Microsoft, hackers, the Internet, the Southeast Asian financial crisis, the euro, as well as the world's final and only superpower—the United States. These are sufficient. They pretty much constitute the main subjects on this planet for the past decade.

However, what we want to say is that all these are related to that war, either directly or indirectly. However, we definitely do not intend to mythicize war, particularly not a lopsided war in which there was such a great difference in the actual power of the opposing parties. Precisely the contrary. In our in-depth consideration of this war, which changed the entire world in merely half a month, we have also noted another fact, which is that war itself has now been changed. We discovered that, from those wars which could be described in glorious and dominating terms, to the aftermath of the acme of what it has been possible to achieve to date in the history of warfare, that war, which people originally felt was one of the more important roles to be played out on the world stage, has at one stroke taken the seat of a B actor.

A war which changed the world ultimately changed war itself. This is truly fantastic, yet it also causes people to ponder deeply. No, what we are referring to are not changes in the instruments of war, the technology of war, the modes of war, or the forms of war. What we are referring to is the function of warfare. Who could imagine that an insufferably arrogant actor, whose appearance has changed the entire plot, suddenly finds that he himself is actually the last person to play this unique role. Furthermore, without waiting for him to leave the stage, he has already been told that there is no great likelihood that he will again handle an A role, at least not a central role in which he alone occupies center stage. What kind of feeling would this be?

Perhaps those who feel this most deeply are the Americans, who probably should be counted as among the few who want to play all the roles, including savior, fireman, world policeman, and an emissary of peace, etc. In the aftermath of "Desert Storm," Uncle Sam has not been able to again achieve a commendable victory. Whether it was in Somalia or Bosnia-Herzegovina, this has invariably been the case. In particular, in the most recent action in which the United States and Britain teamed up to carry out air attacks on Iraq, it was the same stage, the same method, and the same actors, but there was no way to successfully perform the magnificent drama that had made such a profound impression eight years earlier. Faced with political, economic, cultural, diplomatic, ethnic, and religious issues, etc., that are more complex than they are in the minds of most of the military men in the world, the limitations of the military means, which had heretofore always been successful, suddenly became apparent. However, in the age of "might makes right"—and most of the history of this century falls into this period—these were issues which did not constitute a problem. The problem is that the U.S.-led multinational forces brought this period to a close in the desert region of Kuwait, thus beginning a new period.

At present it is still hard to see if this age will lead to the unemployment of large numbers of military personnel, nor will it cause war to vanish from this world. All these are still undetermined. The only point which is certain is that, from this point on, war will no longer be what it was originally. Which is to say that, if in the days to come mankind has no choice but to engage in war, it can no longer be carried out in the ways with which we are familiar. It is impossible for us to deny the impact on human society and its soul of the new motivations represented by economic freedom, the concept of human rights, and the awareness of environmental protection, but it is certain that the metamorphosis of warfare will have a more complex backdrop. Otherwise, the immortal bird of warfare will not be able to attain nirvana when it is on the verge of decline: When people begin to lean toward and rejoice in the reduced use of military force to resolve conflicts, war will be reborn in another form and in another arena, becoming an instrument of enormous power in the hands of all those who harbor intentions of controlling other countries or regions. In this sense, there is reason for us to maintain that the financial attack by George Soros on East Asia, the terrorist attack on the U.S. embassy by Usama Bin Laden, the gas attack on the Tokyo subway by the disciples of the Aum Shinri Kyo, and the havoc wreaked by the likes of Morris Jr. on the Internet, in which the degree of destruction is by no means second to that of a war, represent semi-warfare, quasi-warfare, and sub-warfare, that is, the embryonic form of another kind of warfare.

But whatever you call them, they cannot make us more optimistic than in the past. We have no reason for optimism. This is because the reduction of the functions of warfare in a pure sense does not mean at all that war has ended. Even in the so-called post-modern, post-industrial age, warfare will not be totally dismantled. It has only re-invaded human society in a more complex, more extensive, more concealed, and more subtle manner. It is as Byron said in his poem mourning Shelley, "Nothing has happened, he has only undergone a sea change." War which has undergone the changes of modern technology and the market system will be launched even more in atypical forms. In other words, while we are seeing a relative reduction in military violence, at the same time we definitely are seeing an increase in political, economic, and technological violence. However, regardless of the form the violence takes, war is war, and a change in the external appearance does not keep any war from abiding by the principles of war.

If we acknowledge that the new principles of war are no longer "using armed force to compel the enemy to submit to one's will," but rather are "using all means, including armed force or non-armed force, military and non-military, and lethal and non-lethal means to compel the enemy to accept one's interests."

This represents change. A change in war and a change in the mode of war occasioned by this. So, just what has led to the change? What kind of changes are they? Where are the changes headed? How does one face these changes? This is the topic that this book attempts to touch on and shed light on, and it is also our motivation in deciding to write this book.

[Written on 17 January 1999, the 8th anniversary of the outbreak of the Gulf War]

Part One

On New Warfare

"Although ancient states were great, they inevitably perished when they were fond of war."—Sima Rangju

Technology is the Totem of Modern Man [1]

Stirred by the warm breeze of utilitarianism, it is not surprising that technology is more in favor with people than science is. The age of great scientific discoveries had already been left behind before Einstein's time. However, modern man is increasingly inclined to seeing all his dreams come true during his lifetime. This causes him, when betting on his own future, to prostrate himself and expect wonders from technology through a 1000-power concave lens. In this way, technology has achieved startling and explosive developments in a rather short period of time, and this has resulted in innumerable benefits for mankind, which is anxious for quick success and instant rewards. However, we proudly term this technological progress, not realizing that at this time we have already consigned ourselves to a benighted technological age in which we have lost our hearts [2].

Technology today is becoming increasingly dazzling and uncontrollable. Bell Labs and Sony continue to put out novel toys, Bill Gates opens new "Windows" each year, and "Dolly," the cloned sheep, proves that mankind is now planning to take the place of God the Creator. The fearsome Russian-built SU-27 fighter has not been put to use on any battlefield, and already the SU-35 has emerged to strike a pose [3], but whether or not, once it has exhausted its time in the limelight, the SU-35 will be able to retire having rendered meritorious service is still a matter of considerable doubt. Technology is like "magic shoes" on the feet of mankind, and after the spring has been wound tightly by commercial interests, peo-

1

ple can only dance along with the shoes, whirling rapidly in time to the beat that they set.

The names Watt and Edison are nearly synonymous with great technical inventions, and using these great technological masters to name their age may be said to be reasonable. However, from then on, the situation changed, and the countless and varied technological discoveries of the past 100 years or so makes it difficult for the appearance of any new technology to take on any self-importance in the realm of human life. While it may be said that the formulations of "the age of the steam engine" and "the age of electrification" can be said to be names which reflect the realities of the time, today, with all kinds of new technology continuously beating against the banks of the age so that people scarcely have the time to accord them brief acclaim while being overwhelmed by an even higher and newer wave of technology, the age in which an era could be named for a single new technology or a single inventor has become a thing of the past. This is the reason why, if one calls the current era the "nuclear age" or the "information age," it will still give people the impression that you are using one aspect to typify the whole situation. There is absolutely no doubt that the appearance of information technology has been good news for human civilization. This is because it is the only thing to date that is capable of infusing greater energy into the technological "plague" that has been released from Pandora's box, and at the same time it also provides a magic charm as a means of controlling it [technology]. It is just that, at present, there is still a question of who in turn will have a magic charm with which to control it [information technology]. The pessimistic viewpoint is that, if this technology develops in a direction which cannot be controlled by man, ultimately it will turn mankind into its victim [4]. However, this frightening conclusion is totally incapable of reducing people's ardor for it. The optimistic prospects that it displays itself are intensely seductive for mankind, which has a thirst for technical progress. After all, its unique features of exchanging and sharing represent the light of intelligence which we can hope will lead mankind out of the barbarism of technology, although this is still not sufficient to make us like those futurists who cannot see the forest for the trees, and who use its name to label the entire age. Its characteristics are precisely what keep it from being able to replace the various technologies that we already have in great quantity, that are just emerging, or which are about to be born, particularly those such as biotechnology, materials technology, and nanotechnology, these technologies which have a symbiotic relationship with information technology in which they rely on and promote one another. Over the past 300 years, people have long since become accustomed to blindly falling in love with the new and discarding the old in the realm of technology, and the endless pursuit of new technology has become a panacea to resolve all the difficult questions of existence. Infatuated with it, people have gradually gone astray. Just as one will often commit ten other mistakes to cover up one, to solve one difficult problem people do not hesitate to bring ten more on themselves [5]. For example, for a more convenient means of transportation, people invented cars, but a long string of problems followed closely on the heels of the automobile—mining and smelting, mechanical processing, oil extraction, rubber refining, and road-building, etc., which in turn required a long string of technical means to solve, until ultimately it led to pollution of the environment, destroying resources, taking over farmland, traffic accidents, and a host of thornier problems. In the long run, comparing the original goal of using cars for transportation with these derivative problems, it almost seems unimportant. In this way, the irrational expansion of technology causes mankind to continually lose his goals in the complex ramifications of the tree of technology, losing his way and forgetting how to get back. We may as well dub this phenomenon the "ramification effect." Fortunately, at this time, modern information technology made its appearance. We can say with certainty that this is the most important revolution in the history of technology. Its revolutionary significance is not merely in that it is a brand new technology itself, but more in that it is a kind of bonding agent which can lightly penetrate the layers of barriers between technologies and link various technologies which appear to be totally unrelated. Through its bonding, not only is it possible to derive numerous new technologies which are neither one thing nor the other while they also represent this and that, and furthermore it also provides a kind of brand new approach to the relationship between man and technology. Only from the perspective of mankind can mankind clearly perceive the essence of technology as a tool, and only then can he avoid becoming a slave to technology—to the tool—during the process of resolving the difficult problems he faces in his existence. Mankind is completely capable of fully developing his own powers of imagination so that, when each technology is used its potential is exhausted, and not being like a bear breaking off corncobs, only able to continually use new technology to replace the old. Today, the independent use of individual technologies is now becoming more and more unimaginable. The emergence of information technology has presented endless possibilities for match-ups involving various old and new technologies and among new and advanced technologies. Countless facts have demonstrated that the integrated use of technology is able to promote social progress more than even the discovery of the technology [6].

The situation of loud solo parts is in the process of being replaced by a multi-part chorus. The general fusion of technology is irreversibly guiding the rising globalization trend, while the globalization trend in turn is accelerating the process of the general fusion of technology, and this is the basic characteristic of our age.

This characteristic will inevitably project its features on every direction of the age, and naturally the realm of war will be no exception. No military force that thirsts for modernization can get by without nurturing new technology, while the demands of war have always been the midwife of new technology. During the Gulf War, more than 500 kinds of new and advanced technology of the '80s ascended the stage to strike a pose, making the war simply seem like a demonstration site for new weaponry. However, the thing that left a profound impression on people was not the new weaponry per se, but was rather the trend of systemization in the development and use of the weapons. Like the "Patriots" intercepting the "Scuds," it seemed as simple as shooting birds with a shotgun, while in fact it involved numerous weapons deployed over more than half the globe: After a DSP satellite identified a target, an alarm was sent to a ground station in Australia, which was then sent to the central command post in Riyadh through the U.S. Cheyenne Mountain command post, after which the "Patriot" operators were ordered to take their battle stations, all of which took place in the mere 90-second alarm stage, relying on numerous relays and coordination of space-based systems and C3I systems, truly a "shot heard 'round the world." The real-time coordination of numerous weapons over great distances created an unprecedented combat capability, and this was precisely something that was unimaginable prior to the emergence of information technology. While it may be said that the emergence of individual weapons prior to World War II was still able to trigger a military revolution, today no one is capable of dominating the scene alone.

War in the age of technological integration and globalization has eliminated the right of weapons to label war and, with regard to the new starting point, has realigned the relationship of weapons to war, while the appearance of weapons of new concepts, and particularly new concepts of weapons, has gradually blurred the face of war. Does a single "hacker" attack count as a hostile act or not? Can using financial instruments to destroy a country's economy be seen as a battle? Did CNN's broadcast of an exposed corpse of a U.S. soldier in the streets of Mogadishu shake the determination of the Americans to act as the world's policeman, thereby altering the world's strategic situation? And should an assessment of wartime actions look at the means or the results? Obviously, proceeding with the traditional definition of war in mind, there is no longer any way to answer the above questions. When we suddenly realize that all these non-war actions may be the new factors constituting future warfare, we have to come up with a new name for this new form of war: Warfare which transcends all boundaries and limits, in short: unrestricted warfare.

If this name becomes established, this kind of war means that all means will be in readiness, that information will be omnipresent, and the battlefield will be everywhere. It means that all weapons and technology can be superimposed at will, it means that all the boundaries lying between the two worlds of war and non-war, of military and non-military, will be totally destroyed, and it also means that many of the current principles of combat will be modified, and even that the rules of war may need to be rewritten.

However, the pulse of the God of War is hard to take. If you want to discuss war, particularly the war that will break out tomorrow evening or the morning of the day after tomorrow, there is only one way, and that is to determine its nature with bated breath, carefully feeling the pulse of the God of War today.

Notes

[1] In *Man and Technology*, O. Spengler stated that "like God, our father, technology is eternal and unchanging, like the son of God, it will save mankind, and like the Holy Spirit, it shines upon us." The philosopher Spengler's worship for technology, which was just like that of a theologian for God, was nothing but a manifes-

tation of another type of ignorance as man entered the great age of industrialism, which increasingly flourished in the post-industrial age.

[2]   In this regard, the French philosopher and scientist Jean Ladrihre has a unique viewpoint. He believes that science and technology have a destructive effect as well as a guiding effect on culture. Under the combined effects of these two, it is very difficult for mankind to maintain a clear-headed assessment of technology, and we are constantly oscillating between the two extremes of technical fanaticism and "anti-science" movements. Bracing oneself to read through his *The Challenge Presented to Cultures by Science and Technology*, in which the writing is abstruse but the thinking recondite, may be helpful in observing the impact of technology on the many aspects of human society from a broader perspective.

[3]   Although the improvement of beyond visual range (BVR) weapons has already brought about enormous changes in the basic concepts of air combat, after all is said and done it has not completely eliminated short-range combat. The SU-27, which is capable of "cobra" maneuvers and the SU-35, which is capable of "hook" moves, are the most outstanding fighter aircraft to date.

[4]   F. G. Ronge [as published 1715 2706 1396 2706] is the sharpest of the technological pessimists. As early as 1939, Ronge had recognized the series of problems that modern technology brings with it, including the growth of technological control and the threat of environmental problems. In his view, technology has already become an unmatched, diabolical force. It has not only taken over nature, it has also stripped away man's freedom. In *Being and Time*, Martin Heidegger termed technology an "outstanding absurdity," calling for man to return to nature in order to avoid technology, which posed the greatest threat. The most famous technological optimists were [Norbert] Wiener and Steinbuch. In Wiener's *Cybernetics, God and Robots* and *The Human Use of Human Beings* and Steinbuch's *The Information Society, Philosophy and Cybernetics,* and other such works, we can see the bright prospects that they describe for human society, driven by technology.

[5]   In David Ehrenfeld's book, *The Arrogance of Humanism*, he cites numerous examples of this. In *Too Clever*, Schwartz states that "the resolution of one problem may generate a group of new problems, and these problems may ultimately preclude that kind of resolution." In *Rational Consciousness*, Rene Dibo [as published 3583 0355 6611 0590] also discusses a similar phenomenon.

[6]   In *The Age of Science and the Future of Mankind*, E. Shulman points out that "during the dynamic development of modern culture, which is based on the explosive development of modern technology, we are increasingly faced with the fact of multidisciplinary cooperation ... it is impossible for one special branch of science to guide our practice in a sufficiently scientific manner."

Chapter 1

The Weapons Revolution
Which Invariably Comes First

"As soon as technological advances may be applied to military goals, and furthermore are already used for military purposes, they almost immediately seem obligatory, and also often go against the will of the commanders in triggering changes or even revolutions in the modes of combat."—Engels

The weapons revolution invariably precedes the revolution in military affairs by one step, and following the arrival of a revolutionary weapon, the arrival of the revolution in military affairs is just a matter of time. The history of warfare is continually providing this kind of proof: bronze or iron spears resulted in the infantry phalanx, and bows and arrows and stirrups provided new tactics for cavalry [1]. Black powder cannons gave rise to a full complement of modern warfare modes . . . from the time when conical bullets and rifles [2] took to the battlefield as the vanguard of the age of technology, weapons straightaway stamped their names on the chest of warfare. First, it was the enormous steel-clad naval vessels that ruled the seas, launching the "age of battleships," then its brother the "tank" ruled land warfare, after which the airplane dominated the skies, up until the atomic bomb was born, announcing the approach of the "nuclear age." Today, a multitude of new and advanced technology weapons continues to pour forth, so that weapons have solemnly become the chief representative of war. When people discuss future warfare, they are already quite accustomed to using certain weapons or certain technologies to describe it, calling it "electronic warfare," "precision-weapons warfare," and "information warfare." Coasting along in their mental orbit, people have not yet noticed that a certain inconspicuous yet very important change is stealthily approaching.

No One Has the Right to Label Warfare

The weapons revolution is a prelude to a revolution in military affairs. What is different than in the past is that the revolution in military affairs that is coming will no longer by driven by one or two individual weapons. In addition to continuing to stimulate people to yearn for and be charmed by new weapons, the numerous technological inventions have also quickly eradicated the mysteries of each kind of weapon. In the past, all that was needed was the invention of a few weapons or pieces of equipment, such as the stirrup and the Maxim machine gun [3], and that was sufficient to alter the form of war, whereas today upwards of 100 kinds of weapons are needed to make up a certain weapons system before it can have an overall effect on war. However, the more weapons are invented, the smaller an individual weapon's role in war becomes, and this is a paradox that is inherent in the relationship between weapons and war. Speaking in that sense, other than the all-out use of nuclear weapons, a situation which is more and more unlikely and which may be termed nuclear war, none of the other weapons, even those that are extremely revolutionary in nature, possesses the right to label future warfare. Perhaps it is precisely because people recognize this point that we then have formulations such as "high-tech warfare" and "information warfare" [4], whose intent is to use the broad concept of technology to replace the concept of specific weapons, using a fuzzy-learning approach to resolve this knotty problem. However, it seems that this still is not the way to resolve the problem.

When one delves deeply into this, the term "high technology" [5], which first appeared in the architectural industry in the United States, is in fact a bit vague. What constitutes high technology? What does it refer to? Logically speaking, high and low are only relative concepts. However, using an extremely mutable concept in this irrational manner to name warfare, which is evolving endlessly, in itself constitutes a considerable problem. When one generation's high technology becomes low technology with the passage of time, are we still prepared to again dub the new toys that continue to appear as being high tech? Or is it possible that, in today's technological explosion, this may result in confusion and trouble for us in naming and using each new technology that appears? Not to mention the question of just what should be the standard to determine whether something is high or not? With regard to technology itself, each technology has specific aspects, which therefore means that each has its time limits. Yesterday's "high" is very possibly today's "low," while today's "new" will in turn become tomorrow's "old." Compared to the M-60 tank, the "Cobra" helicopter, and the B-52, the main battle weapons of the '60s–'70s, the

"Abrams" tank, the "Apache" helicopter gunship, the F-117, the "Patriot" missiles, and the "Tomahawk" cruise missiles are high tech. However, faced with the B-2, the F-22, the "Comanche" helicopter, and the "J-Stars" joint-surveillance target-attack radar system, they in turn seem outmoded. It is as if to say there is the concept of high-tech weapons, which is a variable throughout, and which naturally becomes the title of the "bride." Then, as the "flowers bloom each year, but the people change," all that is left is the empty shell of a name, which is continually placed on the head of the girl who is becoming the next "bride." Then, in the chain of warfare with its continuous links, each weapon can go from high to low and from new to old at any time and any place, with time's arrow being unwilling to stop at any point; nor can any weapon occupy the throne of high technology for long. Since this is the case, just what kind of high technology does this so-called high-tech warfare refer to?

High technology, as spoken of in generalities, cannot become a synonym for future warfare, nor is information technology—which is one of the high technologies of the present age and which seems to occupy an important position in the makeup of all modern weapons—sufficient to name a war. Even if in future wars all the weapons have information components embedded in them and are fully computerized, we can still not term such war information warfare, and at most we can just call it computerized warfare [6]. This is because, regardless of how important information technology is, it cannot completely supplant the functions and roles of each technology per se. For example, the F-22 fighter, which already fully embodies information technology, is still a fighter, and the "Tomahawk" missile is still a missile, and one cannot lump them all together as information weapons, nor can war which is conducted using these weapons be termed information warfare [7]. Computerized warfare in the broad sense and information warfare in the narrow sense are two completely different things. The former refers to the various forms of warfare which are enhanced and accompanied by information technology, while the latter primarily refers to war in which information technology is used to obtain or suppress information. In addition, the contemporary myth created by information worship has people mistakenly believing that it is the only rising technology, while the sun has already set on all the others. This kind of myth may put more money in the pockets of Bill Gates, but it cannot alter the fact that the development of information technology similarly relies on the development of other technology, and the development of related materials technology is a direct constraint on information technology break-throughs. For example, the development of biotechnology will determine the future fate of information technology [8]. Speaking of bio-information technology, we may as well return to a previous topic and again make a small assumption: If people use information-guided bio-weapons to attack a bio-computer, should this be counted as bio-warfare or information warfare? I fear that no one will be able to answer that in one sentence, but this is something which is perfectly capable of happening. Actually, it is basically not necessary for people to wrack their brains over whether or not information technology will grow strong and unruly today, because it itself is a synthesis of other technologies, and its first appearance and every step forward are all a process of blending with other technologies, so that it is part of them, and they are part of it, and this is precisely the most fundamental characteristic of the age of technological integration and globalization. Naturally, like the figures from a steel seal, this characteristic may leave its typical imprint on each modern weapon. We are by no means denying that, in future warfare, certain advanced weapons may play a leading role. However, as for determining the outcome of war, it is now very difficult for anyone to occupy an unmatched position. It may be leading, but it will not be alone, much less never-changing. Which is also to say that there is no one who can unblushingly stamp his own name on a given modern war.

"Fighting the Fight that Fits One's Weapons" and "Making the Weapons to Fit the Fight"

These two sentences, "fight the fight that fits one's weapons" and "build the weapons to fit the fight," show the clear demarcation line between traditional warfare and future warfare, as well as pointing out the relationship between weapons and tactics in the two kinds of war. The former reflects the involuntary or passive adaptation of the relationship of man to weapons and tactics in war which takes place under natural conditions, while the latter suggests the conscious or active choice that people make regarding the same proposition when they have entered a free state. In the history of war, the general unwritten rule that people have adhered to all along is to "fight the fight that fits one's weapons." Very often it is the case

that only after one first has a weapon does one begin to formulate tact
to match it. With weapons coming first, followed by tactics, the evolution
of weapons has a decisive constraining effect on the evolution of tactics.
Naturally, there are limiting factors here involving the age and the technology, but neither can we say that there is no relationship between this
and the linear thinking in which each generation of weapons-making specialists only thinks about whether or not the performance of the weapon
itself is advanced, and does not consider other aspects. Perhaps this is one
of the factors why a weapons revolution invariably precedes a revolution in
military affairs.

Although the expression "fight the fight that fits one's weapons" is essentially negative in nature because what it leaves unsaid reflects a kind of
helplessness, we have no intention of belittling the positive meaning that
it has today, and this positive meaning is seeking the optimum tactics for
the weapons one has. In other words, seeking the combat mode which represents the best match for the given weapons, thereby seeing that they perform up to their peak values. Today, those engaged in warfare have now either consciously or unconsciously completed the transition of this rule
from the negative to the positive. It is just that people still wrongfully believe that this is the only initiative that can be taken by backward countries
in their helplessness. They hardly realize that the United States, the fore-
most power in the world, must similarly face this kind of helplessness.
Even though she is the richest in the world, it is not necessarily possible for
her to use up her uniform new and advanced technology weapons to fight
an expensive modern war [9]. It is just that she has more freedom when it
comes to the selection and pairing up of new and old weapons

If one can find a good point of agreement, which is to say, the most
appropriate tactics, the pairing up and use of new and older generation
weapons not only makes it possible to eliminate the weakness of uniform
weaponry, it may also become a "multiplier" to increase the weapons' effectiveness. The B-52 bomber, which people have predicted on many occa-
sions is long since ready to pass away peacefully, has once again become re-
splendent after being coupled with cruise missiles and other precision
guided weapons, and its wings have not yet rested to date. By the use of external infrared guided missiles, the A-10 aircraft now has night-attack capabilities that it originally lacked, and when paired with the Apache helicopter, they complement each other nicely, so that this weapons platform

n the mid-'70s is very imposing. Obviously, "fight the
s weapons" by no means represents passive inaction. For
ncreasingly open weapons market and multiple supply
vided a great deal of leeway with regard to weapons se-
...assive coexistence of weapons which span multiple generations has provided a broader and more functional foundation for trans-
generation weapons combinations than at any age in the past, so that it is
only necessary to break with our mental habit of treating the weapons' generations, uses, and combinations as being fixed to be able to turn something
that is rotten into something miraculous. If one thinks that one must rely
on advanced weapons to fight a modern war, being blindly superstitious
about the miraculous effects of such weapons, it may actually result in turning something miraculous into something rotten. We find ourselves in a
stage where a revolutionary leap forward is taking place in weapons, going
from weapons systems symbolized by gunpowder to those symbolized by
information, and this may be a relatively prolonged period of alternating
weapons. At present we have no way of predicting how long this period
may last, but what we can say for sure is that, as long as this alternation has
not come to an end, fighting the kind of battle that fits one's weapons will
be the most basic approach for any country in handling the relationship between weapons and combat, and this includes the United States, the country which has the most advanced weapons. What must be pointed out is
that the most basic thing is not the thing with the greatest future. Aggressive initiatives under negative preconditions is only a specific approach for
a specific time, and by no means constitutes an eternal rule. In man's hands,
scientific progress has long since gone from passive discovery to active invention, and when the Americans proposed the concept of "building the
weapons to fit the fight," it triggered the greatest single change in the relationship between weapons and tactics since the advent of war. First determine the mode of combat, then develop the weapons, and in this regard,
the first stab that the Americans took at this was "air-land battle," while the
currently popular "digitized battlefield" and "digitized units" [10] which
have given rise to much discussion represent their most recent attempt.
This approach indicates that the position of weapons in invariably preceding a revolution in military affairs has now been shaken, and now tactics
come first and weapons follow, or the two encourage one another, with ad-
vancement in a push-pull manner becoming the new relationship between
them. At the same time, weapons themselves have produced changes with

epoch-making significance, and their development no longer looks only to improvements in the performance of individual weapons, but rather to whether or not the weapons have good characteristics for linking and matching them with other weapons. As with the F-111, which was in a class by itself at the time because it was too advanced, there was no way to pair it up with other weapons, so all they could do was shelve it. That lesson has now been absorbed, and the thinking that tries to rely on one or two new and advanced-technology weapons to serve as "killer weapons" which can put an end to the enemy is now outmoded.

"Building the weapons to fit the fight," an approach which has the distinctive features of the age and the characteristics of the laboratory, may not only be viewed as a kind of active choice, it can also be taken as coping with shifting events by sticking to a fundamental principle, and in addition to being a major breakthrough in the history of preparing for war, it also implies the potential crisis in modern warfare: Customizing weapons systems to tactics which are still being explored and studied is like preparing food for a great banquet without knowing who is coming, where the slightest error can lead one far astray. Viewed from the performance of the U.S. military in Somalia, where they were at a loss when they encountered Aidid's forces, the most modern military force does not have the ability to control public clamor, and cannot deal with an opponent who does things in an unconventional manner. On the battlefields of the future, the digitized forces may very possibly be like a great cook who is good at cooking lobsters sprinkled with butter: when faced with guerrillas who resolutely gnaw corncobs, they can only sigh in despair. The "generation gap" [11] in weapons and military forces is perhaps an issue that requires exceptional attention. The closer the generation gap is, the more pronounced are the battle successes of the more senior generation, while the more the gap opens, the less each party is capable of dealing with the other, and it may reach the point where no one can wipe out the other. Looking at the specific examples of battles that we have, it is difficult for high-tech troops to deal with unconventional warfare and low-tech warfare, and perhaps there is a rule here, or at least it is an interesting phenomenon which is worth studying [12].

Weapons of New Concepts and New Concepts of Weapons

Compared to new-concept weapons, nearly all the weapons that we have known so far may be termed old-concept weapons. The reason they are called old is because the basic functions of these weapons were their mobility and lethal power. Even things like precision-guided bombs and other such high-tech weapons really involve nothing more than the addition of the two elements of intelligence and structural capabilities. From the perspective of practical applications, no change in appearance can alter their nature as traditional weapons, that is, their control throughout by professional soldiers and their use on certain battlefields. All these weapons and weapons platforms that have been produced in line with traditional thinking have without exception come to a dead end in their efforts to adapt to modern warfare and future warfare. Those desires of using the magic of high technology to work some alchemy on traditional weapons so that they are completely remade have ultimately fallen into the high-tech trap involving the endless waste of limited funds and an arms race. This is the paradox that must inevitably be faced in the process of the development of traditional weapons: To ensure that the weapons are in the lead, one must continue to up the ante in development costs; the result of this continued raising of the stakes is that no one has enough money to maintain the lead. Its ultimate result is that the weapons to defend the country actually become a cause of national bankruptcy.

Perhaps the most recent examples are the most convincing. Marshal Orgakov, the former chief of the Soviet general staff, was acutely aware of the trend of weapons development in the "nuclear age," and when, at an opportune time, he proposed the brand-new concept of the "revolution in military technology," his thinking was clearly ahead of those of his generation. But being ahead of time in his thinking hardly brought his country happiness, and actually brought about disastrous results [13]. As soon as this concept—which against the backdrop of the Cold War was seen by his colleagues as setting the pace for the time—was proposed, it further intensified the arms race which had been going on for some time between the United States and the Soviet Union. It was just that at that time no one could predict that it would actually result in the breakup of the Soviet Union and its complete elimination from the superpower contest. A powerful empire collapsed without a single shot being fired, vividly corroborating the lines of the famous poem by Kipling, "When empires perish, it is not with a rumble, but a snicker." Not only was this true for the former Soviet Union, today the Americans seem to be following in the footsteps of their old adversary, providing fresh proof of the paradox of weapons development that we have proposed. As the outlines of the age of technology integration become increasingly clear, they are investing more and more in the development of new weapons, and the cost of the weapons is getting higher and higher. The development of the F-14 and F-15 in the '60s-'70s cost $1 billion, while the development of the B-2 in the '80s cost over $10 billion, and the development of the F-22 in the '90s has exceeded $13 billion. Based on weight, the B-2 [14], which runs $13-$15 billion each, is some three times more expensive than an equivalent weight of gold [15]. Expensive weapons like that abound in the U.S. arsenal, such as the F-117A bomber, the F-22 main combat aircraft, and the Comanche helicopter gunship. The cost of each of these weapons exceeds or approaches $100 million, and this massive amount of weapons with unreasonable cost-effectiveness has covered the U.S. military with increasingly heavy armor, pushing them step by step toward the high-tech weapons trap where the cost stakes continue to be raised. If this is still true for the rich and brash United States, then how far can the other countries, who are short of money, continue down this path? Obviously, it will be difficult for anyone to keep going. Naturally, the way to extricate oneself from this predicament is to develop a different approach.

Therefore, new-concept weapons have emerged to fill the bill. However, what seems unfair to people is that it is again the Americans who are in the lead in this trend. As early as the Vietnam War, the silver iodide powder released over the "Ho Chi Minh Trail" that resulted in torrential rains and the defoliants scattered over the subtropical forests put the "American devils" in the sole lead with regard to both the methods and ruthlessness of new-concept weapons. Thirty years later, with the dual advantages of money and technology, others are unable to hold a candle to them in this area.

However, the Americans are not necessarily in the sole lead in everything. The new concepts of weapons, which came after the weapons of new concepts and which cover a wider area, were a natural extension of this. However, the Americans have not been able to get their act together in this area. This is because proposing a new concept of weapons does not require relying on the springboard of new technology, it just demands lucid and incisive thinking. However, this is not a strong point of the Americans, who are slaves to technology in their thinking. The Americans invariably halt their thinking at the boundary where technology has not yet reached. It cannot be denied that man-made earthquakes, tsunamis, weather disasters, or subsonic wave and new biological and chemical weapons all constitute new concept weapons [16], and that they have tremendous differences with what we normally speak of as weapons, but they are still all weapons whose immediate goal is to kill and destroy, and which are still related to military affairs, soldiers, and munitions. Speaking in this sense, they are nothing more than non-traditional weapons whose mechanisms have been altered and whose lethal power and destructive capabilities have been magnified several times over.

However, a new concept of weapons is different. This and what people call new-concept weapons are two entirely different things. While it may be said that new-concept weapons are weapons which transcend the domain of traditional weapons, which can be controlled and manipulated at a technical level, and which are capable of inflicting material or psychological casualties on an enemy, in the face of the new concept of weapons, such weapons are still weapons in a narrow sense. This is because the new concept of weapons is a view of weapons in the broad sense, which views as weapons all means which transcend the military realm but which can still be used in combat operations. In its eyes, everything that can benefit mankind can also harm him. This is to say that there is nothing in the world today that cannot become a weapon, and this requires that our understanding of weapons must have an awareness that breaks through all boundaries. With technological developments being in the process of striving to increase the types of weapons, a breakthrough in our thinking can open up the domain of the weapons kingdom at one stroke. As we see it, a single man-made stock-market crash, a single computer virus invasion, or a single rumor or scandal that results in a fluctuation in the enemy country's exchange rates or exposes the leaders of an enemy country on the Internet, all can be included in the ranks of new-concept weapons. A new concept of weapons provides direction for new-concept weapons, while the new-concept weapons give fixed forms to the new concept of weapons. With regard to the flood of new-concept weapons, technology is no longer the main factor, and the true underlying factor is a new concept regarding weapons.

What must be made clear is that the new concept of weapons is in the process of creating weapons that are closely linked to the lives of the common people. Let us assume that the first thing we say is: The appearance of new-concept weapons will definitely elevate future warfare to a level which is hard for the common people—or even military men—to imagine. Then the second thing we have to say should be: The new concept of weapons will cause ordinary people and military men alike to be greatly astonished at the fact that commonplace things that are close to them can also become weapons with which to engage in war. We believe that some morning people will awake to discover with surprise that quite a few gentle and kind things have begun to have offensive and lethal characteristics.

The Trend to "Kinder" Weapons

Before the appearance of the atom bomb, warfare was always in a "shortage age" with respect to lethal power. Efforts to improve weapons have primarily been to boost their lethal power, and from the "light-kill weapons" represented by cold steel weapons and single-shot firearms to the "heavy-kill weapons" represented by various automatic firearms, the history of the development of weapons has almost always been a process of continuing to boost the lethal power of weapons. Prolonged shortages resulted in a thirst among military men for weapons of even greater lethal power that was difficult to satisfy. With a single red cloud that arose over the wasteland of New Mexico in the United States, military men were finally able to obtain a weapon of mass destruction that fulfilled their wishes, as this could not only completely wipe out the enemy, it could kill them 100 or 1,000 times over. This gave mankind lethal capabilities that exceeded the demand, and for the first time there was some room to spare with regard to lethal power in war.

Philosophical principles tell us that, whenever something reaches an ultimate point, it will turn in the opposite direction. The invention of nuclear weapons, this "ultra-lethal weapon" [17] which can wipe out all mankind, has plunged mankind into an existential trap of its own making.

Nuclear weapons have become a sword of Damocles hanging over the head of mankind which forces it to ponder: Do we really need "ultra-lethal weapons"? What is the difference between killing an enemy once and killing him 100 times? What is the point of defeating the enemy if it means risking the destruction of the world? How do we avoid warfare that results in ruin for all? A "balance of terror" involving "mutually assured destruction" was the immediate product of this thinking, but its by-product was to provide a braking mechanism for the runaway express of improving the lethal capabilities of weapons, which was continually picking up speed, so that the development of weapons was no longer careening crazily down the light-kill weapons—heavy-kill weapons—ultra-lethal weapons expressway, with people trying to find a new approach to weapons development which would not only be effective but which could also exercise control over the lethal power of the weapons.

Any major technological invention will have a profound human background. The "Universal Declaration of Human Rights" passed by the United Nations General Assembly in 1948 and the more than 50 subsequent pacts related to it have established a set of international rules for human rights in which it is recognized that the use of weapons of mass destruction—particularly nuclear weapons—is a serious violation of the "right to life" and represents a "crime against mankind." Influenced by human rights and other new political concepts, plus the integration trend in international economics, the interlocking demands and political positions involving the interests of various social and political forces, the proposal of the concept of "ultimate concern" for the ecological environment, and particularly the value of human life, have resulted in misgivings about killing and destruction, forming a new value concept for war and new ethics for warfare. The trend to "kinder" [18] weapons is nothing other than a reflection in the production and development of weapons of this great change in man's cultural background. At the same time, technological progress has given us the means to strike at the enemy's nerve center directly without harming other things, giving us numerous new options for achieving victory, and all these make people believe that the best way to achieve victory is to control, not to kill. There have been changes in the concept of war and the concept of weapons, and the approach of using uncontrolled slaughter to force the enemy into unconditional surrender has now become the relic of a bygone age. Warfare has now taken leave of the meat-grinder age of Verdun-like campaigns.

The appearance of precision-kill (accurate) weapons and non-lethal (non-fatal) weapons is a turning point in the development of weapons, showing for the first time that weapons are developing in a "kinder," not a "stronger" direction. Precision-kill weapons can hit a target precisely, reducing collateral casualties, and like a gamma knife which can excise a tumor with hardly any bleeding, it has led to "surgical" strikes and other such new tactics, so that inconspicuous combat actions can achieve extremely notable strategic results. For example, by merely using one missile to track a mobile telephone signal, the Russians were able to still forever the tough mouth of Dudayev, who was a headache, and at the same time eased the enormous trouble that had been stirred up by tiny Chechnya. Non-lethal weapons can effectively eliminate the combat capabilities of personnel and equipment without loss of life [19]. The trend that is embodied in these weapons shows that mankind is in the process of overcoming its own extreme thinking, beginning to learn to control the lethal power that it already has but which is increasingly excessive. In the massive bombing that lasted more than a month during the Gulf War, the loss of life among civilians in Iraq only numbered in the thousands [20], far less than in the massive bombing of Dresden during World War II.

Kinder weapons represent the latest conscious choice of mankind among various options in the weapons arena by which, after the weapons are infused with the element of new technology, the human component is then added, thereby giving warfare an unprecedented kind-hearted hue. However, a kinder weapon is still a weapon, and it does not mean that the demands of being kinder will reduce the battlefield effectiveness of the weapon. To take away a tank's combat capabilities one can use cannons or missiles to destroy it, or a laser beam can be used to destroy its optical equipment or blind its crew. On the battlefield, someone who is injured requires more care than someone who is killed, and unmanned weapons can eliminate increasingly expensive protective facilities. Certainly those developing kinder weapons have already done cold cost-effectiveness calculations of this. Casualties can strip away an enemy's combat capabilities, causing him to panic and lose the will to fight, so this may be considered an extremely worthwhile way to achieve victory. Today, we already have enough technology, and we can create many methods of causing fear which are more effective, such as using a laser beam to project the image of injured followers against the sky, which would be sufficient to frighten those soldiers who are devoutly religious. There are no longer any obstacles to building this kind of weapon, it just requires that some additional imagination be added to the technical element. Kinder weapons represent a derivative of the new concept of weapons, while information weapons are a prominent example of kinder weapons. Whether it involves electromagnetic energy weapons for hard destruction or soft-strikes by computer logic bombs, network viruses, or media weapons, all are focused on paralyzing and undermining, not personnel casualties. Kinder weapons, which could only be born in an age of technical integration, may very well be the most promising development trend for weapons, and at the same time they will bring about forms of war or revolutions in military affairs which we cannot imagine or predict today. They represent a change with the most profound implications in the history of human warfare to date, and are the watershed between the old and the new forms of war. This is because their appearance has been sufficient to put all the wars in the age of cold and hot weapons into the "old" era. Nonetheless, we still cannot indulge in romantic fantasies about technology, believing that from this point on war will become a confrontation like an electronic game, and even simulated warfare in a computer room similarly must be premised upon a country's actual overall capabilities, and if a colossus with feet of clay comes up with ten plans for simulated warfare, it will still not be sufficient to deter an enemy who is more powerful with regard to actual strength. War is still the ground of death and life, the path of survival and destruction, and even the slightest innocence is not tolerated. Even if some day all the weapons have been made completely humane, a kinder war in which bloodshed may be avoided is still war. It may alter the cruel process of war, but there is no way to change the essence of war, which is one of compulsion, and therefore it cannot alter its cruel outcome, either.

Notes

[1]   Engels said, "In the age of barbarism, the bow and arrow was still a decisive weapon, the same as the iron sword in an uncivilized age and firearms in the age of civilization." (*Collected Works of Marx and Engels*, Vol. 4, People's Press, 1972, p. 19)

With regard to how stirrups altered the mode of combat, we can refer to the translation and commentary by Gu Zhun [7357 0402] of an article entitled "Stirrups and Feudalism—Does Technology Create History?" "Stirrups . . . immediately made hand-to-hand combat possible, and this was a revolutionary new mode of combat . . . very seldom had there been an invention as simple as the stirrup, but very seldom did it play the kind of catalytic role in history that this did." "Stirrups resulted in a series of military and social revolutions in Europe." (*Collected Works of Gu Zhun*, Guizhou People's Press, 1994, pp. 293–309)

[2] "Compared to the development of any advanced new weapons technology, the invention of the rifle and the conical bullet between 1850-1860 had the most profound and immediate revolutionary impact. . . . The impact on their age of high-explosive bombs, airplanes, and tanks, which appeared in the 20th century, certainly does not compare to that of the rifle at the time." For details, see T. N. Dupuy's *The Evolution of Weapons and Warfare*, part 3, section 21, "Rifles, Conical Bullets, and Dispersed Formations." (Military Science Publishing House, 1985, pp. 238–250)

[3] In the engagement of the Somme river in World War I, on 1 July 1916 the English forces launched an offensive against the Germans, and the Germans used Maxim machine guns to strafe the English troops, which were in a tight formation, resulting in 60,000 casualties in one day. From that point, mass formation charges gradually began to retreat from the battlefield. (*Weapons and War—The Historical Evolution of Military Technology*, Liu Jifeng [0491 2060 6912], University of Science and Technology for National Defense Publishing House, 1992, pp. 172–173)

[4] If Wiener's views on war game machines are not taken as the earliest discussion of information weapons, then a comment by Tom Luona [as published 5012 6719] in 1976 to the effect that information warfare is a "struggle among decision-making systems" makes him the first to come up with the term "information warfare" (U.S., *Military Intelligence* magazine, 1997, Jan–Mar issue, Douglas Dearth, "Implications, Characteristics, and Impact of Information Warfare") Through independent research, in 1990, Shen Weiguang [3088 0251 0342], a young scholar in China who has over ten years of military service, published *Information Warfare*, which is probably the earliest monograph on information warfare. On the strength of his *Third Wave*, in another best-seller entitled *Power Shift*, Toffler gave information warfare a global look, while the Gulf War happened along to become the most splendid advertisement for this new concept of combat. At that point, discussing "information warfare" became fashionable.

[5] Foreign experts hold that "high technology" is not a completely fixed concept and that it is also a dynamic concept, with different countries emphasizing high technology differently. Military high technology mainly includes military microelectronic device technology, computer technology, optoelectric technology, aerospace technology, biotechnology, new materials technology, stealth technology, and directed-energy technology. The most important characteristic of military high technology is "integration," i.e., each military high technology is made up of various technologies to form a technology group. (For details, see "Foreign Military Data," Academy of Military Sciences, Foreign Military Research Dept., No. 69, 1993.)

[6] Regarding the definition of "information warfare," to date opinions still vary. The definition by the U.S. Department of Defense and the Joint Chiefs of Staff is: Actions taken to interfere with the enemy's information, information processing, information systems, and computer networks to achieve information superiority over the enemy, while protecting one's own information, information processing, information systems, and computer networks. According to U.S. Army Field Manual FM100-6, "the DOD's understanding of information warfare leans toward the effects of information in actual conflicts," while the Army's understanding is that "information has already permeated every aspect, from peacetime to military actions in global warfare" (Military Science Publishing House, Chinese translation, pp. 24–25) "In a broad sense, information warfare constitutes actions which use information to achieve national goals." That is the definition given to information warfare by George Stein, a professor at the U.S. Air University, reflecting a somewhat broader vision than that of the Army. In an article in the 1997 summer edition of *Joint Force Quarterly*, Col. Brian Fredericks proposed that "information warfare is a national issue that goes beyond the scope of national defense," and perhaps this is the most accurate description of information warfare in the broad sense.

[7] Running precisely counter to the situation in which the implications of the concept of "information warfare" are getting broader and broader, some of the smart young officers in the U.S. military are increasingly questioning the concept of "information warfare." Air Force Lt. Col. James Rogers points out that "information warfare really isn't anything new . . . whether or not those who assert that information warfare techniques and strategies will inevitably replace 'armed warfare' are a bit too self-confident." (U.S., *Marines Magazine*, April 1997) Navy Lieutenant Robert Guerli [as published 0657 1422 0448] proposed that "the seven areas of misunderstanding with regard to information warfare are: (1) the overuse of analogous methods; (2) exaggerating the threat; (3) overestimating one's own strength; (4) historical relevance and accuracy; (5) avoiding criticism of anomalous attempts; (6) totally unfounded assumptions; and (7) nonstandard definitions." (U.S., *Events* magazine, Sep 97 issue) Air Force Major Yulin Whitehead wrote in the fall 1997 issue of *Airpower Journal* that information is not all-powerful, and that information weapons are not "magic weapons." Questions about information warfare are definitely not limited to individuals, as the U.S. Air Force document "The Foundations of Information Warfare" makes a strict distinction between "warfare in the information age" and "information warfare." It holds that "warfare in the information age" is warfare which uses computerized weapons, such as using a cruise missile to attack a target, whereas "information warfare" treats information as an independent realm and a powerful weapon. Similarly, some well-known scholars have also issued their own

opinions. Johns Hopkins University professor Eliot Cohen reminds us that "just as nuclear weapons did not result in the elimination of conventional forces, the information revolution will not eliminate guerilla tactics, terrorism, or weapons of mass destruction."

[8]   Macromolecular systems designed and produced using biotechnology represent the production materials for even higher order electronic components. For example, protein molecule computers have computation speeds and memory capabilities hundreds of millions of times greater than our current computers. (*New Military Perspectives for the Next Century*, Military Science Publishing House, 1997 edition, pp. 142–145)

[9]   Even in the Gulf War, which has been termed a testing ground for the new weapons, there were quite a few old weapons and conventional munitions which played important roles. (For details, see "The Gulf War—U.S. Department of Defense Final Report to Congress—Appendix".)

[10]   Starting with "Air-Land Battle," weapons development by the U.S. military has mainly been divided into five stages: Propose requirements, draft a plan, proof of concept, engineering development and production, and outfitting the units. Development regarding the equipping of digitized units is following this same path. (U.S., *Army Magazine*, Oct 1995). In March 1997, the U.S. Army conducted a brigade-size high-level combat test, testing a total of 58 kinds of digitized equipment. (U.S., *Army Times*, 31 March, 7 April, 28 April 1997). According to John E. Wilson, commander of the U.S. Army's Materiel Command, his mission is to cooperate with the Training and Doctrine Command, thinking up and developing bold and novel advanced technology equipment for them which meets their needs. (U.S., *Army Magazine*, October 1997)

[11]   Slipchenko [si li pu qin ke 2448 0448 2528 3830 4430], chairman of the Dept. of Scientific Research at the Russian General Staff Academy, believes that war and weapons have already gone through five ages, and we are now heading toward the sixth. (Zhu Xiaoli, Zhao Xiaozhuo, *The New U.S. and Russian Military Revolution*, Military Science Publishing House, 1996 edition, p. 6)

[12]   The Journal of the National Defense University, No. 11, 1998, carried an article on Chen Bojiang's interview of Philip Odeen, chairman of the U.S. National Defense Panel. Odeen mentioned "asymmetrical warfare" several times, believing that this is a new threat to the United States. Antulio Echevarria published an article in *Parameters* magazine in which he proposed that "in the post-industrial age, the thing that will still be most difficult to deal with will be a 'people's war.'"

[13]   U.S. defense specialists believe that Orgakov already saw that electronic technology would result in a revolution in conventional weapons, and that they would replace nuclear weapons with respect to their effects. However, Orgakov's foresight and wisdom with regard to the issue of a revolution in military affairs

ran aground because of structural problems. "If, in keeping up with the extremely high costs of the revolution in military affairs, a country exceeds the limits that can be borne by its system and material conditions, but it keeps engaging in military power contests with its opponents, the only outcome can be that they will fall further behind with regard to the military forces that they can use. This was the fate of Russia during the czarist and Soviet eras: the Soviet Union undertook military burdens that were difficult to bear, while in turn the military was unwilling to accept the need for strategic retrenchment." (See U.S., *Strategic Review* magazine, spring 1996, Steven Blank, "Preparing for the Next War: Some Views on the Revolution in Military Affairs.")

[14] In 1981, the U.S. Air Force estimated that it could produce 132 B-2s with an investment of $22 billion. However, eight years later, this money had only produced one B-2. Based on its value per unit weight, one B-2 is worth three times its weight in gold. (See *Modern Military*, No. 8, 1998, p. 33, and Zhu Zhihao's *Analysis of U.S. Stealth Technology Policy*.)

[15] The U.S. Dept. of Defense conducted an analysis of the 13 January 1993 air attack on Iraq and believes that there are numerous limitations to high-tech weapons, and that the effect of the combined effect bombs was at times better than that of precision bombs. (U.S., *Aviation Week and Space Technology*, 25 January 93).

[16] New-concept weapons primarily include kinetic-energy weapons, directed-energy weapons, subsonic weapons, geophysical weapons, meteorological weapons, solar energy weapons, and gene weapons, etc. (*New Military Perspectives for the Next Century*, Military Science Publishing House, 1997 edition, p. 3)

[17] The point in substituting the concept of "ultra-lethal weapons" for the concept of "weapons of mass destruction" is to stress that the lethal power of such weapons exceeds the needs of warfare and represents a product of man's extremist thinking.

[18] The "kind" in "kinder weapons" mainly refers to the fact that it reduces slaughter and collateral casualties.

[19] The April 1993 issue of the British journal *International Defense Review* revealed that the United States was energetically researching a variety of non-lethal weapons, including optical weapons, high-energy microwave weapons, acoustic beam weapons, and pulsed chemical lasers. The 6 March 1993 issue of *Jane's Defense Weekly* reported that a high-level non-lethal weapons steering committee at the Dept. of Defense had formulated a policy regulating the development, procurement, and use of such weapons. In addition, according to the 1997 *World Military Yearbook* (pp. 521–522), the U.S. Dept. of Defense has established a "non-lethal weapons research leading group," whose goal is to see that non-lethal weapons appear on the weapons inventory as soon as possible.

[20] See *Military Science Publishing House Foreign Military Data*, 26 March 1993, No. 27, p. 3.

Chapter 2

The War God's Face
Has Become Indistinct

"Throughout the Entire Course of History,
Warfare is Always Changing."—Andre Beaufre

Ever since early man went from hunting animals to slaughtering his own kind, people have been equipping the giant war beast for action, and the desire to attain various goals has prompted soldiers to become locked in bloody conflict. It has become universally accepted that warfare is a matter for soldiers. For several thousand years, the three indispensable "hardware" elements of any war have been soldiers, weapons and a battlefield. Running through them all has been the "software" element of warfare: its purposefulness. Before now, nobody has ever questioned that these are the basic elements of warfare. The problem comes when people discover that all of these basic elements, which seemingly were hard and fast, have changed so that it is impossible to get a firm grip on them. When that day comes, is the war god's face still distinct?

Why Fight and for Whom?

In regard to the ancient Greeks, if the account in Homer's epic is really trustworthy, the purpose of the Trojan War was clear and simple: it was worth fighting a ten-year war for the beautiful Helen. As far as their aims, the wars prosecuted by our ancestors were relatively simple in terms of the goals to be achieved, with no complexity to speak of. This was because our ancestors had limited horizons, their spheres of activity were narrow, they had modest requirements for existence, and their weapons were not lethal enough. Only if something could not be obtained by normal means would our ancestors generally resort to extraordinary measures to obtain it, and then without the least hesitation. Just so, Clausewitz wrote his famous saying, which has been an article of faith for several generations of soldiers and statesmen: "War is a continuation of politics." Our ancestors would fight perhaps for the orthodox status of a religious sect, or perhaps for an expanse of pastureland with plenty of water and lush grass. They would not even have scruples about going to war over, say, spices, liquor or a love affair between a king and queen. The stories of wars over spices and sweethearts, and rebellions over things like rum, are recorded in the pages of history—stories that leave us not knowing whether to laugh or cry. Then there is the war that the English launched against the Qing monarchy for the sake of the opium trade. This was national drug trafficking activity on probably the grandest scale in recorded history. It is clear from these examples that, prior to recent times, there was just one kind of warfare in terms of the kind of motive and the kind of subsequent actions taken. Moving to later times, Hitler expounded his slogan of "obtaining living space for the German people," and the Japanese expounded their slogan of building the so-called "Greater East Asia Co-Prosperity Sphere." While a cursory look at these slogans would suggest that the goals must have been somewhat more complex than the goals of any previous wars, nevertheless the substance behind the slogans was simply that the new great powers intended to once again carve up the spheres of influence of the old great powers and to reap the benefits of seizing their colonies.

To assess why people fight is not so easy today, however. In former times, the ideal of "exporting revolution" and the slogan of "checking the expansion of communism" were calls to action that elicited countless responses. But especially after the conclusion of the Cold War, when the Iron Curtain running all along the divide between the two great camps suddenly collapsed, these calls have lost their effectiveness. The times of clearly drawn sides are over. Who are our enemies? Who are our friends? These used to be the paramount questions in regard to revolution and counterrevolution. Suddenly the answers have become complicated, confusing and hard to get hold of. A country that yesterday was an adversary is in the process of becoming a current partner today, while a country that once was an ally will perhaps be met on the battlefield at the next outbreak of war. Iraq, which one year was still fiercely attacking Iran on behalf of the U.S. in the Iran-Iraq War, itself became the target of a fierce attack by the U.S. military in the next year [1]. An Afghan guerrilla trained by the CIA becomes the latest target for an attack by U.S. cruise missiles overnight.

Furthermore, NATO members Greece and Turkey have nearly come to blows several times in their dispute over Cyprus, and Japan and South Korea, who have concluded a treaty of alliance, have come just short of an open break as a result of their dispute over a tiny island. All of this serves to again confirm that old saying: "all friendship is in flux; self-interest is the only constant." The kaleidoscope of war is turned by the hands of self-interest, presenting constantly shifting images to the observer. Astonishing advances in modern advanced technology serve to promote globalization, further intensifying the uncertainty associated with the dissolution of some perceived self-interests and the emergence of others. The reason for starting a war can be anything from a dispute over territory and resources, a dispute over religious beliefs, hatred stemming from tribal differences, or a dispute over ideology, to a dispute over market share, a dispute over the distribution of power and authority, a dispute over trade sanctions, or a dispute stemming from financial unrest. The goals of warfare have become blurred due to the pursuit of a variety of agendas. Thus, it is more and more difficult for people to say clearly just why they are fighting [2].

Every young lad that participated in the Gulf War will tell you right up front that he fought to restore justice in tiny, weak Kuwait. However, the real reason for the war was perhaps far different from the high-sounding reason that was given. Hiding under the umbrella furnished by this high-sounding reason, they need not fear facing the light directly. In reality, every country that participated in the Gulf War decided to join "Desert Storm" only after carefully thinking over its own intentions and goals. Throughout the whole course of the war, all of the Western powers were fighting for their oil lifeline. To this primary goal, the Americans added the aspiration of building a new world order with "USA" stamped on it. Perhaps there was also a bit of missionary zeal to uphold justice. In order to eliminate a threat that was close at hand, the Saudi Arabians were willing to smash Muslim taboos and "dance with wolves." From start to finish, the British reacted enthusiastically to President Bush's every move, in order to repay Uncle Sam for the trouble he took on their behalf in the Malvinas Islands War. The French, in order to prevent the complete evaporation of their traditional influence in the Middle East, finally sent troops to the Gulf at the last moment. Naturally, there is no way that a war prosecuted under these kinds of conditions can be a contest fought over a single objective. The aggregate of the self-interests of all the numerous countries participating in the war serves to transform a modern war like "Desert Storm" into a race to further various self-interests under the banner of a common interest. Thus, so-called "common interest" has become merely the war equation's largest common denominator that can be accepted by every allied party participating in the war effort. Since different countries will certainly be pursuing different agendas in a war, it is necessary to take the self-interest of every allied party into consideration if the war is to be prosecuted jointly. Even if we consider a given country's domestic situation, each of the various domestic interest groups will also be pursuing its own agenda in a war. The complex interrelationships among self-interests make it impossible to pigeonhole the Gulf War as having been fought for oil, or as having been fought for the new world order, or as having been fought to drive out the invaders. Only a handful of soldiers are likely to grasp a principle that every statesman already knows: that the biggest difference between contemporary wars and the wars of the past is that, in contemporary wars, the overt goal and the covert goal are often two different matters.

Where to Fight?

To the battlefield!" The young lad with a pack on his back takes leave of his family as his daughters and other relatives see him off with tears in their eyes. This is a classic scene in war movies. Whether the young lad is leaving on a horse, a train, a steamship or a plane is not so important. The important thing is that the destination never changes: it is the battlefield bathed in the flames of war.

During the long period of time before firearms, battlefields were small and compact. A face-off at close quarters between two armies might unfold on a small expanse of level ground, in a mountain pass, or within the confines of a city. In the eyes of today's soldier, the battlefield that so enraptured the ancients is a "point" target on the military map that is not particularly noteworthy. Such a battlefield is fundamentally incapable of accommodating the spectacle of war as it has unfolded in recent times on such a grand scale. The advent of firearms led to dispersed formations, and the "point" ["dian" 7820] type battlefield was gradually drawn out into a line of skirmishers. The trench warfare of the First World War, with lines extending hundreds of miles, served to bring the "point" and "line" ["xian"

4775] type battlefield to its acme. At the same time, it transformed the battlefield into an "area" ["mian" 7240] type battlefield which was several dozens of miles deep. For those who went to war during those times, the new battlefield meant trenches, pillboxes, wire entanglements, machine guns and shell craters. They called war on this type of battlefield, where heavy casualties were inflicted, a "slaughterhouse" and a "meat grinder." The explosive development of military technology is constantly setting the stage for further explosive expansion of the battlespace. The transition from the "point" type battlefield to the "line" type battlefield, and the transition from the two-dimensional battlefield to the three-dimensional battlefield did not take as long as people generally think. One could say that, in each case, the latter stage came virtually on the heels of the former. When tanks began roaring over military trenches, prop airplanes were already equipped with machine guns and it was already possible to drop bombs from zeppelins. The development of weapons cannot, in and of itself, automatically usher in changes in the nature of the battlefield. In the history of warfare, any significant advance has always depended in part on active innovating by military strategists. The battlefield, which had been earthbound for several thousand years, was suddenly lifted into three-dimensional space. This was due in part to General J.F.C. Fuller's *Tanks in the Great War of 1914–1918* and Giulio Douhet's *The Command of the Air*, as well as the extremely deep operations that were proposed and demonstrated under the command of Marshall Mikhail N. Tukhachevsky. Erich Ludendorff was another individual who attempted to radically change the nature of the battlefield. He put forth the theory of "total war" and tried to combine battlefield and non-battlefield elements into one organic whole. While he was not successful, he nevertheless was the harbinger of similar military thought that has outlived him for more than half a century. Ludendorff was destined only to fight at battlefields like Verdun and the Masurian Lakes. A soldier's fate is determined by the era in which he lives. At that time, the wingspan of the war god could not extend any farther than the range of a Krupp artillery piece. Naturally, then, it was impossible to fire a shell that would pass through the front and rear areas on its parabolic path. Hitler was more fortunate than Ludendorff; 20 years later, he had long-range weapons at his disposal. He utilized bombers powered by Mercedes engines and V-1 and V-2 guided missiles and broke the British Isles' record of never having been encroached upon by an invader. Hitler, who was neither a strategist nor a tactician, relied on his intuition and made the line of demarcation between the front and rear less prominent in the war, but he never really understood the revolutionary significance of breaking through the partition separating battlefield elements from non-battlefield elements. Perhaps this concept was beyond the ken of an out-and-out war maniac and half-baked military strategist.

This revolution, however, will be upon us in full force soon enough. This time, technology is again running ahead of the military thinking. While no military thinker has yet put forth an extremely wide-ranging concept of the battlefield, technology is doing its utmost to extend the contemporary battlefield to a degree that is virtually infinite: there are satellites in space, there are submarines under the water, there are ballistic missiles that can reach anyplace on the globe, and electronic countermeasures are even now being carried out in the invisible electromagnetic spectrum space. Even the last refuge of the human race—the inner world of the heart—cannot avoid the attacks of psychological warfare. There are nets above and snares below, so that a person has no place to flee. All of the prevailing concepts about the breadth, depth and height of the operational space already appear to be old-fashioned and obsolete. In the wake of the expansion of mankind's imaginative powers and his ability to master technology, the battlespace is being stretched to its limits.

In spite of the situation described above, in military thinking, which is being drawn along by technology, there is still an unwillingness to simply stand still. Since technology has already served to open up more promising prospects for military thought, it is certainly not sufficient to simply expand the area of the battlefield in conventional "mesoscopic" [i.e., between macroscopic and microscopic] space. It is already clear that mechanical enlargement of the existing battlefield will not be the modus operandi for future battlefield change. The opinion that "the future battlefield expansion trend will be reflected in wars that are prosecuted in deeper parts of the oceans and at higher elevations in outer space" is merely a superficial point of view and conclusion that restricts itself to the level of general physics. The really revolutionary battlefield change stems from the expansion of the "non-natural space" ["feiziran kongjian" 7236 5261 3544 4500 7035]. There is no way that the electromagnetic spectrum space can be regarded as a battlespace in the former conventional sense. The electromagnetic spectrum space is a different kind of battlespace that stems from technological creativity and depends on technology. In this type of "man-made space," or "technological space" [3], the concepts of length, width and height, or of land, sea, air and outer space, have all lost their significance. This is because of the special properties of electromagnetic signals whereby they can permeate and control conventional space without occupying any of this space. We can anticipate that every major alteration or extension of the battlespace of the future will depend on whether a certain kind of technological invention, or a number of technologies in combination, can create a brand new technological space. The "network space" is now drawing widespread attention among modern soldiers. Network space is a technological space that is formed by a distinctive combination of electronics technology, information technology and the application of specific designs. If one maintains that a war prosecuted in this space is still a war in which people control the outcome, then the "nanometer space" which is emerging hard on the heels of the network space bodes well for the realization of mankind's dream—a war without the direct involvement of people. Some extremely imaginative and creative soldiers are just now attempting to introduce these battlespaces, comprised of new technologies, into the warfare of the future. The time for a fundamental change in the battlefield—the arena of war—is not far off. Before very long, a network war or a nanometer war might become a reality right in our midst, a type of war that nobody even imagined in the past. It is likely to be very intense, but with practically no bloodshed. Nevertheless, it is likely to determine who is the victor and who the vanquished in an overall war. In more and more situations, this type of warfare will go along hand-in-hand with traditional warfare. The two types of battlespaces—the conventional space and the technological space—will overlap and intersect with each other, and will be mutually complementary as each develops in its own way. Thus, warfare will simultaneously evolve in the macroscopic, "mesoscopic," and microscopic spheres, as well as in various other spheres defined by their physical properties, which will all ultimately serve to make up a marvelous battlefield unprecedented in the annals of human warfare. At the same time, with the progressive breaking down of the distinction between military technology and civilian technology, and between the professional soldier and the non-professional warrior, the battlespace will overlap more and more with the non-battlespace, serving also to make the line between these two entities less and less clear. Fields that were formerly isolated from each other are being connected. Mankind is endowing virtually every space with battlefield significance. All that is needed is the ability to launch an attack in a certain place, using certain means, in order to achieve a certain goal. Thus, the battlefield is omnipresent. Just think, if it's even possible to start a war in a computer room or a stock exchange that will send an enemy country to its doom, then is there non-battlespace anywhere?

If that young lad setting out with his orders should ask today: "Where is the battlefield?" The answer would be: "Everywhere."

Who Fights?

In 1985, China implemented a "Massive Million-Troop Drawdown" in its armed forces. With this as a prelude, every major nation in the world carried out round after round of force reductions over the next dozen or so years. According to many commentators on military affairs, the main factor behind the general worldwide force reductions is that, with the conclusion of the Cold War, countries that formerly were pitted against each other are now anxious to enjoy the peace dividend. Little do these commentators realize that this factor is just the tip of the iceberg. The factors leading to armed forces reductions are by no means limited to this point. A deeper reason for the force reductions is that, as the wave of information technology (IT) warfare ["xinxihua zhanzheng" 0207 1873 0553 2069 3630] grows and grows, it would require too much of an effort and would be too grandiose to set up a large-scale professional military, cast and formed on the assembly lines of big industry and established according to the demands of mechanized warfare. Precisely for this reason, during these force reductions, some farsighted countries, rather than primarily having personnel cuts in mind, are instead putting more emphasis on raising the quality of military personnel, increasing the amount of high technology and mid-level technology in weaponry, and updating military thought and warfighting theory [4]. The era of "strong and brave soldiers who are heroic defenders of the nation" has already passed. In a world where even "nuclear warfare" will perhaps become obsolete military jargon, it is likely that a pasty-faced scholar wearing thick eyeglasses is better suited to be a modern soldier than is a strong young lowbrow with bulging biceps. The best evidence of this is perhaps a story that is circulating in Western military circles regarding a lieutenant who used a modem to bring a naval division to its knees [5]. The contrast between today's soldiers and the soldiers of earlier generations is as plain to see as the contrast which we have already noted between modern weapons and their precursors. This is because modern soldiers have gone through the severe test of an uninterrupted technological explosion throughout the entire 100 years of the twentieth century, and perhaps also because of the salutary influence of the world-wide pop culture; viz., rock and roll, discos, the World Cup, the NBA and Hollywood, etc., etc. The contrast is stark whether we are talking about physical ability or intellectual ability.

Even though the new generation of soldiers born in the '70s and '80s has been trained using the "beast barracks" style of training, popularized by West Point Military Academy, it is difficult for them to shed their gentle and frail natures rooted in the soil of contemporary society. In addition, modern weapons systems have made it possible for them to be far removed from any conventional battlefield, and they can attack the enemy from a place beyond his range of vision where they need not come face to face with the dripping blood that comes with killing. All of this has turned each and every soldier into a self-effacing gentleman who would just as soon avoid the sight of blood. The digital fighter is taking over the role formerly played by the "blood and iron" warrior—a role that, for thousands of years, has not been challenged.

Now that it has come on the stage of action and has rendered obsolete the traditional divisions of labor prevailing in a society characterized by big industry, warfare no longer is an exclusive imperial garden where professional soldiers alone can mingle. A tendency towards civilianization has begun to become evident [6]. Mao Zedong's theory concerning "every citizen a soldier" has certainly not been in any way responsible for this tendency. The current trend does not demand extensive mobilization of the people. Quite the contrary, it merely indicates that a technological elite among the citizenry have broken down the door and barged in uninvited, making it impossible for professional soldiers with their concepts of professionalized warfare to ignore challenges that are somewhat embarrassing. Who is most likely to become the leading protagonist on the terra incognita of the next war? The first challenger to have appeared, and the most famous, is the computer "hacker." This chap, who generally has not received any military training or been engaged in any military profession, can easily impair the security of an army or a nation in a major way by simply relying on his personal technical expertise. A classic example is given in the U.S. FM100-6 Information Operations regulations. In 1994, a computer hacker in England attacked the U.S. military's Rome Air Development Center in New York State, compromising the security of 30 systems. He also hacked into more than 100 other systems. The Korea Atomic Energy Research Institute (KAERI) and NASA suffered damage, among others. What astounded people was not only the scale of those affected by the attack and the magnitude of the damage, but also the fact that the hacker was actually a teenager who was merely 16 years old. Naturally, an intrusion by a teenager playing a game cannot be regarded as an act of war. The problem is, how does one know for certain which damage is the result of games and which damage is the result of warfare? Which acts are individual acts by citizens and which acts represent hostile actions by non-professional warriors, or perhaps even organized hacker warfare launched by a state? In 1994, there were 230,000 security-related intrusions into U.S. DOD networks. How many of these were organized destructive acts by non-professional warriors? Perhaps there will never be any way of knowing [7].

Just as there are all kinds of people in society, so hackers come in all shapes and colors. All types of hackers, with varying backgrounds and values, are hiding in the camouflage provided by networks: curious middle school students; online gold diggers; corporate staff members nursing a grudge; dyed-in-the-wool network terrorists; and network mercenaries. In their ideas and in their actions, these kinds of people are poles apart from each other, but they gather together in the same network world. They go about their business in accordance with their own distinctive value judgments and their own ideas of what makes sense, while some are simply confused and aimless. For these reasons, whether they are doing good or doing ill, they do not feel bound by the rules of the game that prevail in the society at large. Using computers, they may obtain information by hook or by crook from other people's accounts. They may delete someone else's precious data, that was obtained with such difficulty, as a practical joke. Or, like the legendary lone knight-errant, they may use their outstanding online technical skills to take on the evil powers that be. The Suharto government imposed a strict blockade on news about the organized aggressive actions against the ethnic Chinese living in Indonesia. The aggressive actions were first made public on the Internet by witnesses with a sense of justice. As a result, the whole world was utterly shocked and the Indonesian government and military were pushed before the bar of morality and justice. Prior to this, another group of hackers calling themselves "Milworm" put on another fine performance on the Internet. In order to protest India's nuclear tests, they penetrated the firewall of the network belonging to India's [Bhabha] Atomic Research Center (BARC), altered the home page, and downloaded 5 MB of data. These hackers could actually be considered polite. They went only to a certain point and no further, and did not give their adversary too much trouble. Aside from the direct results of this kind of action, it also has a great deal of symbolic significance: in the information age, the influence exerted by a nuclear bomb is perhaps less than the influence exerted by a hacker.

More murderous than hackers—and more of a threat in the real world—are the non-state organizations, whose very mention causes the Western world to shake in its boots. These organizations, which all have a certain military flavor to a greater or lesser degree, are generally driven by some extreme creed or cause, such as: the Islamic organizations pursuing a holy war; the Caucasian militias in the U.S.; the Japanese Aum Shinrikyo cult; and, most recently, terrorist groups like Osama bin Laden's, which blew up the U.S. embassies in Kenya and Tanzania. The various and sundry monstrous and virtually insane destructive acts by these kinds of groups are undoubtedly more likely to be the new breeding ground for contemporary wars than is the behavior of the lone-ranger hacker. Moreover, when a nation state or national armed force (which adheres to certain rules and will only use limited force to obtain a limited goal) faces off with one of these types of organizations (which never observe any rules and which are not afraid to fight an unlimited war using unlimited means), it will often prove very difficult for the nation state or national armed force to gain the upper hand.

During the 1990s, and concurrent with the series of military actions launched by non-professional warriors and non-state organizations, we began to get an inkling of a non-military type of war which is prosecuted by yet another type of non-professional warrior. This person is not a hacker in the general sense of the term, and also is not a member of a quasi-military organization. Perhaps he or she is a systems analyst or a software engineer, or a financier with a large amount of mobile capital or a stock speculator. He or she might even perhaps be a media mogul who controls a wide variety of media, a famous columnist or the host of a TV program.

His or her philosophy of life is different from that of certain blind and inhuman terrorists. Frequently, he or she has a firmly held philosophy of life and his or her faith is by no means inferior to Osama bin Laden's in terms of its fanaticism. Moreover, he or she does not lack the motivation or courage to enter a fight as necessary. Judging by this kind of standard, who can say that George Soros is not a financial terrorist?

Precisely in the same way that modern technology is changing weapons and the battlefield, it is also at the same time blurring the concept of who the war participants are. From now on, soldiers no longer have a monopoly on war.

Global terrorist activity is one of the by-products of the globalization trend that has been ushered in by technological integration. Non-professional warriors and non-state organizations are posing a greater and greater threat to sovereign nations, making these warriors and organizations more and more serious adversaries for every professional army. Compared to these adversaries, professional armies are like gigantic dinosaurs which lack strength commensurate to their size in this new age. Their adversaries, then, are rodents with great powers of survival, which can use their sharp teeth to torment the better part of the world.

What Means and Methods Are Used to Fight?

There's no getting around the opinions of the Americans when it comes to discussing what means and methods will be used to fight future wars. This is not simply because the U.S. is the latest lord of the mountain in the world. It is more because the opinions of the Americans on this question really are superior compared to the prevailing opinions among the military people of other nations. The Americans have summed up the four main forms that warfighting will take in the future as: 1) Information warfare; 2) Precision warfare [8]; 3) Joint operations [9]; and 4) Military operations other than war (MOOTW) [10]. This last sentence is a mouthful. From this sentence alone we can see the highly imaginative, and yet highly practical, approach of the Americans, and we can also gain a sound understanding of the warfare of the future as seen through the eyes of the Americans. Aside from joint operations, which evolved from traditional cooperative operations and coordinated operations, and even Air-Land operations, the other three of the four forms of warfighting can all be considered products of new military thinking. General Gordon R. Sullivan, the former Chief of Staff of the U.S. Army, maintained that information warfare will be the basic form of warfighting in future warfare. For this reason, he set up the best digitized force in the U.S. military, and in the world. Moreover, he proposed the concept of precision warfare, based on the perception that "there will be an overall swing towards information processing and stealthy long-range attacks as the main foundations of future warfare." For the Americans, the advent of new, high-tech weaponry, such as precision-guided weapons, the Global Positioning System (GPS), C4I systems and stealth airplanes, will possibly allow soldiers to dispense with the nightmare of attrition warfare. Precision warfare, which has been dubbed "non-contact attack" by the Americans, and "remote combat" by the Russians [11], is characterized by concealment, speed, accuracy, a high degree of effectiveness, and few collateral casualties. In wars of the future, where the outcome will perhaps be decided not long after the war starts, this type of tactic, which has already showed some of its effectiveness in the Gulf War, will probably be the method of choice that will be embraced most gladly by U.S. generals. However, the phrase that really demonstrates some creative wording is not "information warfare" or "precision warfare," but rather the phrase "military operations other than war." This particular concept is clearly based on the "world's interest," which the Americans are constantly invoking, and the concept implies a rash overstepping of its authority by the U.S.—a classic case of the American attitude that "I am responsible for every place under the sun." Nevertheless, such an assessment does not by any means stifle our praise of this concept because, after all, for the first time it permits a variety of measures that are needed to deal comprehensively with the problems of the 20th and 21st centuries to be put into this MOOTW box, so that soldiers are not likely to be in the dark and at a loss in the world that lies beyond the battlefield. Thus, the somewhat inferior "thought antennae" of the soldiers will be allowed to bump up against the edges of a broader concept of war. Such needed measures include peacekeeping, efforts to suppress illicit drugs, riot suppression, military aid, arms control, disaster relief, the evacuation of Chinese nationals residing abroad, and striking at terrorist activities. Contact with this broader concept of war cannot but lessen the soldiers' attachment to the MOOTW box itself. Ultimately, they will not be able to put the brand new concept of "non-military war operations" into the box. When this occurs, it will represent an understanding that has genuine revolutionary significance in terms of mankind's perception of war.

The difference between the concepts of "non-military war operations" and "military operations other than war" is far greater than a surface reading would indicate and is by no means simply a matter of changing the order of some words in a kind of word game. The latter concept, MOOTW, may be considered simply an explicit label for missions and operations by armed forces that are carried out when there is no state of war. The former concept, "non-military war operations," extends our understanding of exactly what constitutes a state of war to each and every field of human endeavor, far beyond what can be embraced by the term "military operations." This type of extension is the natural result of the fact that human beings will use every conceivable means to achieve their goals. While it seems that the Americans are in the lead in every field of military theory, they were not able to take the lead in proposing this new concept of war. However, we cannot fail to recognize that the flood of U.S.-style pragmatism around the world, and the unlimited possibilities offered by new, high technology, were nevertheless powerful forces behind the emergence of this concept.

So, which [of many kinds of unconventional] means, which seem totally unrelated to war, will ultimately become the favored minions of this new type of war—"the non-military war operation"—which is being waged with greater and greater frequency all around the world?

Trade War: If one should note that, about a dozen years ago, "trade war" was still simply a descriptive phrase, today it has really become a tool in the hands of many countries for waging non-military warfare. It can be used with particularly great skill in the hands of the Americans, who have perfected it to a fine art. Some of the means used include: the use of domestic trade law on the international stage; the arbitrary erection and dismantling of tariff barriers; the use of hastily written trade sanctions; the imposition of embargoes on exports of critical technologies; the use of the Special Section 301 law; and the application of most-favored-nation (MFN) treatment, etc., etc. Any one of these means can have a destructive effect that is equal to that of a military operation. The comprehensive eight-year embargo against Iraq that was initiated by the U.S. is the most classic textbook example in this regard.

Financial War: Now that Asians have experienced the financial crisis in Southeast Asia, no one could be more affected by "financial war" than they have been. No, they have not just been affected; they have simply been cut to the very quick! A surprise financial war attack that was deliberately planned and initiated by the owners of international mobile capital ultimately served to pin one nation after another to the ground—nations that not long ago were hailed as "little tigers" and "little dragons." Economic prosperity that once excited the constant admiration of the Western world changed to a depression, like the leaves of a tree that are blown away in a single night by the autumn wind. After just one round of fighting, the economies of a number of countries had fallen back ten years. What is more, such a defeat on the economic front precipitates a near collapse of the social and political order. The casualties resulting from the constant chaos are no less than those resulting from a regional war, and the injury done to the living social organism even exceeds the injury inflicted by a regional war. Non-state organizations, in this their first war without the use of military force, are using non-military means to engage sovereign nations. Thus, financial war is a form of non-military warfare which is just as terribly destructive as a bloody war, but in which no blood is actually shed. Financial warfare has now officially come to war's center stage—a stage that for thousands of years has been occupied only by soldiers and weapons, with blood and death everywhere. We believe that before long, "financial warfare" will undoubtedly be an entry in the various types of dictionaries of official military jargon. Moreover, when people revise the history books on twentieth-century warfare in the early 21st century, the section on financial warfare will command the reader's utmost attention [12]. The main protagonist in this section of the history book will not be a statesman or a military strategist; rather, it will be George Soros. Of course, Soros does not have an exclusive monopoly on using the financial weapon for fighting wars. Before Soros, Helmut Kohl used the deutsche mark to breach the Berlin Wall—a wall that no one had ever been able to knock down using artillery shells [13]. After Soros began his activities, Li Denghui [Li Teng-hui 2621 4098 6540] used the financial crisis in Southeast Asia to devalue the New Taiwan dollar, so as to launch an attack on the Hong Kong dollar and Hong Kong stocks, especially the "red-chip stocks." [Translator's note: "red-chip stocks" refers to stocks of companies listed on the Hong Kong stock market but controlled by mainland interests.] In addition, we have yet to mention the crowd of large and small speculators who have come en masse to this huge dinner party for money gluttons, including Morgan Stanley and Moody's, which are famous for the credit rating reports that they issue, and which point out promising targets of attack for the benefit of the big fish in the financial world [14]. These two companies are typical of those entities that participate indirectly in the great feast and reap the benefits.

In the summer of 1998, after the fighting in the financial war had been going on for a full year, the war's second round of battles began to unfold on an even more extensive battlefield, and this round of battles continues to this day. This time, it was not just the countries of Southeast Asia (which had suffered such a crushing defeat during the previous year) that were drawn into the war. Two titans were also drawn in—Japan and Russia. This resulted in making the global economic situation even more grim and difficult to control. The blinding flames even set alight the fighting duds of those who ventured to play with fire in the first place. It is reported that Soros and his "Quantum Fund" lost not less than several billion dollars in Russia and Hong Kong alone [15]. Thus we can get at least an inkling of the magnitude of financial war's destructive power. Today, when nuclear weapons have already become frightening mantelpiece decorations that are losing their real operational value with each passing day, financial war has become a "hyperstrategic" weapon that is attracting the attention of the world. This is because financial war is easily manipulated and allows for concealed actions, and is also highly destructive. By analyzing the chaos in Albania not long ago, we can clearly see the role played by various types of foundations that were set up by transnational groups and millionaires with riches rivaling the wealth of nation states. These foundations control the media, control subsidies to political organizations, and limit any resistance from the authorities, resulting in a collapse of national order and the downfall of the legally authorized government. Perhaps we could dub this type of war "foundation-style" financial war. The greater and greater frequency and intensity of this type of war, and the fact that more and more countries and non-state organizations are deliberately using it, are causes for concern and are facts that we must face squarely.

New Terror War in Contrast to Traditional Terror War: Due to the limited scale of a traditional terror war, its casualties might well be fewer than the casualties resulting from a conventional war or campaign. Nevertheless, a traditional terror war carries a stronger flavor of violence. Moreover, in terms of its operations, a traditional terror war is never bound by any of the traditional rules of the society at large. From a military stand-point, then, the traditional terror war is characterized by the use of limited resources to fight an unlimited war. This characteristic invariably puts na-tional forces in an extremely unfavorable position even before war breaks out, since national forces must always conduct themselves according to cer-tain rules and therefore are only able to use their unlimited resources to fight a limited war. This explains how a terrorist organization made up of just a few inexperienced members who are still wet behind the ears can nevertheless give a mighty country like the U.S. headaches, and also why "using a sledgehammer to kill an ant" often proves ineffective. The most recent proof is the case of the two explosions that occurred simultaneously at the U.S. embassies in Nairobi and Dar es Salaam. The advent of bin Laden-style terrorism has deepened the impression that a national force, no matter how powerful, will find it difficult to gain the upper hand in a game that has no rules. Even if a country turns itself into a terrorist ele-ment, as the Americans are now in the process of doing, it will not neces-sarily be able to achieve success.

Be that as it may, if all terrorists confined their operations simply to the traditional approach of bombings, kidnappings, assassinations, and plane hijackings, this would represent less than the maximum degree of terror. What really strikes terror into people's hearts is the rendezvous of terrorists with various types of new, high technologies that possibly will evolve into new superweapons. We already have a hint of what the future may hold—a hint that may well cause concern. When Aum Shinrikyo fol-lowers discharged "Sarin" poison gas in a Tokyo subway, the casualties re-sulting from the poison gas accounted for just a small portion of the terror. This affair put people on notice that modern biochemical technology had already forged a lethal weapon for those terrorists who would try to carry out the mass destruction of humanity [16]. In contradistinction to masked killers that rely on the indiscriminate slaughter of innocent people to pro-duce terror, the "Falange Armed Forces" [Changqiangdang Wuzhuang 7022 2847 7825 2976 5944] group in Italy is a completely different class of high-tech terrorist organization. Its goals are explicit and the means that it employs are extraordinary. It specializes in breaking into the computer networks of banks and news organizations, stealing stored data, deleting programs, and disseminating disinformation. These are classic terrorist op-erations directed against networks and the media. This type of terrorist operation uses the latest technology in the most current fields of study, and sets itself against humanity as a whole. We might well call this type of operation "new terror war."

Ecological War: Ecological war refers to a new type of non-military warfare in which modern technology is employed to influence the natural state of rivers, oceans, the crust of the earth, the polar ice sheets, the air circulating in the atmosphere, and the ozone layer. By methods such as causing earthquakes and altering precipitation patterns, the atmospheric temperature, the composition of the atmosphere, sea level height, and sunshine patterns, the earth's physical environment is damaged or an alternate local ecology is created. Perhaps before very long, a man-made El Niño or La Niña effect will become yet another kind of superweapon in the hands of certain nations and/or non-state organizations. It is more likely that a non-state organization will become the prime initiator of ecological war, because of its terrorist nature, because it feels it has no responsibility to the people or to the society at large, and because non-state organizations have consistently demonstrated that they unwilling to play by the rules of the game. Moreover, since the global ecological environment will frequently be on the borderline of catastrophe as nations strive for the most rapid development possible, there is a real danger that the slightest increase or decrease in any variable would be enough to touch off an ecological holocaust.

Aside from what we have discussed above, we can point out a number of other means and methods used to fight a non-military war, some of which already exist and some of which may exist in the future. Such means and methods include psychological warfare (spreading rumors to intimidate the enemy and break down his will); smuggling warfare (throwing markets into confusion and attacking economic order); media warfare (manipulating what people see and hear in order to lead public opinion along); drug warfare (obtaining sudden and huge illicit profits by spreading disaster in other countries); network warfare (venturing out in secret and concealing one's identity in a type of warfare that is virtually impossible to guard against); technological warfare (creating monopolies by setting standards independently); fabrication warfare (presenting a counterfeit appearance of real strength before the eyes of the enemy); resources warfare (grabbing riches by plundering stores of resources); economic aid warfare (bestowing favor in the open and contriving to control matters in secret); cultural warfare (leading cultural trends along in order to assimilate those with different views); and international law warfare (seizing the earliest opportunity to set up regulations), etc., etc. In addition, there are other types of non-military warfare which are too numerous to mention. In this age, when the plethora of new technologies can in turn give rise to a plethora of new means and methods of fighting war (not to mention the cross-combining and creative use of these means and methods), it would simply be senseless and a waste of effort to list all of the means and methods one by one. What is significant is that all of these warfighting means, along with their corresponding applications, that have entered, are entering, or will enter, the ranks of warfighting means in the service of war, have already begun to quietly change the view of warfare held by all of mankind. Faced with a nearly infinitely diverse array of options to choose from, why do people want to enmesh themselves in a web of their own making and select and use means of warfare that are limited to the realm of the force of arms and military power? Methods that are not characterized by the use of the force of arms, nor by the use of military power, nor even by the presence of casualties and bloodshed, are just as likely to facilitate the successful realization of the war's goals, if not more so. As a matter of course, this prospect has led to revision of the statement that "war is politics with bloodshed," and in turn has also led to a change in the hitherto set view that warfare prosecuted through force of arms is the ultimate means of resolving conflict. Clearly, it is precisely the diversity of the means employed that has enlarged the concept of warfare. Moreover, the enlargement of the concept of warfare has, in turn, resulted in enlargement of the realm of war-related activities. If we confine ourselves to warfare in the narrow sense on the traditional battlefield now, it will very difficult for us to regain our foothold in the future. Any war that breaks out tomorrow or further down the road will be characterized by warfare in the broad sense—a cocktail mixture of warfare prosecuted through the force of arms and warfare that is prosecuted by means other than the force of arms.

The goal of this kind of warfare will encompass more than merely "using means that involve the force of arms to force the enemy to accept one's own will." Rather, the goal should be "to use all means whatsoever—means that involve the force of arms and means that do not involve the force of arms, means that involve military power and means that do not involve military power, means that entail casualties and means that do not entail casualties—to force the enemy to serve one's own interests."

Notes

[1] For more on the close relationship between Iraq and the U.S., the reader may refer to *Desert Warrior: A Personal View of the Gulf War* by the Joint Forces Commander, Junshi Yiwen [6511 0057 6146 2429] Publishing House, p. 212. "Iraq had established extremely close relations with the United States. Iraq had received weapons and valuable intelligence regarding Iranian movements from the U.S., as well as U.S. military support for attacks on Iran's navy."

[2] An article by the then-U.S. Secretary of Defense Les Aspin entitled "On the Sea Change in the Security Environment" was published in the February 1993 issue of *The Officer* magazine, (published in the U.S.):

A Comparison of The New and the Old Security Environments

1. In Regard to the Geopolitical Environment

OLD SECURITY ENVIRONMENT	NEW SECURITY ENVIRONMENT
Bipolar (rigid)	Multipolar (complex)
Predictable	Uncertain
Communism	Nationalism and religious extremism
U.S. the number one Western power	U.S. only the number one military power
Permanent alliances	Temporary alliances
A paralyzed U.N.	A dynamic U.N.

2. In Regard to Threats Faced by the U.S

OLD SECURITY ENVIRONMENT	NEW SECURITY ENVIRONMENT
Single (Soviet)	Diverse
Threat to U.S. survival	Threat to U.S. interests
Clear	Unclear
Deterrable	Non-deterrable
Europe-centered	Other regions
High risk of escalation	Little risk of escalation
Use of strategic nuclear weapons	Terrorists using nuclear weapons
Overt	Covert

3. In Regard to the Use of Military Force

OLD SECURITY ENVIRONMENT	NEW SECURITY ENVIRONMENT
Attrition warfare	Decisive attacks on key targets
War by proxy	Direct reinforcement
Reliance primarily on high technology	Integrated use of high, medium and low technology
Forward deployed	Power projection

| Forward based | Home based |
| Host nation support | Reliance on own strength |

From the table above, one can see the sensitivity of the Americans to the changes in their security environment, and also the various types of forces and factors that are constraining and influencing the formation of the world's new setup since the conclusion of the Cold War.

[3] "Technological space" is a new concept that we are proposing in order to distinguish this type of space from physical space.

[4] According to the U.S. Department of Defense National Defense Report for fiscal year 1998, the number of U.S. military personnel has been cut by 32% since 1989. In addition, the U.S. retired a large amount of obsolete equipment, thus actually increasing combat strength to some degree even while large reductions in U.S. military personnel were being carried out. The U.S. DOD issued its *Quadrennial Defense Review* (QDR) in May of 1997. The QDR emphasized "taking the future into consideration and reforming the U.S. military." It advocated continued personnel cuts and building the U.S. military in accordance with new military affairs theories. However, it also advocated comparatively greater expenditures for the purchase of equipment.

[5] This story first appeared in the British Sunday Telegraph. According to this report, the U.S. military carried out a "Joint Warrior" exercise from Sep 18 until Sep 25, 1995, in order to test the security of its national defense electronics systems. During the exercise, an Air Force officer successfully hacked into the naval command system. (See *The Network is King* by Hu Yong [5170 3144] and *Fan Haiyan* [5400 3189 3601], Hainan Publishing House, pp. 258–259.) There are many similar stories, but there also are some military experts who believe that these are cases of "throwing up a confusing mist before someone's eyes."

[6] In their book *War and Anti-War*, Alvin and Heidi Toffler wrote: "If the tools of warfare are no longer tanks and artillery, but rather computer viruses and microrobots, then we can no longer say that nations are the only armed groups or that soldiers are the only ones in possession of the tools of war." In his article entitled "What the Revolution in Military Affairs is Bringing—The Form War Will Take in 2020," a Colonel in the Japanese Self-Defense Forces by the name of Shoichi Takama has noted that the civilianization of war will be an important characteristic of 21st century warfare.

[7] Many hackers are adopting a new tactic which might be styled "network guerrilla warfare."

[8] Precision warfare is a new form of warfighting. It came about as a result of combining increased weapons accuracy with increased battlefield transparency. (See "From Gettysburg to the Gulf and Beyond," by Colonel Richard J. Dunn III

[McNair Paper 13, 1992], quoted in *World Military Affairs Yearbook for 1997*, [1997 Nian Shijie Junshi Nianjian], published by the PLA in Chinese, pp. 294–295.)

[9]   "Joint Vision 2010," a document prepared by the [Chairman of the] U.S. Joint Chiefs of Staff/Joint Staff. See *Joint Force Quarterly*, Summer 1996.

[10] See the U.S. Army's 1993 edition of *Operations Essentials* [translator's note: this probably refers to FM 100-5, "Operations," Department of the Army, June 1993]. Consult *Army Magazine* (U.S.), June 1993.

[11] After his research on the Gulf War, the Russian tactical expert I.N. Vorobyev pointed out that remote combat is a warfighting method that has great potential. (*Military Thought*, in Russian, 1992, #11.)

[12] There was an article entitled "Financial Markets are the Biggest Threat to Peace" in the August 23, 1998, issue of the *Los Angeles Times*. The article noted: "At present, financial markets constitute the biggest threat to world peace, not terrorist training camps." (See *Reference News* [Cankao Xiaoxi 0639 5072 3194 1873], Beijing, September 7, 1998.)

[13] *Who Has Joined the Fray?—Helmut Kohl*, by Wang Jiannan [3769 0494 0589], China Broadcasting Publishing House [in Chinese], 1997, pp. 275, 232, 357.

[14] An article entitled "A New York Corporation that Affects Economies" in the July 29, 1998, issue of *The Christian Science Monitor* disclosed how Moody's credit rating reports influence and even manipulate economic trends in Italy, South Korea, Japan and Malaysia. See *Reference News*, August 20, 1998.

[15] Soros pours out all his bitterness in his book, *The Crisis of Global Capitalism*. On the basis of a ghastly account of his investments in 1998, Soros analyzes the lessons to be learned from this economic crisis.

[16] Some security experts in the U.S. have suggested to the government that it lay up large stores of antidotes, in order to guard against a surprise chemical attack by a terrorist organization.

Chapter 3

A Classic That Deviates
From the Classics

*"Did the special nature of the Gulf War . . . trigger 'a revolution
in military affairs' or not? This is ultimately a question of
perspective."—Anthony H. Cordesman, Abraham R. Wagner*

Compared to any war in history, the Gulf War can be considered a major war. More than 300 warships from six carrier groups, 4,000 aircraft, 12,000 tanks and 12,000 armored vehicles, and nearly two million soldiers from more than 30 nations took part in the war. Of the 42-day war, 38 days were air strikes, while the ground war lasted only 100 hours. The U.S.-led multinational force crushed 42 Iraqi divisions, and the Iraqi forces suffered 30,000 casualties and 80,000 prisoners; 3,847 tanks, 1,450 armored vehicles, and 2,917 artillery pieces were destroyed, while the U.S. forces only lost 184 people, but incurred the enormous cost of $61 billion. [1]

Perhaps because victory was achieved so easily, to this day there are very few people in Uncle Sam's wildly jubilant group that have accurately evaluated the significance of the war. Some hotheads used this to ceaselessly fabricate the myth that the United States was invincible, while some who could still be considered cool-headed—most of whom were commentators and generals unable to take part in "Desert Storm" in a complex and subtle frame of mind—believed that "Desert Storm" was not a typical war [2] and that a war conducted under such ideal conditions cannot serve as a model. When one listens to such talk it smacks somewhat of sour grapes. Actually, viewed from a traditional perspective, "Desert Storm" was not a classic war in the typical sense but since it was a war conducted just as the greatest revolution in military affairs in the history of man to date was arriving it cannot be measured with traditional or even outmoded standards. At a time when new warfare required a new classic, the U.S.-led allied forces created it right on time in the Gulf, and only those who were

fettered by the old conventions could not see its classic significance for future warfare. This is because the classics for future warfare can only be born
by departing from traditional models. We have no intention of helping the
Americans create a myth, but when "Desert Storm" unfolded and concluded for all to see, with its many combatant countries, enormous scale,
short duration, small number of casualties, and glorious results startling the
whole world, who could say that a classic war heralding the arrival of warfare in the age of technical integration-globalization had not opened wide
the main front door to the mysterious and strange history of warfare—even
though it was still just a classic created by U.S. technology and the U.S.
style of fighting?

When we attempt to use wars that have already occurred to discuss
what constitutes war in the age of technical integration-globalization, only
"Desert Storm" can provide ready-made examples. At present, in any sense
it is still not just the only [example], but the classic [example], and therefore it is the only apple that is worthy of our close analysis [the authors return to the analysis of analyzing an apple later in the chapter].

The "Overnight" Alliance

From Saddam's perspective, annexing Kuwait seemed more like a house-
hold matter in the extended Arab family compared to the taking of American hostages during the Iranian revolution, and besides, he had given notice ahead of time. However, he overlooked the differences between the
two. When Iran took the hostages, it was certainly a slap in the Americans'
face, but Iraq had seized the entire West by the throat. Lifelines are naturally more important than face, and the United States had no choice but to
take it seriously, while other countries which felt threatened by Iraq also
had to take it seriously. In their alliance with the United States, what most
of the Arab countries had in mind was rooting out the Islamic heresy represented by Saddam to keep him from damaging their own interests were
he to grow stronger unopposed, and it is very difficult to really say that they
wanted to extend justice to Kuwait. [3] The common concerns about their
interests enabled the United States to weave an allied network to catch Iraq
very quickly. The Western powers are already thoroughly familiar with
modern international political skills, and the anti-Iraq alliance was assem-
bled under the United Nations banner. The halo of justice successfully dis-

pelled the Arab people's religious complex, so that Saddam was playing the role of a modern-day Saladin, whose plan to launch a "holy war" against the Christians fell through. Numerous countries volunteered to be responsible nodes in this alliance network. Although they were unwilling, Germany and Japan finally seemed actually happy to open their purses, and what was more important than providing money was that neither of them lost the opportunity to send their own military personnel, thereby taking a stealthy and symbolic step toward again becoming global powers. Egypt persuaded Libya and Jordan to be neutral in the war and no longer support Iraq, so that Saddam became thoroughly isolated. Even Gorbachev, who wanted to get the Americans' support for his weak position domestically, ultimately tacitly recognized the military strikes of the multinational forces against his old ally. Even powers such as the United States must similarly rely on the support of its allies, and this support was primarily manifested in providing legitimacy for its actions and in logistical support, not in adding so many troops. The reason that President Bush's policies were able to get widespread approval from the American public was to a great extent due to the fact that he had established an international alliance, thereby getting the people to believe that this was not a case of pulling someone else's chestnuts out of the fire, and it was not just the Americans who were funding the war and preparing to have their blood spilled. They went so far as to send the VII Corps from Germany to Saudi Arabia, mobilizing 465 trains, 312 barges, and 119 fleets from four NATO countries. At the same time, Japan also provided the electronics parts urgently needed by U.S. military equipment, and this further demonstrated the increasing reliance of the United States on its allies. In the new age, "going it alone" is not only unwise, it is also not a realistic option. [4] For example, the alliance formed a kind of common need. From the Security Council's Resolution 660 calling for Iraq to withdraw from Kuwait to Resolution 678 which authorized the member countries to take any actions, international society broadly identified itself with the alliance which was temporarily cobbled together. One hundred and ten countries took part in the embargo against Iraq, and more than 30 countries took part in the use of force, including numerous Arab countries! Obviously, every country had fully estimated where its interests were prior to this action.

The full-scale intervention of the United Nations was not sufficient to make it possible for this fragile and dew-laden spider-web-like alliance, which was formed in a very short period of time, to easily withstand the impact of a war. It can be said that, as far as the politicians were concerned, the alliance was only a single high-level meeting following a careful weighing of interests, a single contract signing, or even a verbal promise via a hotline. However, for the troops carrying out the allied warfare, no detail could be overlooked. To avoid having U.S. soldiers violate Muslim commandments, in addition to stipulating that they must abide strictly by the customs of the country in which they were stationed, the U.S. military even leased a "Cunard Princess" yacht and anchored it at sea to provide Western-style amusements for the U.S. troops. To prevent the Israelis from retaliating against the "Scud" missile attacks and throwing the camp which was assaulting Iraq into disorder, the United States made a tremendous effort to provide the Israelis with air support, taking great pains to look after the alliance network.

More profoundly, the appearance of the "overnight" alliance brought an era to a close. That is, the age of fixed-form alliances which had begun with the signing of the military alliance between Germany and Austria-Hungary in 1879. Following the Cold War, the period in which alliances were formed on the basis of ideology faded away, while the approach in which alliances are built on interests rose to primacy. Under the general banner of realpolitik, in which national interests are paramount, any alliance can only be focused more nakedly on interests, and at times they don't even feel like raising the banner of morality. Without a doubt, the alliance phenomenon will continue to exist, but in more cases they will be loose and short-term interest coalitions. Which is also to say that there will no longer be any alliances where only morality, not interests, are involved. Different periods have different interests and goals, and that will be what determines whether there are alliances or not. Increasingly pragmatic and unconstrained by any moral fetters, this is the characteristic feature of modern alliances. All forces are united by a network of interests, and they may be very short-lived but extremely effective. The interest relationships of modern states, as well as among trans-national organizations and even among regional forces have thus begun to be increasingly transitory. As the rock and roll singer Cui Jian sings, "It's not that I don't understand, it is that this world is rapidly changing." Today's mode of ever-changing combinations of force, along with the age of ever-changing technological integration and globalization, has given rise to certain tacit alliances which are by no means fortuitous. Therefore, the "overnight" alliance that was formed by the Gulf War formally opened the curtain to a new alliance era.

Timely "Reorganization Act"

The supercilious Americans often engage in actions which cause them to reflect on their mistakes, and this disposition, which would seem to be a contradiction, time and again amazes those who want to witness the presumptuous Americans suffering. At the same time it also enables the Americans to time and again reap considerable benefits. It truly seems as if the Americans are always able to find the key to open the door of the next military action among the lessons of each military action. Struggles between the views and interests of factions in the armed services have been around for a long time, and this is so in every country. The competition by the various armed services in the U.S. military to protect their own interests and strive for glory is well known to all, and they are not equaled in this respect. In this regard, what leaves a particular deep impression is that sixty years ago in combat with Japan, to emphasize the roles of their own service arms, MacArthur and Nimitz each came up with a Pacific strategy. Even President Roosevelt, who was circumspect and farsighted, had trouble balancing between the two. Another thing that demonstrates this point is that the U.S. aircraft which bombed Vietnam 30 years ago actually had to listen to commands from four different headquarters at the same time, which is truly hard to believe. Up until about 15 years ago, there were separate and independent command systems and it was not clear who was in authority, and this had disastrous consequences for U.S. troops stationed in Beirut, as it led directly to approximately 200 Marines losing their lives. However, even after he was made commander-in-chief of the allied forces during "Desert Storm," the problem that was exposed in Grenada was still fresh in the memory of General Norman Schwarzkopf. When he was deputy commander of the joint task force during the "Grenada" action, each of the service arms of the U.S. forces taking part in the action went its own way. The question [raised by this action] was, during joint operations, just who listens to whose commands?

It is somewhat ironic that this problem, which had troubled the U.S. military for several decades, was not overcome by generals who had experienced extensive combat or experts who were steeped in statecraft, but was resolved by two congressmen named Goldwater and Nichols. The "DOD Reorganization Act" [5] proposed by these two, which was passed by Congress in 1986, used the legislative approach to resolve the problem of unified command of the various armed services during joint combat.

Next, there were issues left over which required a war. Neither too soon nor too late but just at this time, Saddam foolishly launched his invasion of Kuwait and this was simply a heaven-sent opportunity for the Americans who were anxious to test whether or not the "Reorganization Act" would work. In that sense, rather than saying that the "Reorganization Act" was timely, it would be better to say that the arrival of the Gulf War was timely.

Powell and Schwarzkopf were the lucky earliest beneficiaries of the "Reorganization Act" and at the same time they also became the two most powerful generals in the history of American warfare. As the Chairman of the Joint Chiefs of Staff (JCS), Powell for the first time had clearly attained the position of the President's chief military adviser, which enabled him to take orders directly from the President and the Secretary of Defense, as well as issue orders to the three services based on that; and he no longer had to serve as the coordinator for the endless wrangling that took place among the chiefs of staff of the armed services. As the battlefield commander, Schwarzkopf was spared the nagging and held the real power in his hands. As for the incessant chatter coming from the Pentagon, he was free to choose what to listen to and to do what he wanted to do with the air of a general who is outside the country and somewhat beyond the command of the monarch, while the great army swarming over the Gulf, as well as the satellites in space and the frogmen under the water, all the way to each roll-on roll-off ship, had to submit to his orders. This made it possible for him to exercise the trans-service authority granted to the commander of the joint headquarters by the "DOD Reorganization Act" without any hesitation when necessary. For example, when the front line Marine commanders urgently requested to carry out an amphibious landing on the shores of Kuwait, he looked at the overall situation and resolutely exercised his veto power, continuing to concentrate on operation "Left Hook," the well-thought-out plan he had from the start.

That a law which had not been in effect for five years could be implemented so thoroughly in a war that came along at the same time must be attributed to the contractual mentality of the people in the legal society represented by the United States. Furthermore, the new pattern of command which was derived from this became the most successful and fitting application of military command since the services were divided. Its direct result was to reduce the levels of command, implementing true entrusted command and causing the old deeply rooted tree-structure command system to start to evolve toward a network structure; and a side effect of this evolution was to enable more combat units to share first-time battlefield information. If the "Reorganization Act" is considered against the wider backdrop of the age, it is not difficult to discover that this reorganization of the U.S. military was by no means a chance coincidence, but was timely and in conformity with the natural demands the new age posed for the old military command relations, that is, by recombining the service arm authority which was originally dispersed, then on that basis generating a super-authority that overrode the authority of all the service arms and which was concentrated on certain temporary goals, it became possible to be more than equal to the task in any battlefield contest. The emergence of the "Reorganization Act" in the United States and the effects it produced in the U.S. military are food for thought, and any country which hopes to win a war in the 21st century must inevitably face the option of either "reorganizing" or being defeated. There is no other way.

Going Further Than Air-Land Battle

"Air-land battle" was originally a strategy devised by the U.S. military to stymie the enemy when dealing with the masses of Warsaw Pact tanks that could come pouring out like a flood at any time onto the plains of Europe, but the military suffered from never having a chance to show what it could do. The Gulf War provided a stage for a full performance by those in the U.S. military, who were full of creativity and bloodlust, but the actual battlefield conditions were quite a bit different from what people had envisioned beforehand. "Desert Storm" was basically an "all-air," "no-ground" campaign that lasted several dozen days, and they barely got to use "Desert Sword," which was displayed at the last moment, including that beautiful "left hook," for only 100 hours before wrapping things up in a huff. The ground war did not become the next-to-last item on the program as hoped for by the Army, but was like a concerto which winds up hastily after the first movement is played. [6] Douhet's prediction that "the battlefield in the air will be the decisive one" seems to have achieved belated confirmation. However, everything that happened in the air over the Gulf far exceeded the imagination of this proponent of achieving victory through the air. Whether in Kuwait or Iraq, none of the air combat involved gallant duels for air supremacy, but represented an integrated air campaign that blended all the combat operations, such as reconnaissance, early-warning, bombing, dogfights, communications, electronic strikes, and command and control, etc., together, and it also included the struggle for and occupation of outer space and cyberspace.

At this point, the Americans who proposed the "air-land battle" concept have already gone quite a bit further than Douhet, but even so, they will still have to wait several years before they understand that, once they resort to the theory of integrated operations in real combat, the scope will go far beyond what they initially envisioned, extending over a broad and all-inclusive range that covers the ground, sea, air, space, and cyber realms. Although it will still require some time to assimilate the results of the Gulf War, it is already destined to become the starting point for the theory of "omni-dimensional combat" proposed by the elite of the U.S. Army when they suddenly woke up.

The interesting thing is that, while one may believe that the Americans' insight came somewhat late, this actually had no effect on their early acquisition of the key to "omni-dimensional combat." This is the famous "air tasking order." [7] The "air tasking order," which ran up to 300 pages every day, was drafted jointly by the Army, the Navy, and the Air Force and enabled Schwarzkopf, the supreme commander of the allied forces who was from the Army himself, to issue commands to the entire allied air force. It was the soul of the air campaign, and every day selected the optimum strike targets for all the aircraft in keeping with the overall operational strike plan. Every day upwards of 1,000 aircraft took off from the Arabian Peninsula, Spain, England, and Turkey and, in keeping with the computer-processed "air tasking order," launched trans-service, transborder, precise and coordinated air strikes. Although in the eyes of the Navy this command program was overly "Air Force-oriented"—and because of this they even took the petty approach of stealthily keeping behind some of their aircraft so they could be put to good use when an opportunity for the Navy to shine presented itself (even though it never came)—

ultimately this program successfully organized the most massive and most complex air campaign in the history of warfare.

Not only that, but the "air tasking order" also provided a model for a kind of organizational command for all subsequent combat operations. One "order" represented an optimal scheme for combining the combat forces among the service arms, and the complexity and success of its transnational combinations was where it really shone. In this respect alone, it was already far beyond the range of what was envisioned by the architects of the "air-land battle" theory. This is to say that the U.S. soldiers unintentionally ushered the God of War into an open area in which she had never set foot.

Who is the King of Land Warfare?

Isoroku Yamamoto was doubtless the most innovative and "extraordinarily talented" military man of his age, and the use of aircraft carriers in the sneak attack on Pearl Harbor and the great victory he achieved represent the stroke of genius he left on the history of naval combat. What is hard to understand is that the same Yamamoto actually was unable to grasp the epoch-making significance of his own creative tactics. After commanding the combined fleet in dealing a severe blow to the U.S. Navy, he still held to the belief that only battleships were the main decisive force at sea, once again throwing the key that would open the door to victory and that was already in his grasp back into the vast waves of the Pacific ocean. While the first person to make a mistake can still be an object of pity, the second person to make the same mistake is simply incredibly stupid, particularly those people who make mistakes which have already been made but which they are just unable to anticipate. What is regrettable is that in the history of war there are frequent examples like this in which thinking lags behind acting. Just as with Isoroku Yamamoto at that time, although the U.S. Army used helicopters to smash the Iraqi armored and mechanized units, once the gunsmoke in the Gulf cleared it inexplicably reverted to its pre-war level of thinking, shunting aside the helicopters which by all rights should have been the new favorites in the war. It is said that during the entire ground war, other than one desperate fight put up by the "Medina" armored division of the Republican Guard when it was surrounded south of Basra by the U.S. VII Corps, there was hardly any tank warfare worthy of the name.

However, the Americans, who had clearly already used helicopters to inaugurate a new age in ground warfare, [proceeded to] increase development outlays for other weapons, including tanks, while appropriations for helicopters was the only thing cut back. Sticking to their outmoded ways, they are still treating tanks as the decisive weapon in future ground warfare. [8]

Actually, as early as the Vietnam War, helicopters had begun to display their abilities in the hands of the Americans, and soon afterward, the Soviet Union let helicopters show their exceptional skills in the hilly regions of Afghanistan, as did the British in the Falkland Islands. However, because their opponents were mainly guerrillas and non-armored infantry, it delayed the challenge that helicopters would pose to tanks a full 20 years. The Gulf War finally gave helicopters an opportunity to show what they could do. This time, not counting the helicopter units of the allied forces, the U.S. military alone deployed 1,600 helicopters of various models to the Gulf, and this enormous group of helicopters was sufficient to form one complete helicopter army. However, at this time the Americans, who had all along boasted of their innovative spirit, showed no originality at all, but just like the French who in World War II dispersed their tanks and assigned them to the infantry, they had the helicopters serve as a force attached to the armored and mechanized units and other troops. Fortunately, the helicopters, which were destined to establish their name in this war, did not allow this to mask their royal demeanor. Just as the Americans were praising the "Patriot," the F-117, the "Tomahawk" missiles, and other battlefield stars to the skies via CNN, the helicopters were unfairly given the cold shoulder (with just the "Apache," which was a favorite, getting passing marks). Other than the "Final Report to Congress" written by the Department of Defense after the war, very few people still recall that it was the helicopters, not some of the other favorite new weapons, that performed first-rate service in "Desert Storm." In the 20 minutes preceding the start of the continuous bombing, which lasted more than a month, following a ground-hugging flight of several hours, the MH-53J and AH-64 helicopters used "Hellfire" missiles to carry out advance destruction of Iraqi early-warning radar, opening a safe passage for the bomber groups and showing the incomparable penetration capabilities of helicopters. As the most flexible flying platform on the battlefield, they also undertook a large number of the supply transport, medical evacuation, search and rescue, battlefield reconnaissance, and electronic countermeasures missions, etc., and during the battle of Khafji, the main force which rapidly checked the Iraqi offensive and finally drove back the Iraqi military was again helicopters. During the war, the thing which truly left a deep impression and demonstrated the deep potential of the helicopters was "Operation Cobra." The 101st [Airborne] Division used more than 300 helicopters to perform the single most far-reaching "leapfrog" operation in the history of war, establishing the "Cobra" forward operations base more than 100 kilometers inside Iraq. Subsequently they relied on the base in cutting off the only escape route for the Iraqi military scattered behind the Euphrates River valley, as well as intercepting the Iraqi troops fleeing along the Hamal [as published] dike road. This was definitely the most deeply significant tactical operation of the ground war during the war. It proclaimed that, from this point, helicopters were perfectly capable of conducting large-scale operations independently. When the throngs of Iraqi soldiers ran from the fortifications destroyed by the helicopters and knelt to beg to surrender, they were in turn herded into a group by the helicopters just like a cattle drive on the Western plains, and the view that "only the infantry can ultimately resolve a battle" has now been radically shaken by these American "flying cowboys." Originally, however, the initial intent of the leapfrog operation by the helicopters was just to provide support for the armored units that were to handle the main offensive, but the unexpected success of the helicopter units caused the plan to fall far behind the developments in the battle situation. Because of this, Schwarzkopf had to order the VII Corps to attack 15 hours ahead of time, and although under the command of General Franks the speed of the advance of the VII Corps through the desert was far faster than that of Gudarian, who became famous at the time for launching tank blitzkriegs, he [Franks] did not win the good "blitzkrieg" reputation that the previous generation did, but actually was rebuked for "moving forward slowly, one step at a time, like an old lady." Following the war, General Franks refuted the criticism that came from the allied headquarters in Riyadh, based on the reason that the Iraqi military still had fighting capabilities. [9] In reality, however, neither the critics nor those who refuted them had grasped the essence of the problem. The reason that the mobility of the tanks under General Franks' command was criticized was precisely because of the comparison with the helicopters. To this day, there has still been no example of combat which has demonstrated that any kind of tanks can keep up with the combat pace of helicopters. Actually, this did not just involve mobility. As the former "kings of land warfare," the tanks are being challenged by the helicopters on all fronts. Compared to the tanks, which have to constantly labor to overcome the coefficient of friction of the earth's surface, the helicopters' battlespace is at treetop level, so they are totally unaffected by any surface obstacles and their excellent mobility is sufficient to cancel out the flaw of not having heavy armor. Similarly, as mobile weapons platforms, their firepower is by no means inferior to that of the tanks, and this represents the greatest crisis encountered by tanks since they ascended the stage of warfare with the nickname of "tanks." What is even tougher for the tanks is the energy required to organize a sizable tank group assault (transporting a given number of tanks to a staging area alone is a massive headache) and the risks one runs (when tanks are massed, they are extremely vulnerable to preemptive strikes by the enemy), so they really have no advantages to speak of when compared to helicopters, which are good at dispersed deployment and concentrated strikes, and which can be massed to engage in conventional warfare or dispersed to fight guerrilla warfare. In fact, tanks and helicopters are natural enemies, but the former is far from a match for the latter, and even the outmoded AH-1 "Cobra" helicopters, not to mention the AH-64 "tank-killer" helicopters, destroyed upwards of 100 tanks during the Gulf War while sustaining no casualties at all of their own. Faced with the powerful strike capabilities of the helicopters, who can still maintain that "the best weapon to deal with tanks are tanks?" [10]

We can now say that helicopters are the true tank terminators. This new star, which rose gradually over the waves of the Gulf, is in the process of achieving its own coronation through the illustrious battle achievements during the Gulf War, and there is no doubt that it is just a question of time before it drives the tank from the battlefield. It may not take very long before "winning a land battle from the air" is no longer an overdramatized slogan, and more and more ground force commanders are reaching a consensus on this point. Furthermore, the new concepts of a "flying army" and "flying ground warfare" in which the helicopter is the main battle weapon may become standard military jargon and appear in every military dictionary.

Another Player Hidden Behind the Victory

Leaving aside the point that as commander in chief of the three services Bush certainly knew the time the attack was to begin, when viewed simply in terms of the CNN television broadcasts, the whole world was the same as the U.S. president in that they saw at the same time the soul-stirring start of the war. In the information-sharing age, a president doesn't really have much more in the way of special privileges than an ordinary citizen. This is where modern warfare differs from any wars of the past, with real-time or near real-time reports turning warfare into a new program that ordinary people can monitor directly via the media, and thus the media has become an immediate and integral part of warfare, and no longer merely provides information coming from the battlefield.

Unlike a direct broadcast of a World Cup soccer match, everything that people saw, other than that which was first limited by the subjective perspective of the television reporters (the 1,300 reporters sent to the front lines were all aware of the "Revised Regulations Regarding Gulf War News Reports" that had just been issued by the Pentagon, so each person in his own mind exercised restraint about what could and could not be reported), also had to go through the security reviews at the joint news offices set up in Dhahran and Riyadh. Perhaps U.S. military circles and the media had both learned the lesson during the Vietnam War when the discord between the two was so great, but this time the news agencies and the military got along very well. There is one figure that perhaps can illustrate this issue very well. Of the more than 1,300 news items released throughout the entire period of the war, only five were sent to Washington for review, and of these four received approval within several hours, while the remaining item was canceled by the press unit itself. With the concerted assistance of the news reporters, the battlefield commanders successfully influenced the eyes and ears of the entire world, getting people to see everything that the military wanted them to see, while no one was able to see anything that they did not want people to know. The U.S. press uniformly abandoned its vaunted neutrality, enthusiastically joining the anti-Iraq camp and coordinating with the U.S. military just like an outstanding two-man comic act, quite tacitly and energetically arriving at the same script for the war, with the force of the media and that of the allied army forming a joint force regarding the attack on Iraq. [11] Not long after Iraq invaded Kuwait, reports quickly appeared in the various media that a massive U.S. force was streaming into Saudi Arabia, causing the Iraqi military on the Kuwait-Saudi Arabia border to flinch and quietly creating the momentum for a "hobbling" operation. The day before the start of "Desert Storm," the Western media again trumpeted the news of a U.S. carrier fleet passing through the Suez Canal, which served to confuse Saddam and have him believe that, with disaster looming, the U.S. forces had still not completed their deployment. Similarly, without the support of the embellishment by the media, none of the so-called high-tech weapons sent to be used in the Gulf War would have been as awesome as people believed. In the upwards of 98 press conferences held throughout the entire course of the war, people saw images of how the precision-guided missiles could penetrate the air vents in a building and explode, of "Patriots" intercepting "Scuds," and numerous other shots that left a profound impression. All these things represented an intense visual shock to the entire world, including the Iraqis, and it was from this that the myth about the unusual powers of the U.S.-made weapons was born, and it was here that the belief was formed that "Iraq would inevitably lose, and the U.S. was bound to win." Obviously, the media helped the Americans enormously. We might as well say that, intentionally or otherwise, the U.S. military and the Western media joined hands to form a noose to hang Saddam's Iraq from the gallows. In the "Operational Outline" that was revised after the war, the Americans took pains to suggest that "the force of the media reports was able to have a dramatic effect on the strategic direction and the scope of the military operations," while the newly drafted field manual FM100-6 (Information Operations) goes even farther in using the example of the media war during the Gulf War. It would appear that, in all future wars, in addition to the basic method of military strikes, the force of the media will increasingly be another player in the war and will play a role comparable to that of military strikes in promoting the course of the war. Unlike battlefield propaganda, which has an excessively subjective tinge and is easily rejected by an opponent or neutral individuals, because it is cleverly cloaked as objective reporting the media has a quiet impact that is hard to gauge. In the Gulf, in the same manner that the U.S.-led allied forces deprived Iraq of its right to speak militarily, the powerful Western media deprived it politically of its right to speak, to defend itself, and even of its right to sympathy and support, and compared to the weak voice of Iraqi propaganda, which portrayed Bush as the "great Satan" who was wicked beyond redemption, the image of Saddam as a war-crazed aggressor was played up in a much more convincing fashion. It was precisely the lopsided media force together with the lopsided military force that dealt a vicious one-two blow to Iraq on the battlefield and morally, and this sealed Saddam's defeat.

However, the effects of the media have always been a two-edged sword. This means that, while it is directed at the enemy, at the same time on another front it can similarly be a sharp sword directed at oneself. Based on information that was disclosed following the war, the reason that the ground war abruptly came to a halt after 100 hours was actually because Bush, influenced by a hasty assessment of the course of the war that was issued on television by a battlefield news release officer, later came to a similarly hasty decision of his own, "dramatically shortening the time from strategic decision-making to concluding the war." [12] As a result, Saddam, whose days were numbered, escaped certain death, and it also left a string of "desert thunder" operations, which were ultimately duds, for Clinton, who came to power later. The impact of the media on warfare is becoming increasingly widespread and increasingly direct, to the point where even major decisions by the president of a superpower such as this one involving the cessation of hostilities are to a very great extent rooted in the reaction to a single television program. From this, one can perceive a bit of the significance that the media carries in social life today. One can say entirely without exaggeration that an uncrowned king has now become the major force to win any battle. After "Desert Storm" swept over the Gulf, no longer would it be possible to rely on military force alone without the involvement of the media to achieve victory in a war.

An Apple With Numerous Sections

As a war characterized by the integration of technology that concluded the old era and inaugurated the new one, "Desert Storm" is a classic war that can provide all-encompassing inspiration to those in the military in every country. Any person who enjoys delving into military issues can invariably draw some enlightenment or lessons from this war, regardless of which corner of the war one focuses on. Based on that, we are terming this war, which has multiple meanings with regard to its experiences and lessons, a multi-section apple. Furthermore, the sectional views of this apple are far from being limited to those that we have already discussed, and it is only necessary for one to approach it with a well-honed intellect to have an unexpected sectional view appear before one's eyes at any moment.

When President Bush spoke with righteous indignation to the United States and the whole world about the moral responsibility being undertaken for Kuwait, no responsible economist could have predicted that, to provide for the military outlays of this war, the United States would propose a typical A-A "shared responsibility" program, thereby launching a new form for sharing the costs of international war—fighting together and splitting the bill. Even if you aren't a businessman, you have to admire this kind of Wall Street spirit. [13]

Psychological warfare is really not a new tactic, but what was novel about the psychological warfare in "Desert Storm" was its creativity. After dropping an extremely powerful bomb, they would then have the airplanes drop propaganda leaflets, warning the Iraqi soldiers several kilometers away who were quaking in their boots from the bombing that the next bomb would be their turn! This move alone was sufficient to cause the Iraqi units which were organized in divisions to collapse. In the prisoner of war camp, one Iraqi division commander admitted that the impact of the psychological war on Iraqi morale was second only to the bombing by the allied forces. [14]

When the war began, the A-10 was viewed by the Americans as an outmoded ground attack aircraft, but after forming what was dubbed a "lethal union" with the "Apache" helicopter, by eliminating Iraqi tanks on a large scale it staved off its own elimination, reaching the point where it became one of the myriad dazzling stars in the air over the Gulf. By matching a weapon that was far from advanced with other weapons, they actually achieved miraculous results like this, and the design and use of these weapons can be an inspiration that is hard to express in a few words. With regard to General McPeak, who was hastily given the job of the Air Force chief of staff not long before the war started, the toothmarks he left in "this apple" were during the war, when he was able to achieve his dream of breaking down the barriers between the strategic and tactical air forces and establish mixed air force wings, as well as his use of the "subtract seven and add four" approach following the war to bring about the most richly original reform of the Air Force command structure in its history. That is, following the elimination of seven Air Force commands, including the strategic, tactical, transport, logistics, systems, communications, and security commands, he organized them into the four air combat, mobility, materiel and intelligence commands. [15] It is hard to imagine how General Mc-Peak's colleagues would have taken such a bold innovation had there been no Gulf War. [16] However, those of us who were outsiders during the Gulf War have no way of achieving enlightenment and lessons from it, et cetera, et cetera.

If we pursue this to the limit, we will see that there are even more aspects to this apple, but not all of them are by any means things that can be pointed out or circled everywhere. To tell the truth, its flaws and questionable aspects are nearly as numerous as its strengths, but nonetheless this cannot cause us to treat it with the slightest contempt. Although this was a war that is rich with implications, it still cannot be treated as the encyclopedia of modern warfare, at least it does not provide us with any completely ready-made answers regarding future warfare. However, after all, it does represent the first and most concentrated use of a large number of new and advanced weapons since their appearance, as well as a testing ground for the revolution in military affairs triggered by this, and this point is sufficient to earn it the position of a classic in the history of warfare, as well as providing a completely new hotbed for our budding thoughts.

Notes

[1]   See "The Gulf War—Final Report of the Department of Defense to Congress," "Defense in the New Age: Experiences and Lessons from the Gulf War," and other research reports.

[2]   The first chapter ("A Unique War") in the research report *Military Experiences and Lessons of the Gulf War* put out by the U.S. Center for Strategic and International Studies holds that "Actually, the uniqueness of the Gulf War to a very great extent keeps us from being able to draw lessons and experiences from it . . . in fact, just how much in the way of important, long-term experiences and lessons can be drawn from the Gulf War is a major issue." (*The Gulf War*, Vol. 2, Military Science Publishing House, 1992 internal publication, p 155) Following the Gulf War, people in the Chinese military, who had been shaken intensely, from the very beginning accepted the views of Western military circles almost completely, and at this point there are quite a few of them who are beginning to rethink the lessons and experiences of the Gulf War. (Conmilit, Nov. 1998, No. 262)

[3] The anti-Saddam alliance in the Arab world was centered around Saudi Arabia, Egypt, and Syria. According to General Khalid, who was a commander of the allied forces in "Desert Storm," Iraq posed an enormous threat to them, so "we have no other choice but to ask for the assistance of friendly forces, particularly the United States." (see *Desert Warrior*, Military Translations Publishing House, p. 227) The Americans also took the alliance very seriously. For details, see "Attachments to the Final Report of the Department of Defense to Congress," No 9, "Alliance Construction, Coordination, and Combat".

[4] Chapter 2 ("U.S. Military Reliance") of the research report *Military Experiences and Lessons of the Gulf War* put out by the U.S. Center for Strategic and International Studies points out that "this war demonstrated without a doubt that, whether with regard to politics or logistical support, the U.S. military must rely on friendly states and allies. Without the considerable help of other countries, the United States has no way to carry out any major emergency operation. Other than in small operations, the option of 'going it alone' is basically unworkable, and all diplomatic and defense policy decisions must be based on this understanding." (Ibid.)

[5] In the research report on the Gulf War done for the House of Representatives by L. Aspin and W. Dickinson, there is high praise for the "Goldwater - Nichols DOD Reorganization Act," writing that "the Goldwater - Nichols DOD Reorganization Act ensured that the three military services would pull together to fight the same war." The report also quoted Secretary of Defense Cheney, saying that the said act "is the legislation with the most far-reaching impact on the Department of Defense since the 'National Security Act.'" The generals in the military also had high praise for it, with Navy Admiral Owens, who was formerly vice chairman of the Joint Chiefs of Staff terming the "Goldwater - Nichols DOD Reorganization Act" "one of the three great revolutions in military affairs in the United States," and "this act stipulated that in all conflicts, the fight would be conducted using a joint force, and it also clarified that chiefs of staff of the services are no longer combat commanders. The combat commanders are the five theater commanders in chief." (Journal of the National Defense University, No. 11, 1998, pp. 46–47; Conmilit, No. 12, 1998, p. 24).

[6] General Merrill McPeak, who was Air Force chief of staff during the Gulf War, stated that this was "a war which involved the massive use of air power and a victory achieved by the U.S. and multinational air force units," and "it was also the first war in history in which air power was used to defeat ground forces" (Air Force Journal (U.S.), May 1991). In a statement prior to the war, his predecessor Michael J. Dugan noted that "the only way to avoid much bloodshed in a ground war is to use the Air Force." Although Dugan was seen to have overstepped his authority and was removed from his post, his views were not at all mistaken.

[7]   Whether it is the report from the DOD or L. Aspin's report to the House of Representatives, both give a high assessment of the "air tasking order," holding that "the air tasking order orchestrated a precisely-planned, integrated air battle."

[8]   According to predictions by Russian and Western military specialists, "today, the lifespan of a tank as an individual target on the battlefield does not exceed 2–3 minutes, and its lifespan in the open as part of a battalion/company formation is 30–50 minutes." This kind of estimate by the experts notwithstanding, most countries still have tanks serving as a main weapon (*Soldier* (Russia), No. 2, 1996). In an article entitled "The Future of Armored Warfare," Ralph Peter states that " 'Flying tanks' are something that people have wanted for a long time, but when one considers the rational use of fuel and the physical and psychological factors during battle, the future need is still for ground systems. Seeing that attack helicopters are already a concentration of the various features that we envisioned for flying tanks, we believe that attack helicopters can complement armored vehicles, but cannot replace them." (*Parameters*, Fall 1997).

[9]   *Into the Storm: A Study in Command* is the book that General Franks wrote after retiring. In it he mentions that the speed with which the VII Corps crossed the desert was not a mistake, and that the criticism from Riyadh was unreasonable. (See *Army Times* (U.S.), 18 August 1997.)

[10] See "Appendix to the Final Report of the Department of Defense to Congress," p. 522.

[11] See "Appendix to the Final Report of the Department of Defense to Congress," Section 19, "News Reports."

[12] U.S. Army Field Manual FM100-6, Information Operations, discloses the details of this dramatic event (See pp. 68–69). The television news reports on the "expressway of death" also had an effect on the overly-early conclusion of the war. (*Joint Force Quarterly*, Fall-Winter edition, 1997–98).

[13] Section 16 of the "Appendix to the Final Report of the Department of Defense to Congress" has a special discussion of the issue of "shared responsibility." Contrary to the general belief, the main reason for the U.S. to get their allies to share the costs of the war was not the economic factor, but rather political considerations. In *21st Century Rivalries*, Lester Thurow notes that, with regard to the $61 billion that the war cost, "compared to its annual GDP of six trillion dollars, this expense was hardly worth mentioning. The reason that they wanted those countries which did not send combat personnel to the war to provide fiscal assistance was entirely to convince the U.S. public that the war was not America's alone, but was a joint operation."

[14] In the magazine *Special Operations*, Major Jake Sam [as published] reviews the circumstances of the psychological warfare conducted by the 4th Psyops Group

during the Gulf War. (See *Special Operations*, October 1992). In the December 1991 issue of the U.S. military's *Journal of Eastern Europe and Middle Eastern Military Affairs* there is also an article devoted to psychological warfare during the Gulf War.

[15]   Air Force chief of staff McPeak advocated the use of "mixed wings" made up of several kinds of aircraft to replace the wings made up of just one kind of aircraft. He said that "if we were to do something else in Saudi Arabia today, we would no longer use wings outfitted with 72 F-16s, but rather a wing made up of some attack airplanes, air defense fighters, jamming aircraft flying outside the air defense zone, "Wild Weasels," and refueling aircraft, etc. . . . This tactic may be of use when an armed conflict breaks out in some region of the world." (Air Force (U.S. journal), February 1991.

[16]   Secretary of the Air Force Donald Rice held that "the Gulf War explained this point (experience) very thoroughly: Air power can make the greatest contribution during the unified and integrated planning and implementation of combat operations." General Michael Lowe [as published], commander of the Tactical Air Command, pointed out that "using various terminology such as 'strategy' and 'tactics' to limit the types and missions of aircraft is impeding the efforts to develop air power, and at this point, we must carry out organizational and structural reforms." (See Air Force Manual AFM1-1 Basic Aerospace Theories of the U.S. Air Force, p. 329, footnote 8). Deputy Chief of Staff for programs and operations Jenny V. Adams [as published] believes that the lesson to be drawn from the Gulf War is "to modify, not review, our combat regulations." USAF Deputy Chief of Staff for logistics and engineering Henry Weiqiliao [as published] also approves of carrying out reforms to reduce the weak links in the support area. See *Jane's Defense Weekly*, 9 March 1991.

Chapter 4

What Do Americans Gain By Touching the Elephant?

"Aerial combat was the decisive factor for victory in the war against Iraq. . . .
High technology weapons were effectively used, and not only were they
the key reason that air and ground troops demonstrated remarkably in
combat, they also were the key reason United Nations forces were
able keep their casualties and fatalities so low.—L. Aspin

The Gulf War has been the United States military's biggest war catch in the past few decades. When the war had just ended, the American military, members of Congress, and various civic organizations began to carry out a detailed examination of this catch from different points of view. From each of the reports submitted by them and each of the steps subsequently taken by the American military, the tremendous achievements of this examination can be seen. These achievements, moreover, are all extremely valuable to armies and military personnel throughout the world, and there must be no delay in looking at them. Because the nationalistic instincts of the Americans I especially admire are particularly prominent in the long-standing sectarianism that exists among the military services, theoretical blind spots and thought errors are bound to occur in the research, to the extent that a grand warfare investigation has been turned into a blind person trying to size up an elephant. This is a topic that requires our clear re-examination and should not be treated as an excuse to deny its value. But what is it, after all, that Americans want to feel on this big beast? Let's first take a look at it.

The Hand Extended Under the Military Fence
[Each Armed Service Views War Differently]

The fence erected between the U.S. Army and the Navy since the time of the Civil War not only could not be eliminated after the birth of the U.S. Air Force, it instead became the fence separating the three branches of the military. It became the historical chronic disease giving headaches to the President and the Pentagon. Even though there was an effective "reorganization method" during the Gulf War, it was not so much a clever way for getting to the root of the problem as it was an expedient measure for bringing about a temporary solution in light of this invisible obstacle. As soon as things had settled down and all the troops had returned home, the doors were closed as before and everyone went their own way. Nevertheless, the high-ranking officers at the head of each of the three military branches are certainly not a mediocre generation of stupidly unchanging leaders. The course and outcome expected from the Gulf War at the time when it shocked the whole world also deeply shook these "Desert Storm" policymakers. The dumbfounded feelings of having lost an adversary that came as a result of the dissolution of the Soviet Union along with the renewed motivation to establish the United States at the forefront of the new world order made these leaders clearly realize the urgency with which they must reform the armed forces even though they still had no intention of abandoning their prejudices. In view of each of the successive military combat regulations in the 1990s, its starting points have without exception been established on the basis of the many fresh experiences and lessons gained in the Gulf War. Just as "in the eyes of a thousand people, there are a thousand views," what unfolded in the eyes of the three branches of the U.S. military were three different Gulf Wars. In this war, which not only was the last war of old times, but also the inaugural war of modern times, each of the three branches stuck to its own arguments and made every effort to find the evidence most advantageous to its respective branch, hardly realizing that the hand outstretched from behind the military wall could not possibly make heads or tails of such a big elephant as the Gulf War.

General Sullivan felt what may have been an inflexible elephant's leg. Though in the eyes of this officer, who at the time of the Gulf War was Assistant Army Chief of Staff and became Chief of Staff only after the war had been over for a few months, the U.S. Army's show was not unremarkable during "Desert Storm," but it certainly could not be called outstanding. Especially when compared with the 38 days of wanton and indiscriminate bombing by the Air Force, four days of a ground warfare clean sweep were unable to bring long expected glory to his armed forces. As someone who intimately knows each key link of the Army, he understood better than anyone wherein lay the crux of these age-old armed services in this landmark war. Even though the U.S. Army's prestige was at its apex when he took his position in "Desert Storm," it turned into an even stronger military force with no one to battle because the Soviet Army had declined and the facts were known. He still farsightedly conveyed, however, prophetic concern for the common people. His greatest concern was that after the tension of the Cold War had suddenly relaxed, the Army structure would exhibit signs of aging, and the politicians who were eager to take part in the dividends of peace would render his Army unable to cross the threshold of the 21st century and preserve its leading position among the armies of the world at the start of the new millennium. Its only way of reviving was to swallow some very strong medicine and carry out a complete remolding of itself. To this end, he advanced tentative plans for building a completely new "21st century Army" in which the U.S. Army would be redesigned at every segment," from the foxholes to the factories." [1] In order to reduce to the greatest possible extent the spread of the effect of bad bureaucratic practices at the various organizational levels, he initially established a "Louisiana Drill Task Force" of only 1,100 people under his direct command which used the experience and lessons drawn from the Gulf War to mold this special force often referred to as the "digitized force." Additionally, he used its successfully clever maneuverings to take the Army to the edge of informational warfare, striding to the forefront of the armed forces in one step, thus taking the Army down a road of bold innovation as well as difficult future expectations. During the entire process, what he did not make clear was that in carrying out such a completely attractive reform there still were the selfish motives of the armed forces hidden within—the size of the military expenditure pie had shrunk during the past few decades and the piece cut out for the Army was bigger than that of the other military branches. Sullivan's successor, General Reimer, also knew this path well and furthered these reforms on the basis of the blueprints drawn up by his predecessor. [2] Everyone knows that there was great expense in establishing a digitized force, but what made this more shrewd on the part of Sullivan and Reimer was that spending more money was precisely in the interest of acquiring more money. From the "21st century Army" to the "post-2010 Army" and then to the "Army of the future," it took two steps to make three flights. Using a rather convincing development objective as bait, they attracted the support of Capitol Hill and even more military expenditure to build up the Army. Regarding those politicians who were totally ignorant of military issues and who could not necessarily draw new conclusions and methods for victory in the face of the generals, they mostly feared making fools of themselves, and so none dared make irresponsible remarks to a man who might well be the next president. Actually, no matter how much hubbub the "digitized force" caused, the time when anyone will make a final conclusion on the validity of this plan is still far off. What others do not say is that it is just a standard method according to the U.S. Army, like a new weaponry purchase that goes from a proposed requirement of the military to manufacture by the industrial sector and then back to the military for testing, a process that can take as long as 10 years. However, the two rhythms that cannot work together—the "18-month rule" for computer development and the "60-day rule" for network technology—make it very difficult for the "digitized force" to finalize a technology design and establish a military force, thereby turning it into a top spun by the continually changing new technology. In the tired course of dealing with these things, not only is it not known what course to take, nothing is attempted and nothing is accomplished. [3] On this point alone, linking an armed force's fate to the popularity of a certain type of technology, a bold plan with leading characteristics, makes it difficult truly to become the only road marker guiding the Army's future development. Moreover, who now dares state with certainty that in future wars this heavy spending will not result in an electronic Maginot line that is weak because of its excessive dependence on a single technology? [4]

Regarding the Air Force, the straightforward General Dugan was relieved of his post, and the Air Force troops under the command of an Army general during the entire "Desert Storm" operation were not prevented from becoming the big winners in the Gulf War. [5] "Global presence, global power," the founding principle of the military, has for the first time withstood the test of war, and the Air Force has been a force which could by itself succeed in strategy and battle attack missions on any battle front, its position having never been as illustrious as it is now. [6] This has made the smug General McPeak and his successor determined to go even further. They feel that one victory is enough to allow them to take the leading role within the armed forces from this point on. The Air Force, which was molded 50 years ago from an appendage of the Army, is no longer ignorant—it had suddenly grown wings when it touched the elephant in the

Gulf. Even though Air Force Chief of Staff Fogleman and Army Chief of Staff Reimer were of the same mind and, having gone through the Gulf War, "the two branches of the military both had deep understanding of military wartime operations for the 21st century," "relations between the Army and the Air Force became strained when the two branches tried to work out details and uses for the lessons gained from the Gulf War." [7] The reason is very simple—neither the Air Force, whose wings were growing increasingly strong, nor the Army, which regarded itself as the number one authority under heaven, were willing to hand over the right to control operational command to the other. Those keeping to each respective stand were seemingly justified, but upon surmounting it, one would discover that it was a completely unbeneficial military struggle, with the result that each meeting of military leaders to study joint operations became a mere formality and none of the new experience obtained from the Gulf War was fully and effectively shared between them. One need only look at the successive compendia and regulations issued by the Air Force and Army following the end of the war to understand this point.

What needs to be pointed out is that after the war, what the Air Force did was of course not limited to scrambling for power and profit with the other branches of the military. The main component of "Desert Storm" was the response to the successful experience of the air attack campaigns—they reorganized all the air combat troops into mixed wings in accordance with effective models that had already been proven. They then used a method of subtracting seven and adding four to completely reorganize the entire Air Force command mechanism. They are currently in the middle of testing the formation of an Air Force expeditionary force that can reach any war zone in the world within 48 hours and maintain combat capability during the entire course of any crisis and conflict. The Air Force, which all along has demonstrated tremendous enthusiasm for electronic warfare and even information warfare, had taken the lead in establishing an Air Force information warfare center even before Sullivan established the digitized force. These actions clearly are directly related to the results of the Gulf War. What is regrettable is that such a good attempt was unable to break free of the military's boundaries with the result that the old cry for "joint military operations" was still just a slogan as before. But then all of this did not prevent the generals of the U.S. Air Force from following the example of their Army colleagues and using the positive changes within the armed forces and the positive struggle outside the armed forces as the two wheels that would advance their own branch's interests. A stagnant military with no fresh plans is one that could not steal a good portion from the pockets of the congressmen who administer military funds appropriation. In this regard, the Air Force has its own multiplication table [xiaojiujiu 1420 0046 0046] [8]. In the military's intensifying budgetary struggle, space flight weapons systems are a powerful trump card held by the Air Force. Even though the "Star Wars" system advanced by President Reagan appeared to be a bluff at the very beginning, and two presidents later it still has not developed true combat capability, the enthusiasm of Americans for establishing space combat power has never cooled. [9] Relying on this enthusiasm, many Air Force Chiefs of Staff have striven for the most possible military funding for their own armed forces. Probably only heaven knows whether American space flight power will be as General Estes said, "What space flight troops demonstrated in the Gulf War proved that they had the potential for independent service."

If the Gulf War is really seen as a big elephant, then it can be said that the U.S. Navy's front fin is hardly touching the fur of the elephant, which is just the same as saying it is not touching the elephant at all. Perhaps it is precisely because of this that the U.S. Navy's historically most painful transformation of strategic theory has begun from the homebound voyage of the proud and arrogant seamen who slid down from the cold bench of the "Gulf War." This suffering has fully tormented for a year and a half those servicemen growing gills. After that, a White Paper called "From Sea to Land" put forward by several lieutenant colonels and colonels was placed on the desk of the Naval Commander. This document clearly deviated from the creed and altogether old regulations of the U.S. Navy's spiritual mentor, Mahan. Decisive battles on the ocean striving for command of the seas must never again be treated as the Navy's eternally unchanging sacred mission. For the first time, rather, support of coastal and land-based combat would rank as its chief responsibility. This is as good as turning the long-tailed sharks cruising the deep oceans into short-mouthed crocodiles rolling about in the mire. What is even more surprising is that unorthodox opinions like these have gone so far as to obtain the joint signatures of the heads of the Navy, battle commanders, and Marine Corps commanders to become the most significant naval document since Mahan's "The Effect of Naval Power on History." Sudden bold strategic changes have provided an important turn for the better to this force which has been in search of a regenerative road against the backdrop of great change in world structure. Although the objectives that the Navy has established for itself are not as radical as those of the Army nor as ambitious as the Air Force, its transformation is obviously more fundamental and more complete. In doing its calculations, the Navy, which is not one bit inferior to the Army and the Air Force, of course wants to kill two birds with one stone in the areas of transforming itself and vying for military funding. An armed force that did not play any significant role in a major war, however, must put forward a very attractive plan and carry out the most thorough reforms if it wants to be sure to get a fixed piece of post-war benefit pie as well as ambitiously attempt to get a bigger piece. Therefore, two years after putting forward "From Sea to Land," the Navy again issued a new White Paper, "Forward Position . . . From Sea to Land" [10], and poured new hormones such as the more vigorous "Existence of the Forward Position," "Deployment of the Forward Position," "Combat of the Forward Position" into the Navy's strategy. Another two years later, Navy battle commander Admiral Boorda put forward "Naval Concepts for the Year 2020." After Boorda killed himself to redeem his soldiers' honor which he had ruined, his successor, Admiral Johnson, followed established rules and promoted the reforms begun by all his predecessors. He classified "deterrence and prevention of conflict in peacetime, and winning victory in wartime" as the three major responsibilities of the U.S. Navy in the 21st century. What never changed was that he was also the same as his predecessors in that all of the plans he proposed treated the Navy as the axis without exception. His reasoning this time is that among the many foreign combat tasks that the U.S. military shoulders, the Army needs to draw support from many areas to launch a deployment, and the Air Force is exceedingly dependent on the bases of other countries. Only the Navy possesses cruise freedom in any maritime space. Using the capability of multiple means for penetrating battle, the result naturally is that the Navy should become the core of a joint combat force. The thinking of this admiral is extremely clear. With consensus for his theory from the three military commanders and the Department of Defense, followed by logical thought, the probable outcome would be the preference of his branch in getting budgetary allocations. According to what has been divulged about the 1998 U.S. national defense budget, during the past ten years in the course of a steady trend of U.S. military spending reductions, the Navy and the Marine Corps are the two areas in the whole military that have had the least reduction in spending. The naval commanders have always gotten what they wanted. [11]

What is analyzed and outlined above is the general direction of the U.S. military since the end of the Gulf War and the current situation of fracture between the branches of the armed services. Perhaps you will be moved by all the hard work done by the U.S. military to summarize this war, and perhaps you will be influenced by the various methods adopted by the U.S. military to defend the interests of the armed services. At the same time, however, you may also have deep sympathy that so many outstanding soldiers and remarkable minds went so far as to be separated inside the military fence, pinning each other down and counteracting each other to the point that each of these armed services with strong outlooks in the end still formed an American military that had its entire pace disrupted by uncertain bugle calls.

The Illness of Extravagance, and Zero Casualties

Large-scale use of costly weapons in order to realize objectives and reduce casualties without counting costs—this kind of warfare which can only be waged by men of wealth is a game that the American military is good at. "Desert Storm" manifested once again the Americans' unlimited extravagance in war and has already become an addiction. Airplanes which cost an average of US$25 million each carried out 11,000 wanton and indiscriminate bombings in a 42-day period, destroying the general headquarters of the renewed Socialist Party with each US$1.3 million Tomahawk guided missile, taking aim at foxholes with precision guided bombs worth tens of thousands of U.S. dollars . . . even if the American generals knew as soon as they began that they need not spend so much on this unrestrained battle banquet costing US$61 billion, using such an ostentatious battle style of "attacking birds with golden bullets," their over-extravagance would still not have been prevented. An American-made bomber is like a flying mountain of gold, more costly than many of its targets. Shouldn't hitting a quite possibly insignificant target with tons of American dollars arouse people's suspicions? Aside from this, during the long duration of 161 days, more than 52,000 personnel and over 8,000,000 tons of goods and materials were brought over day and night to the front line from America and all over Europe, including thousands of sun hats long since scrapped in some warehouse and crates of American fruit rotting in Riyadh. Major General Pagonis, the commanding officer in charge of logistic support, calls such large-scale chaotic and extravagant safeguarding activities "possibly historically unheard of" naval operations. However, according to the vivid statements of the U.S. Department of Defense, this is analogous to having moved all of the living facilities of Mississippi's capital city, Jackson, to Saudi Arabia. Of all the soldiers in the world, probably only the Americans would consider this a necessary extravagance in order to win one war. [12] It is just this point that strikes people strangely. However, the Pentagon, which was completely remolded by McNamara in the spirit of commerce, all along could only estimate the innumerable costs of luxury style war. [13] Even the Armed Services Committee of the House of Representatives, an organization that frequently conducts verbal warfare with four-star generals over money, did not even utter a word regarding the astonishing expenditures of this war. In the respective investigation reports done on the Gulf War, the key effect of high-technology weaponry was given almost all equally high appraisals. Secretary of Defense Cheney said "we lead fully one generation in the area of weapon technology," and Congressman Aspin responded "the benefits demonstrated by high-tech weaponry have exceeded our most optimistic estimates." If you cannot make out the overtones of my praises and only think they are proud of the American military for having fully realized their war objectives by defeating Iraq with the aid of high-technology weapons, then you may think that this however is the typical nonsense spoken by two who have different opinions regarding the ability of technology to bring success, and you also are not yet fully aware of the meaning of American-style warfare. What you must know is that this is a nationality that has never been willing to pay the price of life and, moreover, has always vied for victory at all costs. The appearance of high-technology weaponry can now satisfy these extravagant hopes of the American people. During the Gulf War, of 500,000 troops, there were only 148 fatalities and 458 wounded. Goals that they long since only dreamt were almost realized—"no casualties." Ever since the Vietnam War, both the military and American society have been sensitized to human casualties during military operations, almost to the point of morbidity. Reducing casualties and achieving war objectives have become the two equal weights on the American military scale. These common American soldiers who should be on the battlefield have now become the most costly security in war, like precious china bowls that people are afraid to break. All of the opponents who have engaged in battle with the American military have probably mastered the secret of success—if you have no way of defeating this force, you should kill its rank and file soldiers. [14] This point, taken from the *U.S. Congressional Report*'s emphasis on "reducing casualties is the highest objective in formulating the plan," can be unequivocally confirmed. "Pursuit of zero casualties," this completely compassionate simple slogan, has actually become the principal motivating factor in creating American-style extravagant warfare. Therefore, unchecked use of stealth aircraft, precision ammunition, new tanks, and helicopters, along with long-distance attack and blanket bombing—for all of these, weapons are okay as are tricks, so that there are no dual objectives that at the same time carry contradictions—there must be victory without casualties.

Warfare framed on this basis can only be like killing a chicken with a bull knife. Its high-technology, high-investment, high-expenditure, and high-payback features make its requirements for military strategy and combat skill far lower than its requirements for the technological performance of weaponry. Even in successful wars of this dimension, there is not one outstanding battle that is laudable. Compared with the advanced technology that they possess, the American military clearly is technologically stagnant and it is not good at seizing opportunities provided by new technology for new military tactics. Aside from effective use of advanced-technological weaponry, we are not sure how much of a disparity exists between the military thought revealed in this war by Americans and other countries. The difference at least cannot be any bigger than that between their weaponry. Perhaps it is precisely because of this that this war was unable to become a masterpiece of military skill. Instead it became, to a great extent, a sumptuous international fair of high-technology weapons with the United States as the representative and, as a result, began the spread of the disease of American-style war extravagance on a global scale. At the same time as huge amounts of U.S. dollars were trampling Iraq, it also muddled soldiers all over the world for a time. As the world's leading arms dealers, Americans naturally are overjoyed. In the face of this typical war with its advanced-technology, dull warfare, and huge spending, just as with a Hollywood movie, with its simple plot, complex special effects, and identical patterns, for a long time after the war people could not understand the main threads of this complicated affair and believed that modern warfare is fought in just this way, leaving those who cannot fight such an extravagant war feeling inadequate. This is why the military forums in every country since the Gulf War are full of a faction yearning for high technology weapons and calling for high technology wars.

In discussing the talented American inventor, Thomas Edison, poet Jeffers writes, "We . . . are skilled in machinery and are infatuated with luxuries." Americans have a strong inborn penchant for these two things as well as a tendency to turn their pursuit of the highest technology and its perfection into a luxury, even including weapons and machinery. General Patton, who liked to carry ivory-handled pistols, is typical of this. This inclination makes them rigidly infatuated with and therefore have blind faith in technology and weapons, always thinking that the road to getting the upper hand with war can be found with technology and weapons. This inclination also makes them anxious at any given time that their own leading position in the realm of weaponry is wavering, and they continually alleviate these concerns by manufacturing more, newer, and more complex weapons. As a result of this attitude, when the weapons systems which are daily becoming heavier and more complicated come into conflict with the terse principles required of actual combat, they always stand on the side of the weapons. They would rather treat war as the opponent in the marathon race of military technology and are not willing to look at it more as a test of morale and courage, wisdom and strategy. They believe that as long as the Edisons of today do not sink into sleep, the gate to victory will always be open to Americans. Self-confidence such as this has made them forget one simple fact—it is not so much that war follows the fixed race course of rivalry of technology and weaponry as it is a game field with continually changing direction and many irregular factors. Whether you wear Adidas or Nike cannot guarantee you will become the winner.

It appears that Americans, however, do not plan to pay attention to this. They drew the benefit of the Gulf War's technological victory and obviously have resolutely spared no cost to safeguard their leading position in high technology. Even though the many difficulties with funding have brought them up against the embarrassment of having difficulty continuing, they have not been able to change their passion for new technology and new weapons. The detailed list of extravagant weapons constantly being drawn up by the U.S. military and approved by Congress will certainly get longer and longer [15], but the list of American soldier casualties in future wars may not necessarily be "zero" because of wishful thinking.

Group. Expeditionary Force. Integrated Force.

"What kind of army does the U.S. Army need in the 21st century?" This is a question that has puzzled the U.S. Army for the last 10 years of the 20th century. [16] During the Gulf War, the effect of the Army's mediocre show along with the high-technology weapons on the rhythm of battle formed a clear contrast. The U.S. Army, which all along has been more conservative than the Navy and the Air Force, finally became conscious of the need to work out a system for carrying out reforms. What is interesting is that the role of resistance in this instance was not the Army's upper echelon. Rather, it was the new division commanders who had just climbed up to higher positions from command levels and the new commanders who replaced them. The views of those of the "brigade faction" wearing the eagle insignia and the sign of the maple leaf, however, are in complete contradiction. They believe that it is the Army troops that have been unable to pass the test of war and therefore must undergo a major operation. The "crack troops," "model troops," and "primary brigade," these three programs, have been handed over to General Sullivan. Even though this Army Chief of Staff has admiringly embodied the third program's "new thinking for future operations," he has still not been able to persuade the majority of generals to accept it. The result has been that, after he was relieved of his office, there was a change of heart between the conservatives and the reformists and the Army made the Fourth Mechanized Unit the foundation in January 1996 to organize a new experimental brigade of 15,800 men. [17] The position of the "divisional faction" clearly prevailed. The members of the "brigade faction," however, were not willing to just let the matter drop. They staunchly believed that a "military force that is excessively massive and cumbersome will be difficult to suit to the combat requirements of the 21st century." The military force which began to be implemented during the period of short range to complex guns must be completely rescinded, and five to six thousand new-type combat troops should be substituted to form the new Army type for basic combat. In order to relieve the generals' feelings of disgust, they displayed experience in the ways of the world and retained equally high-ranking military positions as the old-style Army in the new program. [18] At just the critical moment of the incessant debate between the "divisional" and "brigade" factions, the director of the U.S. Army Battle Command Laboratory, Army Lieutenant Colonel Maigeleige [transliteration as printed 7796 2706 7191 2047] sounded another new call. In his book, "Break the Factional Position," he advocated simultaneously abandoning the systems of divisions and brigades and replacing them with 12 battle groups of about 5,000 men each. Its new position is determined by the ousted establishment's set pattern of large and small, and the human numbers of many and few. It could adopt building-block methods according to wartime needs and put into practice mission-style group organization. The reverberations that his viewpoint has brought in the Army has somewhat exceeded expectations, to the point that General Reimer has required all generals to read this book. [19] Perhaps the current Army Chief of Staff has exceptional insight and recognizes that even though the lieutenant colonel's key points may not find miracle cures for the difficult issues, they can yet be regarded as the magical cure for sloughing off the thought-cocoons of those old soldiers in general's clothes.

Originally, the concept of a "group" was certainly not new to the Army. The reform of the "five-group atomic troops" [20] in the 1950s and 1960s was generally considered to be an unsuccessfull attempt and even criticized as having been an indirect cause leading to the U.S. military's poor show in the Vietnam War. In the eyes of Maigeleige, however, a prematurely delivered child may be unable to grow to manhood. If it is said that the birth of the "group" 30 years ago was unlucky, then today it can be said that it is a good time. Modernized weaponry has been enough to make any relatively small-scale force not be inferior to previously much larger armed forces in the areas of firepower and mobility. The appearance of the C4I has especially brought armed forces which have a mutual superiority advantage to unite in battle, becoming the new growing point in fighting power. If this time still embraces the 18-type weapons-ready divisional system or brigade system, then it can truly be said that it is incompatible with present needs. However, even if military technological development is the emergence of new high technology, it also is a turning point and certainly will not automatically bring on advanced military thought and institutional establishments. One good feature hides one hundred bad—the leading position with military technology and weaponry has hidden from view this fact: The U.S. military is no different in the institutional establishment as in military ideology, and is clearly behind the advanced military technology it possesses. In this sense, using the "group" to destroy the position formed by the divisions and the brigades is the most damaging concept in the institutional establishment of the U.S. Army since the Gulf War and has represented the new thought wave of the U.S. military system establishment reform. Unlike the Army, the Air Force and the Navy do not have deep-rooted "positional" traditions. The pace of their adjustments clearly are comparatively light. The Air Force particularly made opportune use of the momentum of Desert Storm to completely eliminate the divisional system in one blow, and they took advantage of the opportunity to change all of the combat flight wings into integrated wings and took the lead in achieving the first round of system establishment reforms. After "global arrival, global power" was defined as the new objective for Air Force strategy, it continued to flap the wings of reform and began testing the plan for establishing an "Air Force Expeditionary Force" advanced by Air Force Wing Commander John Jiangpo [transliteration as printed 3068 3789]. According to this commander's idea, the so-called "Air Force Expeditionary Force" is a capable and vigorous force of 1,175 men and 34 aircraft put together to aim at striving for superiority in the air, carrying out air attacks, suppressing enemy air defense power, and air-to-air refueling, etc., that can reach a theatre of operations within 48 hours of having received the order, and that can maintain air combat capability throughout the entire course of a conflict. In this regard, it can be said that the actions of the U.S. Air Force are supersonic. They currently have established three "Air Force Expeditionary Forces" and also have completed real troop deployment. When the fourth and fifth of these forces began to be set up, its three predecessor "Air Force Expeditionary Forces" were already outstanding in such military operations as the "Southern Watch" and "Desert Thunder." [21]

Regarding the Navy, since there already has been a new strategy of "Forward Position . . . From Sea to Land," formation of an expeditionary force from a combination of the naval fleet and ground forces is logical. Unlike the Army, which is taking strides to protect against difficulties, and the Air Force, which is like a charging hurricane, the Navy is more willing to go through repeated maneuvers and actual combat in order to polish the concept of the "Naval Expeditionary Force." From [the advent] of the "Ocean Risk" of the Atlantic Ocean general headquarters, of the "Double Assault" of the European general headquarters, of the "Silent Killer" of the Pacific Ocean general headquarters, and of the ground force's "Sea Dragon" maneuver since May of 1992, to the establishment of the "Southern Watch" no-fly zone in southern Iraq, the "Vigilant Warrior" to deter Iraq, as well as the "Hope Renewal" in Somalia, Bohei's [3134 7815] "Capable Guard," and Haiti's "Preservation of Democracy"—in each of these operations the Navy has been diligently testing its new organization. [22] The mission that they stipulate for this "Naval Expeditionary Force" of one battleship group, one amphibious guard force, and Marine Corps task forces is rapid control of the seas along with combat in coastal regions. What amazes and pleasantly surprises the Navy most is that the amphibious landing equipment needed by this expeditionary force actually obtained Congressional budgetary approval. [23] The partiality that the American politicians have towards the Navy caused the Navy and especially the Marines to be treated with coldness upon their return from the Gulf War. Moreover, after establishing the new naval system establishment, they were fully confident of occupying the number one position in the American armed forces.

The institutional reforms that began after the Gulf War not only adjusted the internal structure of the U.S. military, but also gave impetus to changes in weapons development and tactics, and even had a far-reaching effect on America's national strategy. The small-scale, flexible, and quick "Expeditionary Force," not only used for military attacks but also able to carry out non-warfare tasks, has become the new style of establishment striven for by each military branch as well as a convenient and effective tool in the hands of the U.S. government. We have discovered that, because there are these highly proficient "killer mace" [sha shou jian 3010 2087 9505] forces and a dangerous, worrisome trend has even been brought about, in handling international affairs the U.S. government has become increasingly fond of using force, makes moves more quickly, and seeks revenge for the smallest grievances. These mutual moves between the armed forces and the government, military and politics, is causing the U.S. military to begin undergoing a deep yet quite possibly disastrous change from system establishment to strategic thinking. Currently, the U.S. Department of Defense is trying to set about organizing the ground, air, and sea expeditionary forces into an integrated "Allied Task Force." This is the newest move in this change. [24] It is still difficult to foresee whether this completely integrated force will drag the U.S. military and even the United States using the same special characteristics into a troublesome mire while nimbly achieving the global mission bestowed on the U.S. government.

From Joint Campaigns to Total Dimensional War—
One Step to Thorough Understanding

When we say that American military theory is behind, it is only behind relative to its advanced military technology. Compared to the servicemen of other countries, the fully technological aspect of Americans' military thinking naturally occupies an insurmountable leading position on the scale of high-tech war in hypothetical future wars. Perhaps the Soviet Arjakov [Ao'er jiakefu 1159 1422 0502 4430 1133] school of thought which was the first to advance the "new military revolution" is the only example that has come to light.

The "new military revolution" is vividly portrayed by the anvil forged in the Gulf War. Not only with the American military but also with servicemen of the whole world, these words have become a blindly ludicrous and popular slogan. It is not a matter requiring great effort due to yearning for the technology of others and following certain slogans. The only ones using a great effort are the Americans. If they want to guarantee their own leading position in a field of military reforms that has already begun and will be completed right away, then the first thing that must be resolved is to eliminate the lag that exists between U.S. military thinking and military technology. Actually, the war dust has only settled [zhan chen fu ding 2069 1057 3940 1353]. The U.S. military has not yet completed troop withdrawal from the Persian Gulf and has already begun top-to-bottom "thought exchange transfusion." This means that, after military technological reforms are initiated, they will not be able to be make up missed lessons of synchronized follow-up for military thought reform. Even though in the final analysis they are also unable to completely break away from their penchant for technology, Americans still are in this unusual encirclement from which they are unable to break free. They have achieved certain results that are equally beneficial for American service-men as well as servicemen all over the world—first is formation of the "joint campaign" concept, second is forging "total dimensional warfare" thinking.

Formulation of the "joint campaign" originally came from the Number One Joint Publication in November 1991 of the "United States Armed Forces Joint Operations" regulations issued by the U.S. Military Joint Conference. This is clearly brimming with new concepts of the Gulf War and has broken through the confines of the popular "cooperative war" and "contractual war" which are already dated, and even surpassed the "air/ground integrated battle" theory seen by Americans as the magic weapon. This regulation exposes the four key elements of the "joint campaign"—centralized command, equality of the armed forces, complete unification, and total depth while doing battle. It has made clear for the first time the command control authority of the battle zone unified commander; it has stipulated that any one military branch can take the leading battle role based on different situations; it has expanded "air/ground integrated battle" into ground, sea, air, and space integrated battle; and it has emphasized implementation of total depth while doing battle on all fronts. Under the strong impetus of the American Joint Chiefs of Staff meeting, each military branch is successively setting about formulating and unifying mutually matching military regulations in order to make public this new tactic representative of the direction of future wars. [While the services have formally accepted this new concept], in private they still constantly bear in mind the prominent core functions of their branches, and they especially hope to carry out a unification that is clearly demarcated—that is a unification that makes clear each domain and authority, including regulations, laws, and the differentiation among each other's military honors. Chairman of the Joint Chiefs of Staff Shalikashvili feels that this does not intend to indicate a compromise between each of the Chiefs of Staff. Adopting the publication called "The Plan for a Joint Force in 2010," The "Model" for Leading the United States Military to Joint Operations [25], he resolutely plays the part of a modern Moses, leading the U.S. military to dismantle the fences separating the branches of the military, and stride along the difficult path of really bringing about integrated unified operations in the midst of a twilight which brings doubt.

Even though it is in the United States, a country which easily propagates and accepts new things, the situation is still far more difficult than Shalikashvili thought. In the wake of his retirement, criticism of the "joint plan" for the U.S. military has gradually increased, and skepticism has again gained ground. The Marine Corps believes that they "must not worship the 'joint [plan]' and stifle relevant future discussions on troop organization," that "the uniformity of the joint [plan] will lead to the loss of the distinctiveness of the armed forces," and that this is mutually contrary to the American spirit of "emphasizing competition and diversification." The Air Force tactfully expressed the opinion that the "2010 unification plan must develop in practice and encourage mutual emulation between the armed services," that "in this era of change and experimentation our thinking must be flexible and cannot become rigid." [26] The views of the Navy and the Army in this regard are similar and have plenty of power to destroy Shalikashvili's painstaking efforts in an instant. It is thus evident that it is not only in Eastern reforms that the situation occurs where policies shift with a change of the person in charge. As onlookers, we of course can simply sacrifice a valuable ideology for the narrow benefit of a group. Because the essence of "joint campaigns" and "joint plans" certainly is not in the confirmation or expropriation of military advantage, rather its intention is to enable each branch of the military to achieve unification of operations within a centralized battleground space, and reduce to the greatest possible extent the negative effects of each branch going its own way. Before a way is found to truly integrate the forces, this is obviously a conceivable tactic of high order. The limitation of this valuable thinking, however, lies in that its starting point and ending point have both fallen onto the level of armed force and have been unable to expand the field of vision of "joint" to all of the realms in which humans can produce confrontational behavior. The drawback of this thinking at the very end of the 20th century, a time when an inkling of the broad sense of war has already emerged, is that it appears to attract attention to such an extent that if the concept of "total dimensional warfare" had not been set forth in the 1993 U.S. Army publication *The Essentials of War*, we would be simply astounded at the "anemic" realm of U.S. military thinking.

Following the 13th revision of this programmatic document, there was a penetrating insight into the various challenges that the U.S. military might face in the following years and for the first time a completely new concept of "non-combat military operations" was advanced. It was because of this concept that people saw the possibility of carrying out total positional warfare, and it brought the American Army to find an extremely lofty new name for its war theory—"total dimensional warfare." What is interesting is that the person in charge of revising the U.S. Army's 1993 publication of *The Essentials of War* and who displayed a fiercely innovative spirit was General Franks, the man who was criticized by people as an operational conservative when the Navy commanded the Seventh Fleet. If not for later circumstances that changed the direction of thinking of Americans, this commander of the U.S. Army Training and Doctrine Headquarters who first took his post after the war would have brought the history of American military thinking to a historical breakthrough. Although General Franks and the officers who compiled his military regulations were unable to reconcile the tremendous discrepancy between the two sentences, "implementation of centralized air, ground and sea operations supported by the entire theatre of operations" and "mobilization of all mastered methods in each possible operation, both combat and non-combat, so as to resolutely complete any mission assigned at the least price" in this publication *The Essentials of War*, they were even less able to discover that, apart from war as a military operation, there still exists the possibility for far vaster non-military war operations. However, it at least pointed out that "total dimensional warfare" should possess the special characteristics of "total depth, total height, total frontage, total time, total frequency, and multiple methods," and this precisely is the most revolutionary feature of this form of battle that has never been seen in the history of war. [27]

It is too bad that the Americans, or more specifically the American Army, discontinued this revolution too early. In one case of dissension, Holder, one-time regimental commander under General Franks, who later held the post of Combined Arms Commander of the Army Training and Doctrine Headquarters, strongly cross-examined his superior officer's idea. The then-Lieutenant General Holder already was not the out-and-out vigorous Colonel Holder on the battlefield. This time he was playing the part of the Army mouthpiece for conservative tradition. His view was that "the belief that non-combat operations has its own set of principles is not welcomed among combat troops and many commanding officers are opposed to differentiating between non-combat operations and the original meaning of military operations." After Holder's death, "the Army had formed a common consensus to handle differentiation of non-combat operations as a wrong practice." They believe that if "non-combat military operations" are written into the basic regulations, it will weaken the armed forces' trait of emphasis on military affairs and also could lead to confusion in armed forces operations. With the situation going in this direction, General Franks' revolution ended in an unavoidable miscarriage. Under the inspiration of the next commander of the Army Training and Doctrine Headquarters, General Hartzog, General Holder and the editorial group for the 1998 publication of *The Essentials of War* finally made a major amendment to the new compendium with "a single principle covering all types of the Army's military operations" as the fundamental key. Their practice is to no longer distinguish between non-combat operations and general military operations, but to differentiate battle operations into four types—attack, defense, stabilization, and support—and return the original manuscript to such responsibilities of non-combat operations as rescue and protection and reassembling the old set of combat operations in order to enable it to put centralized combat principles on the right course and altogether discard the concept of "total dimensional warfare." [28] At face value, this is a move of radical reform and simplification by simply cutting out the superfluous. In reality, however, this is an American edition of poor judgment. At the same time as the theoretical confusion brought by the unripe concept of "non-combat military operations" was eliminated, the rather valuable ideological fruits that they had accidentally picked were also abandoned on account of the newly revised compendium. It appears that in doing the one step forward, two steps back dance, all nationalities are self-taught.

Nevertheless, pointing out the U.S. Army's lack of foresight is not equivalent to saying that the "total dimensional warfare" theory cannot be criticized. Quite the opposite, there are clear flaws in this theory from both its conceptual denotation and connotation. Indeed, "total dimensional war's" understanding of battle is already much broader than any previous military theory, but as far as its innate character is concerned, it still has not escaped the "military" category. For example, the "non-military combat operations" concept we raised above is much broader in meaning than military combat operations and can at least be placed along with comparable war realms and patterns outside the field of vision of American servicemen—it is precisely this large domain that is the area for future servicemen and politicians to develop imagination and creativity—with the result that it also cannot count as truly meaning "total dimensional." Not to mention the phrase "total dimensional" in the U.S. Army, which also has not in the end reconciled how many dimensional spaces are referred to, whether it is that each [space] is an interrelated element of war or it is that there are two simultaneously. This is to say, it still has not been elaborated on and is in a state of chaos. If, however, what total dimension is referring to cannot be reconciled, then the nature of the relationship between each dimension, this original concept with its rich potential, can of course not be fully launched. Actually, there is no one who can launch a war in 360-degree three-dimensional space with time and other non-physical elements of total dimensionality added, and any particular war will always have its particular emphasis and is always launched within a limited dimension as well as terminated within a limited dimension. The only difference is that in the predictable future, military operations will never again be the entire war, rather they are one dimension within the total dimension. Even adding "non-combat military operations" as proposed by General Franks cannot count as total dimensionality. Only by adding all "non-military combat operations" aside from military operations can total dimensional war's complete significance be realized. What needs to be pointed out is that this ideology has never emerged in all of the theoretical research of the U.S. military since the Gulf War. [29] Even though these concepts of "non-combat military operations" and "total dimensional warfare" are full of original ideas and are already fairly close to a military ideological revolution that started from the military technology revolution, it can be said that it has already arrived under the last precipice on the rugged mountain path, and the mountain peak of the great revelation is still far away. Here, however, the Americans have stopped, and the American hares who have always been ahead of every other country in the world in military technology and military ideology have begun to gasp for breath. No matter that Sullivan or Franks let out "running hare" breaths in so many military theses after the Gulf War, they still cannot leave all the tortoises behind.

Perhaps now this is the time when Lieutenant Colonel Lonnie Henley [30] and these Americans who have called into question the capability of other countries' military revolutions should examine their consciences:

Why has there not been a revolution?

Notes

[1]   *The 21st Century Army* is written by Sullivan. From the time he took his post until after he left it, he has always been unabatedly enthusiastic about this issue. Even though many people within the U.S. military and the forces of other countries have equated The 21st Century Army with The Digitized Force, Sullivan certainly does not see it this way. He believes that the U.S. Army should continually promote "integration" reforms, and that The 21st Century Army should be treated more as "an attitude and a direction" rather than an "ultimate plan." "Integration of a 21st century includes such aspects as battle theory, system of organization, training, commanding officer development, equipment and soldier issues, and base facilities, etc." (*United States Military Theory*, May–June 1995) According to the general view currently held by the U.S. Army, "The 21st century force is the current Army force carrying out information-age field operations experiments, theoretical research, and equipment purchasing plans, to enable the ground combat troops to handle preparations for carrying out missions from now until 2010." (Army Training and Doctrine Headquarters Assistant Chief of Staff, Colonel Robert Jilibuer [transliteration as printed 1015 0448 1580 1422], *Armed Forces Journal*, October 1996)

[2]   General Dennis J. Reimer said, " 'The 2010 Army Concept' is also the theoretical link between 'The 21st Century Army' and 'The Army of Tomorrow'. 'The 21st Century Army' is the plan that the Army is carrying out right now . . . 'The Army of Tomorrow' is the Army's long-range plan that is currently under deliberation . . . mutual coordination between the three has determined a complete set of continuous and orderly changes, so as to guarantee that the Army can develop along a methodical direction." (See "The 2010 Army Concept" report, 1997.)

[3]   Technological renewal is a far faster phenomenon than weaponry, hiding deeper disparities: "It is easier for forerunners to fall behind." (This point can be verified from the development of the telecommunications industry and changes in computers.) This perhaps is the single most difficult disparity to bring into line for the professional military and information technology established along the lines of big industry. It is for this reason that Americans have a morbid sensitivity to the spread of all new military high technology and even new civilian technology.

[4]   There are also many people within the United States who are questioning this. Colonel Allen Campen believes that "hastily adopting new tactics that people do not fully understand and that have not been tested is risky" and "quite possibly will turn a beneficial military revolution into a gamble with national security." (*United States Signal Magazine*, July 1995)

[5]   Even though the Joint Force Air Squadron Headquarters commanded by Air Force General Charles Horner had to take orders from Schwarzkopf, in the final analysis he received the most publicity during the Gulf War.

[6]   Global Arrival, Global Power was the strategic plan of the U.S. Air Force after the Cold War, published in June 1990 in White Paper format. Six months later, the basic principle of this plan was tested and verified in the Gulf War.

[7]   See *United States Army Magazine*, December 1996, "Army and Air Force Joint War."

[8]   In 1997, the United States again proposed a new development strategy, Global Participation—The Plan for the United States Air Force in the 21st Century. "Our strategic plan can be summarized in one sentence: 'the United States Air Force will become the outstanding air and space force in the world . . . it will be a global force enabling the United States to show itself everywhere'." (See *Global Participation—The Plan for the United States Air Force in the 21st Century*)

[9]   Even though President Clinton announced the elimination of the "Star Wars" plan, in reality the United States military has never relaxed the pace of space militarization. Global participation —21st Century United States Air Force Concept especially points out that "the first step of this revolutionary change is to turn the U.S. Air Force into an air and space force, then to remold it into an air and space force." The sequence of these changes has obviously embodied the core revisions. The space flight headquarters is putting even more emphasis on the function of space flight troops (specifically see United States Military Space Flight Troops and Unified Space Flight Theory). In April 1998, the U.S. space flight headquarters issued a long-range plan, "Tentative Plan For 2020," and advanced four war concepts for military space flight—space control, global war, total force consolidation, and global cooperation. By 2020, space control must have achieved the following five objectives: ensure entry into space; keep watch over space; protect the space systems of the United States and its allies; prevent enemies from utilizing the space systems of the United States and its allies; and stop enemies from utilizing space systems. (See *Modern Military Affairs*, 1998, No. 10, pp. 10–11.)

[10] "The White Paper, 'From Sea to Land', issued in 1992 by the Navy and Navy ground forces, marks changes in the core and emphasis of strategy . . . emphasis on naval implementation of forward deployment, this is the most essential difference reflected between 'Forward Position . . . From Sea to Land' and 'From Sea to Land'." (Navy Admiral J.M. Boorda, *Marine Corps Magazine*, March 1995) This admiral also bluntly demanded the "Navy's preference in budgetary matters."

[11] See the U.S. Department of Defense's *National Defense Report* for the fiscal year 1998.

[12]   See *The Gulf War—Final Report* of the U.S. Department of Defense to Congress and Appendix 6.

[13]   McNamara, who went from president of the Ford Motor Company to head of the Department of Defense, introduced the business accounting system of private enterprise and the concept of "cost comparison" to the United States military. He has made the forces learn how to spend less money when purchasing weapons, but they have other standards for how to fight. "The Department of Defense must achieve the following objective: exchange our country's security for the least amount of risk, least amount of expenditure, and, in the event of a entering a war, the least number of casualties." (McNamara, *Looking Back on the Tragedy and the Lessons of the Vietnam War*, pp. 27–29)

[14]   Colonel Xiaochaersi Denglapu [transliteration as printed 1420 2686 1422 2448 6772 2139 2528] points out that "casualties are an effective way to weaken America's strength . . . For this reason, enemies can bring about our casualties by dashing ahead recklessly without regard to losses or by achieving a blind tactical victory." ("Analysis From the Standpoint of the Enemy 'Unification Concept for 2010'," *Joint Force Quarterly*, 1997–1998 Fall/Winter)

[15]   According to the U.S. Department of Defense's National Defense Report for the fiscal year 1997, there are 20 advanced technological items that obtained Congressional approval: "1, rapid force delivery systems; 2, precision attack multi-barrel launch systems; 3, high altitude maximum range unmanned vehicles; 4, medium altitude maximum range unmanned vehicles; 5, precision target capture signal systems; 6, cruise missile defense; 7, simulated battlefields; 8, joint counter (submarine) mines; 9, ballistic missile interception with kinetic energy weaponry; 10, advanced technology utilized to formulate a high-level joint plan; 11, battlefront understanding and data transmission; 12, anti large-scale destruction weapons; 13, air bases (ports) for the biological weapons defense; 14, advanced navigational systems; 15, combat discernment; 16, joint rear service; 17, combat vehicle survivability; 18, short life expectancy and low cost medium-scale transport helicopters; 19, semi-automatic image handling; 20, small-scale air-fired false targets."

[16]   "What Kind of Army Does the U.S. Army Need in the 21st Century?" Xiao'en Neile [transliteration as printed 5135 1869 0355 0519] in *Army Times*, October 16, 1995, reviews this issue in detail.

[17]   According to the United States *Army Times*, "After five years of analysis, study, and military internal discussion, Army authorities in the end finally formulated a new establishment for armored units and mechanized mobile units. The new plan is called 'The 21st Century Establishment'. . . . a support headquarters composed of troop units, one armored division, two mechanized mobile units, artillery units (brigade level), one aviation unit, and one unit for rear services

management and support. The entire division consists of 15,719 men (containing 417 reserve duty personnel)." The personnel putting this establishment together explain that "this newly planned establishment does not count as a revolutionary establishment . . . actually it is seen as a relatively conservative establishment." (See *Army Times*, June 22, 1998, Jimu Taisiwen [transliteration as printed 0679 1191 3141 2448 2429].)

[18] See John R Brinkerhoff, "The Brigade-based New Army," *Parameter Quarterly*, Winter 1997.

[19] For the detailed viewpoint of the book *Break Localized Fronts*, see the article by Xiao'en Neile in the *United States Army Times*, June 9, 1997.

[20] In order to suit the needs of nuclear war and to try to enable troops to carry out combat in the nuclear battlefield as well as enable survivability, in 1957 the U.S. Army reorganized the atomic divisions with the group divisions. The entire division was between 11,000 and 14,600 men, divided into five combat groups with strong motorization, and all with tactical nuclear weapons. However, this division's attack capability on a non-nuclear battlefield was relatively low.

[21] For the U.S. Air Force expeditionary force concept, see the article by Air Force Brigadier General William Looney in *Air Power Journal*, Winter 1996.

[22] Just as the Head of the Naval War Office, Kaiersuo [transliteration as printed 0418 1422 4792], and Army Commander Wangdi [transliteration as printed 5345 6611] said, under the circumstances of the continual cutting of military spending and fewer and fewer bases abroad, "the United States needs a unified combat force that is relatively small in scale but rapidly deployed and easy to assemble and train." (May 1993, *Naval Institute Journal*) For the "Naval Expeditionary Force," see *Marine Corps Magazine*, March 1995.

[23] See November 1995, *Sea Power*, "From Over the Horizon to Over the Beach": "More Than Expected Budget Funds—The U.S. Congress recently agreed to allocate funds in the fiscal year 1996 to build the seventh multi-use amphibious attack vessel, making the Navy very happy. Because of budgetary limitations, the U.S. Navy plans to wait until 2001 to apply for allocation for this ship . . . the Navy originally decided to put off requesting allocation to build the first LPD-17 amphibious dock transport until the 1998 fiscal year rather than 1996. However, What exceeded expectations was that Congress voted to approve allocation of US $974 million for this warship."

[24] In 1993, the United States Report on the Complete Investigation of Defense proposed, "The following troop 'package' is enough to handle a large-scale regional conflict: four to five Army units; four to five ground force expeditionary units; 10 Air Force combat mechanized forces; 100 Air Force heavy bombers; four to five Naval warship combat troops; special combat forces . . . other than this, we have proposed a new concept for troops abroad—'self-adapted special

establishment unified troops'. According to the requirements of the battle zone command, it is organized from specially designated Air Force troops, ground troops, and special type combat troops and Navy troops."

[25] For the "Joint Doctrine for 2010" put forward in 1996 by the United States joint military meeting, see *Joint Force Quarterly*, Summer 1996. In the Winter 1996 edition of *Joint Force Quarterly*, Naval War Commander Johnson and Air Force Chief of Staff Fogleman both expressed support for the "Joint Doctrine for 2010." Army Chief of Staff Reimer also immediately put forward the "Army Concept for 2010" in response to the "Joint Doctrine for 2010."

[26] See the article, "Reform Will Not Be Smooth Sailing," by Commander Huofuman [transliteration as printed 7202 1133 2581] in the *United States Naval Institute Journal*, January 1998.

[27] There is a detailed introduction to "Total Dimensional Warfare" in the 1997 *World Military Almanac*. (pp. 291–294)

[28] According to the article "Changes to the Newly Published Draft of 'Essentials of War'," by Xiaoen Neile in the *United States Army Times*, August 18, 1997.

[29] There probably is only the article, "A Military Theoretical Revolution: The Various Mutually Active Dimensions of War," by Antuli'ao Aiqieweiliya [transliteration as printed 1344 0956 0448 1159 1002 0434 4850 6849 0068], that has pointed out that the "various dimensions" of war should not be such things as length, breadth, and depth indicated in geometric and space theory. Instead, it is such factors that are intimately related to war as politics, society, technology, combat, and logistics. It is too bad, however, that he still centers on the military axis to look at war and has not formed a breakthrough in war denotation.

[30] At the Strategy Conference held by the United States Army War College in April 1996, Army Lieutenant Colonel Lonnie Henley wrote a paper for a report entitled "21st Century China: Strategic Partner . . . or Opponent." The conclusion was: "In at least the first 25 years of the next century, China will be unable to carry out a military revolution." (See the Foreign Military Data of the Military Science Academy Foreign Military Research Department, June 1997.)

Part Two

A Discussion of New Methods of Operation

"Therefore, soldiers do not have a constant position, water does not have a constant shape, and to be able to attain victory in response to the changes of the enemy is called miraculous."—Sun Zi

"The direction of warfare is an art similar to a physician seeing a patient."—Fu Le

The expression of "military revolution" is as fashionable as Jordan's NBA fans. Aside from the appearance of each new thing having its factors of necessity, I am afraid that even more essential is that it is related to Americans being adept at creating fashions. The Americans, who have always liked to hold a leading position in the world in terms of various questions, are very good at putting pretty packaging on each prospective thing and then afterwards dumping it on the whole world. Even though many nations have been anxious about and resisted the invasion of American culture, yet most have followed suit and completely imitated their views in terms of the issue of the military revolution. The results are not difficult to predict, and so when the Americans catch a cold, the entire world sneezes. Because Perry, the former Secretary of the Department of Defense of the United States, emphasized stealth technology and was renowned as the "father of the stealth," when answering the question, "what have been the important achievements and theoretical breakthroughs in the military revolution of the United States" that was posed by a visiting scholar from China, he answered without thinking, "it is naturally stealth and information technology." Perry's answer represented the mainstream view of American military circles—the military revolution is the revolution in military technology. From the view of those like Perry, it is only necessary to resolve the problem from the technical standpoint of allowing the soldiers in front of the mountain to know "what was in back of the mountain" and then this is equivalent to accomplishing this military revolution. [1] Observing, considering, and resolving problems from the point of view of technology is typical American thinking. Its advantages and disadvantages are both very apparent, just like the characters of Americans. This type of idea which equates the technology revolution with the military revolution was displayed through the form of the Gulf War and had a powerful impact and effect on the militaries throughout the world. There were hardly any people who were able to maintain sufficient calm and clarity within this situation, and naturally there could also not be any people who discovered that the misunderstanding begun by the Americans is now causing a misunderstanding by the entire world of a widespread global revolution. The slogan of "building the military with high technology" is like a typhoon of the Pacific Ocean, wherein it lands in more and more countries [2], and even China, which is on the western coast of the Pacific, also appears to have splashed up a reverberation during the same period.

It cannot be denied that the military technology revolution is the cornerstone of the military revolution, and yet it is unable to be viewed as the entirety of the military revolution, for at best it is the first step of this wild whirlwind entering the course. The highest embodiment and final completion of the military revolution is summed up in the revolution of military thought, for it cannot stay on this mundane level of the transformation of military technology and system formulation. The revolution in military thought is, in the final analysis, a revolution in fighting forms and methods. The revolution of military technology is fine, as is the reform of the formulated system, but their final results are based upon changes in fighting forms and methods. Only the completion of this change will be able to signify the maturation of the military revolution. [3] If the revolution of military technology is called the first stage of the military revolution, then we are now in the essentially important second stage of this revolution. Approaching the completion of the revolution of military technology is to a very large degree a foreshadowing of the beginning of the new stage, which also to a very great extent presents problems in carrying out ideological work in the first stage: while the revolution of military technology has allowed one to be able to select measures within a larger range, it has also made it so that one is threatened by these measures within the same range (this is because the monopolizing of one type of technology is far more difficult than inventing a type of technology). These threats have never been like they are today because the measures are diverse and infinitely changing, and this really gives one a feeling of seeing the enemy behind every tree. Any direction, measure, or person always possibly becomes a potential threat to the security of a nation, and aside from being able to clearly sense the existence of the threat, it is very difficult for one to be clear about the direction from which the threat is coming.

For a long time both military people and politicians have become accustomed to employing a certain mode of thinking, that is, the major factor posing a threat to national security is the military power of an enemy state or potential enemy state. However, the wars and major incidents which have occurred during the last ten years of the 20th century have provided to us in a calm and composed fashion proof that the opposite is true: military threats are already often no longer the major factors affecting national security. Even though they are the same ancient territorial disputes, nationality conflicts, religious clashes, and the delineation of spheres of power in human history, and are still the several major agents of people waging war from opposite directions, these traditional factors are increasingly becoming more intertwined with grabbing resources, contending for markets, controlling capital, trade sanctions, and other economic factors, to the extent that they are even becoming secondary to these factors. They comprise a new pattern which threatens the political, economic and military security of a nation or nations. This pattern possibly does not have the slightest military hue viewed from the outside, and thus they have been called by certain observers "secondary wars" or "analogous wars." [4] However, the destruction which they do in the areas attacked are absolutely not secondary to pure military wars. In this area, we only need mention the names of lunatics such as George Soros, bin Laden, Escobar, [Chizuo] Matsumoto, and Kevin Mitnick [5]. Perhaps people already have no way of accurately pointing out when it first began that the principal actors starting wars were no longer only those sovereign states, but Japan's Shinrikyo, the Italian Mafia, extremist Muslim terrorist organizations, the Colombian or "Golden New Moon" drug cartel, underground figures with malicious intent, financiers who control large amounts of powerful funds, as well as psychologically unbalanced individuals who are fixed on a certain target, have obstinate personalities, and stubborn characters, all of whom can possibly become the creators of a military or non-military war. The weapons used by them can be airplanes, cannons, poison gas, bombs, biochemical agents, as well as computer viruses, net browsers, and financial derivative tools. In a word, all of the new warfare methods and strategic measures which can be provided by all of the new technology may be utilized by these fanatics to carry out all forms of financial attacks, network attacks, media attacks, or terrorist attacks. Most of these attacks are not military actions, and yet they can be completely viewed as equal to warfare actions which force other nations to satisfy their own interests and demands. These have the same and even greater destructive force than military warfare, and they have already produced serious threats different from the past and in many directions for our comprehensible national security.

Given this situation, it is only necessary to broaden the view slightly, wherein we will be able to see that national security based upon regionalism is already outmoded. The major threat to national security is already far from being limited to the military aggression of hostile forces against the natural space of one's country. In terms of the extent of the drop in the national security index, when we compare Thailand and Indonesia, which for several months had currency devaluations of several tens of percentage points and economies near bankruptcy, with Iraq, which suffered the double containment of military attacks and economic boycott, I fear there was not much difference. Even the United States, which is the only superpower which has survived after the Cold War, has also realized that the strongest nation is often the one with the most enemies and the one threatened the most. In the National Defense Reports of the United States for several consecutive fiscal years, aside from listing "the strong regional nations hostile to American interests" in order of ten major threats, they also consider "terrorism, subversive activities and anarchistic conditions which threaten the stability of the federal government, threats to American prosperity and economic growth, illegal drug trade, and international crimes" as threats to the United States. As a result, they have expanded the multi-spatial search range of possible threats to security. [6] Actually, it is not only the United States but all nations which worship the view of modern sovereignty that have already unconsciously expanded the borders of security to a multiplicity of domains, including politics, economics, material resources, nationalities, religion, culture, networks, geography, environment, and outer space, etc. [7] This type of "extended domain view" is a premise for the survival and development of modern sovereign nations as well as for their striving to have influence in the world. By contrast, the view of using national defense as the main target of security for a nation actually seems a bit outmoded, and at the least is quite insufficient. Corresponding to the "extended domain view" should be the new security concept of omnibearing inclusion of national interests. What it focuses on is certainly not limited to the issue of national security but rather brings the security needs in many areas including the political security, economic security, cultural security, and information security of the nation into one's own target range. This is a "large security view" which raises the traditional territorial domain concept to the view of the interest domain of the nation.

The increased load of this type of large security view brings with it complications of the target as well as the means and methods for realizing the target. As a result, the national strategy for ensuring the realization of national security targets, namely, what is generally called grand strategy, also necessitates carrying out adjustments which go beyond military strategies and even political strategies. Such a strategy takes all things into consideration that are involved in each aspect of the security index of the interests of the entire nation, as well as superimposes political (national will, values, and cohesion) and military factors on the economy, culture, foreign relations, technology, environment, natural resources, nationalities, and other parameters before one can draw out a complete "extended domain" which superposes both national interests and national security—a large strategic situation map.

Anyone who stands in front of this situation map will suddenly have a feeling of lamenting one's smallness before the vast ocean: how can one type of uniform and singular means and method possibly be used to realize such a voluminous and expansive area, such complex and even self-conflicting interests, and such intricate and even mutually repelling targets? For example, how can the military means of "blood letting politics" spoken of by Clausewitz be used to resolve the financial crisis of Southeast Asia? Or else how can hackers who come and go like shadows on the Internet be dealt with using the same type of method? The conclusion is quite evident that only possessing a sword to deal with national security on a large visible level of security is no longer sufficient. One log cannot prop up a tottering building. The security vault of a modern national building is far from being able to be supported by the singular power of one pillar. The key to its standing erect and not collapsing lies in whether it can to a large extent form composite force in all aspects related to national interest. Moreover, given this type of composite force, it is also necessary to have this type of composite force to become the means which can be utilized for actual operations. This should be a "grand warfare method" which combines all of the dimensions and methods in the two major areas of military and non-military affairs so as to carry out warfare. This is opposite of the formula for warfare methods brought forth in past wars. As soon as this type of grand warfare method emerged, it was then necessary to bring forth a totally new form of warfare which both includes and surpasses all of the dimensions influencing national security. However, when we analyze its principle, it is not complex and is merely a simple matter of combination. "The Way produced the one, the one produced the two, the two produced the three, and the three produced the ten thousand things." Whether it is the two or the three or the ten thousand things, it is always the result of combination. With combination there is abundance, with combination there are a myriad of changes, and with combination there is diversity. Combination has nearly increased the means of modern warfare to the infinite, and it has basically changed the definition of modern warfare bestowed by those in the past: warfare carried out using modern weapons and means of operation. This means that while the increase of the measures shrinks the effects of weapons, it also amplifies the concept of modern warfare. I am afraid that most of the old aspirations of gaining victory through military means when confronted with a war, wherein the selection of means to the range of the battlefield is greatly extended, will fall into emptiness and "be marginally within the mountain" [zhi yuan shen zai ci shan zhong 0662 4878 6500 0961 2974 1472 0022]. What all those military people and politicians harboring wild ambitions of victory must do is to expand their field of vision, judge the hour and size up the situation, rely upon adopting the major warfare method, and clear away the miasma of the traditional view of war—go to the mountain and welcome the sunrise.

Notes

[1] When Senior Colonel Chen Bojiang, a research fellow at the Institute of Military Science, was visiting scholars in the United States, he visited a group of very important persons in the American military. Chen Bojiang asked Perry: "What are the most important achievements and breakthroughs that have been brought on by the American military revolution?" Perry answered: "The most important breakthrough is of course the stealth technology. It is a tremendous breakthrough. However, I want to say that in a completely different area something of equal importance is the invention of information technology. Information technology has

resolved the problem which has needed to be resolved by soldiers for several centuries, namely: what is behind the next mountain? The progress on solving this problem has been very slow for several centuries. The progress of technology has been extremely rapid over the last ten years, wherein there have been revolutionary methods for resolving this problem." (*National Defense University Journal*, 1998, No. 11, p. 44) As a professor in the College of Engineering of Stanford University, Perry is naturally more willing to observe and understand the military revolution from the technical viewpoint. He is no doubt a proponent of technology in the military revolution.

[2]   It was pointed out in the "Summary of the Military Situation" in the *1997 World Military Yearbook* that: "A special breakthrough point in the military situation in 1995–1996 was that some major nations began to stress "using high technology to build the military" within the framework of the quality building of the military. The United States used the realization of battlefield digitization as the goal to establish the policy of using high technology to build the military. Japan formulated the new self-defense troop reorganization and outfitting program and required the establishment of a "highly technological crack military force." Germany brought forth the De'erpei [transliteration as printed 1795 1422 5952] Report seeking to realize breakthroughs in eight sophisticated techniques. France proposed a new reform plan so as to raise the "technical quality" of military troops. England and Russia have also taken actions; some medium and small nations have also actually purchased advanced weapons attempting to have the technical level of the military "get in position in one step." (*1997 World Military Affairs Yearbook*, People's Liberation Army Press, 1997, p. 2)

[3]   Aside from the view which equates the military technology revolution with the military revolution, many people are even more willing to view the military revolution as the combined product of new technology, the new establishment of the military, and new military thought. For example, Steven Maizi [transliteration as printed 7796 5417] and Thomas Kaiweite [transliteration as printed 0418 4850 3676] said in their report entitled *Strategy and the Military Revolution: From Theory to Policy*: "The so-called military revolution is composed of the simultaneous and mutually promoting changes in the areas of military technology, weapon systems, combat methods and the troop organization system, wherein there is a leap (or sudden change) of the fighting efficiency of the military." (Research report of the Strategic Institute of the American Army Military College entitled *Strategy and the Military Revolution: From Theory to Policy*) It is also considered in a research report of the American Research Center for Strategy and International Issues related to the military revolution that the military revolution is the combined result of many factors. Toffler equates the military revolution with the substitution of civilization being somewhat large and impractical.

[4] See Zhao Ying's *The New View of National Security.*

[5] George Soros is a financial speculator; bin Laden is an Islamic terrorist; Escobar is a notorious distant drug smuggler; [Chizuo] Matsumoto is the founder of the heterodox "Aum Shinrikyo" in Japan; and Kevin Mitnick is the renowned computer hacker.

[6] The Secretary of Defense of the United States mentioned the various threats confronting the United States in each National Defense Report for the 1996, 1997, and 1998 fiscal years. However, this type of wide angle view is actually not a standard of observation which Americans can self-consciously maintain. In May of 1997, it was pointed out in "The Global Security Environment," the first section of the *Four-Year Defense Investigation Report* published by the Department of Defense of the United States, that the security of the United States will be facing a series of challenges. First will be the threats coming from Iraq, Iran, the Middle East, and the Korean Peninsula; second is the spread of sensory technology such as nuclear, biological and chemical weapons as well as projection technology, information warfare technology, stealth technology, etc.; third is terrorist activity, illegal drug trade, crimes by international organizations, and out-of-control immigration; fourth is the threat of large-scale antipersonnel weapons. "Nations which will be able to rival the United States will not possibly appear prior to the year 2015, and yet after 2015, there will possibly appear a regionally strong nation or a global enemy well-matched in strength. Some consider that even if the prospects of Russia and China are unforeseeable, yet it is possible that they could become this type of enemy." This report, which is a joint effort by the office of the Secretary of the Department of Defense and the Joint Chiefs of Staff, is naturally still wallowing in the so-called military threat which is half-real and half-imaginary. In analyzing the threats of the 1997 United States' National Military Strategy formed from this report, there is a special section which mentions "unknown factors" and shows that the Americans are anxious and fearful of future threats.

[7] Xiaomohan Malike [transliteration as printed 1420 5459 3352 7456 0448 0344] of Australia pointed out that the seven tendencies which will influence national security during the 21st century are: globalized economy; the globalized spread of technology; the globalized tide of democracy; polarized international politics; changes in the nature of international systems; changes in security concepts; and changes in the focal points of conflicts. The combined effects of these tendencies form the sources of the two categories of conflict threatening security in the Asian-Pacific Region. The first category is the source of traditional conflicts: the struggle for hegemony by large nations; the expansion of nationalism by successful nations; disputes over territorial and maritime rights and interests; economic competition; and the proliferation of large-scale destructive weapons. The second category is the new sources of future conflicts: nationalism (racism) in declining

nations; conflicts in cultural religious beliefs; the spread of lethal light weapons; disputes over petroleum, fishing, and water resources; the tide of refugees and population flows; ecological disasters; and terrorism. All of these pose multiple threats to nations in the 21st century. The view of this Australian regarding national security is slightly higher than that of the American officials. (See the *United States' Comparative Strategies*, 1997, No. 16, for details.)

Chapter 5

New Methodology of War Games

The great masters of warfare techniques during the 21st century will be those who employ innovative methods to recombine various capabilities so as to attain tactical, campaign and strategic goals.—Yier Tierfude

Everything is changing. We believe that the age of a revolution in operating methods, wherein all of the changes involved in the explosion of technology, the replacement of weapons, the development of security concepts, the adjustment of strategic targets, the obscurity of the boundaries of the battlefield, and the expansion of the scope and scale of non-military means and non-military personnel involved in warfare are focused on one point, has already arrived. This revolution is not seeking operating methods which coordinate with each type of change, but rather is finding a common operating method for all of these changes. In other words, finding a new methodology which uses one method to deal with the myriad changes of future wars. [1]

Flicking Away the Cover of the Clouds of War

Who has seen tomorrow's war? No one. However, its various scenes have already passed through the mouths of many prophets and have been frozen on our mental screens like a vulgar cartoon. From the strangling warfare of satellites in space orbits to the angular pursuits of nuclear submarines in the deep areas of the oceans; from the precision bombs released by stealth bombers to the cruise missiles fired from a Zeus Shield Cruiser, they cover the heavens and the earth, and they can be said to be too numerous to enumerate. The most representative of them is the description of a field maneuver exercise with troops carried out by a digitized unit of the American military at the Fort Irwin National Training Center:

With the command center's digitized units acting as the "blue troops," the computer was continuously inputting and processing information transmitted from satellites and "Joint Star" aircraft; the early warning planes monitored the entire air space; the fighter bombers guided by satellites and early warning planes used precision missiles to attack targets; the armored forces and armored helicopters alternated initiating three-dimensional attacks against the enemy; the infantry soldiers used laptop computers to receive commands and used automatic weapons fired with sighting devices carried on helmets; and the most splendid scene was actually one soldier who successively attacked five mice and led the strong fire power of his own artillery and airmen towards a group of enemy tanks on another side of the ridge. His computer screen displayed [the results]: the enemy tanks had already been hit.

Called the "21st Century Army" and "blue troops" with fully digitized equipment and conducted in the Mojave Desert, the final result of this exercise was one win, one draw, and six losses, but the "21st Century Army" and "blue troops" lost to the traditionally equipped "red troops." However, this did not prevent Secretary of Defense Cohen from announcing in a news release after the conclusion of the exercise that: I consider that you are all witnessing a military revolution here. . . . [2]

It is obvious that the military revolution referred to by Cohen is identical to the warfare understood by those prophets that we previously mentioned. The winner always likes to coast on the path of victory. Like the French military which relied upon climbing out of the trenches at Verdun to win World War One and hoped that the next war would be carried out the same as the Maginot Line, the American military which won a victory in the Gulf War also hopes to continue the "Desert Storm" type addiction during the 21st century. Although each calculation won glory like that of Schwarzkopf, all of the American generals understand that it is not possible for wars in the next century to be simple replays of the Gulf War. It was for this reason that they began to carry out replacements of the weaponry of the United States' military even before the smoke cleared, and they also made adjustments to the original combat theories and organizational system. Military people throughout the world saw the framework of the future American military and the concept of American style warfare from The Concept of Joint Forces in the Year 2010 to The Army of the Future.

Taking into consideration the loftiness of the hall, then this is quite out of the ordinary [that is, the superiority of the American military force, like a majestic hall, is overwhelming]. It was little imagined that the blind spot in the visual field of the Americans would just appear here.

To date, the trends of the development of the weaponry of the United States military, the changes in defense policies, the evolution of combat theories, the renewal of ordinances and regulations, and the views of high-level commanders are all following along quickly on one path. They affirm that military means are the final means for resolving future conflicts, and the disputes between all nations will ultimately end up with two large armies meeting on the battlefield. Given this premise, the American military is requiring itself to nearly simultaneously win wars in two battle areas, and they have done a great deal of preparation for this. [3] The problem is who is there in the Pentagon, like the former Chief of the Joint Chiefs of Staff General Bower, who so clearly recognized that the United States was focusing most of its energies in again fighting a "cold type war which would never come again" and was very possibly using its own strength in the wrong direction? [4] This is because the international trend at the end of the 20th century is clearly displayed. As practically existing, the age of wars being a matter of moving weapons and soldiers has still not been translated into history, but as a concept it has already begun to noticeably fall behind. Following the increase in the number of international treaties limiting the arms race and the proliferation of weapons, the United Nations and regional international organizations have enlarged their intervention power in local wars and regional conflicts and relatively decreased the military threat to national security; on the contrary, the springing up of large amounts of new high technology will actually greatly increase the possibility of non-military measures threatening national security, and the international community, which is at a loss of what to do upon being confronted with non-military threats with such destruction no less than that of a war, at the least lacks necessary and effective limitations. This has objectively accelerated the occurrence of non-military wars, and at the same time it has also resulted in the old concepts and systems of national security being on the brink of collapse. Aside from the increasingly intense terrorist attacks, as well as the hacker wars, financial wars and computer virus wars which will dominate the future, there are also the present various types of "new concept wars" to which it is difficult to fix a name and are already sufficient to have the security view of "resisting the enemy outside of one's national gate" become something of the past in the space of an evening.

It is not the case that American military circles have not noticed this advantage of eliminating the enemy against military and non-military threats (we have already referred above to several National Defense Reports for several fiscal years by the Defense Department of the United States), and yet they have pushed the resolution of the latter problem on to the politicians and the Central Intelligence Agency so that they have retreated from the existing all-dimensional wars, non-combatant military operations, and other new views. They have tightened up more and more so that they have shrunk into a watching tree hung full with various types of sophisticated weapon fruits waiting alone for a muddle-headed and idiotic rabbit to come and knock into it. However, after Saddam knocked himself dizzy at the bottom of this tree, who else is there who would become the second type of this rabbit?

Given their state of mind of "looking around in the dark with daggers drawn," the American soldiers who had lost their opponent due to the collapse of the former Soviet Union are vehemently searching for a reason not to allow themselves to be "unemployed." This is because from the generals to the common soldiers, from the spear of attack to the shield of defense, from major strategies to minor methods of operation, everything that the American military does is done in preparation of gaining victory in a major war. It should not be said that as soon as there were no longer two armies facing off against each other that American military circles and even the American Congress would produce an empty feeling at having lost their goal. The result was that without an enemy, one still had to be created. Therefore, even if it is a tiny area such as Kosovo, they cannot pass up an opportunity to try out their frosty blades. American military circles, which are digging deeper and deeper into the insoluble problem of either using force or not using any at all, seems, after stretching their own tentacles from war regions to the realm of non-combat military actions, to no longer be willing to extend themselves to a far distance, and are now in the realm of forming non-military warfare. This is possibly owing to a lack of sensitivity to new things and also possibly a result of work habit, and even more so possibly due to limitations in thinking. Regardless of the reason, the American soldier always locks his own field of vision in the range covered by war clouds, and this is an indisputable fact.

Even though the United States bears the brunt of being faced with the threat of this type of non-military war and has been the injured party time after time, yet what is surprising is that such a large nation unexpectedly does not have a unified strategy and command structure to deal with the threat. What makes one even more so wonder whether to laugh or cry is that unexpectedly they have 49 departments and offices responsible for anti-terrorist activities, but there is very little coordination and cooperation among them. Other nations are not that much better than the United States in this area. The allocations and basic investment directions of various nations for security needs are still only limited to the military and intelligence and political departments, but there are few and pitiful investments in other directions. Again using the United States as an example, it uses seven billion dollars in funds for anti-terrorism, which is only 1/25 of the US$250 billion military expenditure.

Regardless of how each nation turns a deaf ear to the pressing threat of non-military warfare, this objective fact is encroaching upon the existence of mankind one step at a time, expanding and spreading based on its own pattern and speed. It is not necessary to point it out as people will discover that when mankind focuses more attention on calling for peace and limiting wars, many of the origins are the things in our peaceful lives which all begin one after another to change into lethal weapons which destroy peace. Even those golden rules and precious precepts which we have always upheld also begin to reveal a contrary tendency and become a means for some nations to be able to launch attacks against other nations or certain organizations and individuals to do so against the entire society. It is similar to [the following scenarios]: when there is a computer then there is a computer virus, and when there is currency there is monetary speculation, freedom of faith and religious extremism and heretical religions, common human rights and national sovereignty, free economics and trade protection, national autonomy and global unification, national enterprises versus transnational corporations, information liberalization and information boundaries, and the sharing of knowledge and the monopoly of technology. It is possible for each field that at any moment tomorrow there will break out a war where different groups of people are fighting at close quarters. The battlefield is next to you and the enemy is on the network. Only there is no smell of gunpowder or the odor of blood. However, it is war as before, because it accords with the definition of modern warfare: forcing the enemy to satisfy one's own interests. It is very obvious that none of the soldiers in any one nation possesses sufficient mental preparation against this type of new war which completely goes beyond military space. However, this is actually a severe reality which all soldiers must face.

The new threats require new national security views, and new security views then necessitate soldiers who first expand their fields of vision prior to expanding their victories. This is a matter of wiping away the long narrow cloud covering of war cast over one's eyes.

The Destruction of Rules and the Domain of Losing Effectiveness

As an extreme means for resolving conflicts of survival and interests, war has always been the beast truly tamed by mankind. On the one hand, it is the street cleaner of the ecological chain of society, and on the other hand, it is also the directly formed threat facing the survival of mankind. How can we order it about without being harmed by it? Over the last several thousand years, and especially in the 20th century, during the intervals between the fires of war, there has always been one matter pursued: making efforts to lock the beast in the cage. It is for this reason that people have formulated innumerable treaties and rules. From the famous Geneva Convention to the United Nations and to the present, they have begun to continuously make various resolutions concerning war, erected one railing after another on the roads of crazy and bloody wars, and have wanted to utilize international laws and regulations to control the harm of war to mankind to the lowest level, from specifically not allowing the use of biochemical weapons, not allowing the indiscriminate killing of civilians, not allowing the mistreatment of prisoners, and limiting the use of land mines, etc., to the widespread opposition to the use of military force or the threat of the use of force in handling national relations issues. All of these regulations are gradually becoming accepted by each nation. The most commendable of these is a series of treaties on nuclear non-proliferation, the banning of nuclear testing, bilateral and multilateral reduction of nuclear weapons, etc., which have to date resulted in mankind avoiding entrance into a nuclear winter. At the conclusion of the Cold War, the entire world was overjoyed and considered that a "fearful peace" was being entered from this. After Schwarzkopf used a "storm" fist to down Saddam on the Gulf fighting stage, President Bush was elated with success: "The new order of the world has already withstood its first test." He was like Chamberlain returning from Munich announcing that mankind will "get together in a world having the hope of peace." What was the result? Like Chamberlain, he also boasted too early. [5]

Regardless of whether it is the end of the Cold War or the Gulf War, neither was able to bring about the promises of politicians to the world and the new international order anticipated by all of mankind. The collapse of the polarized world resulted in the beasts of local wars roaring out of their cages one by one, drenching the nations and regions of Rwanda, Somalia, Bohei, Chechen, Congo and Kosovo in pools of blood. People had again discovered by this time how the efforts for peace over several thousand years could collapse at one single blow!

The appearance of this type of situation is related to the practical attitude embraced by each nation concerning the establishment of international rules. Whether or not each nation acknowledges the rules often depends on whether or not they are beneficial to themselves. Small nations hope to use the rules to protect their own interests, while large nations attempt to utilize the rules to control other nations. When the rules are not in accord with the interests of one's own nation, generally speaking, the breaking of the rules by small nations can be corrected by large nations in the name of enforcers of the law. However, when large nations break the rules, for example the United States enforcing supranational laws in Panama, wherein it grabbed the head of another nation and brought him to be tried in their own nation. Another example is India's disregard of the nuclear test ban treaty, wherein it swallowed up the Himalayan nation of Sikkim, which was a similar action to Iraq swallowing up Kuwait. The international community time and again only sighed in despair, being at a loss of what to do. [6] However, in any matter, there is always its unbeatable rival and natural enemy, which is aptly reflected in the Chinese popular saying: brine forms the bean curd, and one thing always overcomes another. In the international community, the participation by large nations, when facing the weak and powerless, in the formulation and the utilization of rules as well as the disregard and even destruction of rules when the rules are not advantageous to them, form a fresh contrast with the springing up of those non-state forces who do not acknowledge any rules and specialize in taking the existing national order as their goal of destruction. As the natural enemy of the international community, and especially large nations, while they threaten the survival of mankind, they also produce minute effects on the balance of society and the ecology. In other words, these non-state forces serve as a type of socially destructive force which both destroys the normal international order and restrains the destruction of the international community by those large nations. For example, there were the warning intrusions of nameless hackers [7] to the web site of the National Defense Ministry of India after it carried out nuclear tests and the terrorist act by the rich Moslem Osama bin Laden because of his dissatisfaction with the presence of the United States in the Middle East. Even though it is still difficult for us now to delineate the positive and negative effects of these actions, yet it can be determined that all of these actions carry irresponsible and destructive characteristics which disregard rules.

The direct result of the destruction of rules is that the domains delineated by visible or invisible boundaries which are acknowledged by the international community lose effectiveness. This is because all principals without national power who employ non-military warfare actions to declare war against the international community all use means that go beyond nations, regions and measures. Visible national boundaries, invisible internet space, international law, national law, behavioral norms, and ethical principles have absolutely no restraining effects on them. They are not responsible to anyone, nor limited by any rules, and there is no disgrace when it comes to the selection of targets, nor are there any means which are not used. Owing to the surreptitious nature of their movements, they have very strong concealment, create widespread damage because of their extreme behavior, and appear unusually cruel as a result of their indiscriminate attacks on civilians. All of this is also broadcast through real time via continuous coverage by the modern media which very much strengthens the effects of terrorism. When carrying out war with these people, there is no declaration of war, no fixed battlefield, no face-to-face fighting and killing, and in the majority of situations, there will be no gunpowder smoke, gun fire, and spilling of blood. However, the destruction and injuries encountered by the international community are in no way less than those of a military war.

Following the gradual fading out of the old terrorists who specialized in kidnapping, assassination, and hijacking, new forces of terrorism quickly appeared and very rapidly filled in the vacuum left by their predecessors. During a short period of over ten years, they transformed from being persons of nameless origins to world public nuisances, with the chief among them being computer hackers. The popularization of personal computers, and especially the formation of the internet, has resulted in the malicious acts of hackers increasingly endangering the existing social order. The hackers we speak of here refer to those network killers who steal information, delete and change files, release viruses, transfer capital, and destroy programs on the network. In order to differentiate them from the non-malicious hackers, we should perhaps call the former "network bandits" or "network tyrants" which would be much more accurate. Their powers of destroying the present world are shocking. Early, in 1988, when the hackers were first beginning their activities and people did not know anything about their danger, the very small "worm" designed by Robert Morris completely paralyzed 6,000 computers of the military and civilian computer systems throughout the United States, including the "Long-Range Planning Office" of the United States' Department of Defense, the Research Center of the Rand Corporation, and Harvard University. Afterwards, this type of event began to appear one after another in the internet connections of nations and regions. Since the United States government began to seriously attack network crimes in 1990, not only have hacker activities not witnessed any decrease, but on the contrary, they have spread globally and have the great force of a forest fire. It is worth noting that following the "Information Warfare" ordinance of the American military, which placed enemy nation armies or world opponents on a par with non-approved users, inside personnel, terrorists, non-national organizations, and foreign intelligence organizations as the six sources of network threats, hackers with national or military backgrounds had already begun to reveal clues. [8] This not only greatly strengthened the battle formations of the hackers so that the actions of the disbanded and straggling hackers quickly escalated into national (network tyrant) actions, it also resulted in the increasing enlargement of the internet threat faced by all nations (including those nations with national or military hackers), and is becoming increasingly difficult to predict and guard against. The only thing which could be predicted was that the damage of this type of threat to the large network nation of the United States would certainly be greater than for other nations. Faced with these prospects, even J. Saiteerdou [as printed 1049 3676 1422 6757], who is responsible for the investigation of computer crimes in the FBI of the United States, said with both self-confidence and worry: "Give me ten carefully chosen hackers, and within 90 days I would then be able to have this nation lay down its arms and surrender." When compared with "network bandits"—these network terrorist hackers—the terror of the bombs of bin Laden are closer to the traditional terrorism in legacy. However, this does not prevent us from considering him to be within the ranks of new terrorism. This is because aside from the religious or even heterodox teaching background and tendency to oppose control by large nations, from the person of bin Laden himself, we can see the shadows of those old fighters who make loud and empty boasts, are so fond of the limelight, and make use of light weapons and a single method, but in other areas they cannot be spoken of in the same breath. Prior to the major bombings at the American embassies in Nairobi and Dar es Salaam which shocked the world, the name of bin Laden was still not listed in the name list of the 30 terrorist organizations published by the International Anti-Terrorist Organization, and even though earlier he already had many murder cases attributed to him, he was only a "nameless hero" in the Islamic world, owing to his having not boasted of them. Even after the Americans had already launched cruise missiles at him and issued an arrest warrant, he still repeatedly denied that he was personally connected with the bombing cases. "Concealing oneself and shielding," having weightier results, and unexpectedly gaining an undeserved reputation are perhaps the first major characteristics of the new bin Laden-type terrorist organizations. In addition, having learned how to use economic means and taking advantage of the loopholes in the free economics initiated by the West, they set up management-type companies and banks and engage in large-scale drug trafficking and smuggling, the resale of munitions, the printing of large amounts of forged currency, and rely on the contributions of religious followers to attain stable capital resources. [9] On this basis, the tentacles of these new terrorist organizations extend to even wider areas, and the means are also diversified, such as widely using religious and heretical organizations to develop their own media for propaganda, setting up anti-government militia organizations, etc. The easy accomplishment of raising funds guarantees that they will be able to attain and master large amounts of high technology means so that they will be able to kill even more people with great ease. Even though the vast majority of the attacks they have launched to date have been aimed at the rich nations and Western nations, especially the large nations which have the capability to control other nations, yet they are a common threat to the existing order, the destruction of commonly acknowledged rules, and to the international community. It can be seen from known conditions that these new developing terrorist organizations are merely several black waves turning over within the new global terrorist activities. It can be confirmed that there are even greater turbid currents which we do not know about surging under the water surface. Newly converging into this counter current are the international financial speculators. Although there is still no one at present listing these immaculately dressed and dapper fellows in the ranks of terrorists, yet in terms of their actions and the calamitous consequences they have caused in England, Mexico and Southeast Asia, none of those types, such as the "bandits" and bin Laden, can even hold a candle to them. Taking the big financial crocodiles as represented by Soros, on the strength of a daily business volume exceeding US$120 billion in floating capital, he used financial derivative methods as well as free economic regulations to repeatedly change his attitude and play tricks to foment trouble, so as to bring about one financial upheaval after another. As a result, the area of harmed nations gradually enlarged from Southeast Asia to Russia and then to Japan, and finally to Europe and the United States, which were watching from the sidelines and were also unable to escape by sheer luck, so that the existing world financial system and economic order were fundamentally shaken and it had already become another new disaster threatening human society and international security. [10] The typical characteristics of terrorism, including being transnational, concealed, without rules, and tremendously destructive, have given us reason to call it financial terrorism.

Before the tremendous state apparatus, terrorists and their organizations are perhaps not worth mentioning in terms of numbers of peoples and methods, but in fact there is not one country which dares to look at them lightly. The reason is that this is a group of maniacs which does not act according to the rules. A terrorist organization which possesses nuclear weapons is definitely much more dangerous than a nation with the same nuclear weapons. The creed of bin Laden is "If I die, then I will also not let others live," and therefore, he would then stop at nothing, so that in order to kill over ten Americans he would also drench several thousand innocent people in a pool of blood. Soros's logic is "I entered the room to steal money because your door was not locked." In this way, he does not have to be responsible for destroying the economies of other nations and throwing the political order of others into disarray.

For bin Laden who hides under the hills of Islamic fundamentalism, Soros who conceals himself within the forests of free economics, and the computer hackers who hide themselves in the green curtains of networks, no national boundaries exist, and borders also are ineffective. What they want to do is carry out wanton destruction within a regulated sphere and act wildly and run amuck within an unregulated sphere. These new terrorist forces have formed an unprecedented serious challenge to the existing world order, and in turn they have made us doubt to a certain degree the logical production of a fixed order. Perhaps those who check the destruction of rules and those who revise the rules are both necessary. This is because any destruction of rules always brings on new problems which need to be rigorously dealt with. In an age when an old order is about to be removed, those in the lead are frequently those who are the first to destroy the rules or those who are the earliest to adapt to this situation. Naturally, in this respect, the new terrorists have already walked to the head of the international community.

The most ideal method of operation for dealing with an enemy who pays no regard to the rules is certainly just being able to break through the rules. Recently, in coming to grips with enemies which appear and disappear in the domain of non-military warfare, the Americans have utilized cruise missiles, the Hong Kong government has used foreign currency reserves and administrative measures, and the British government has broken conventions so as to allow their secret service organizations to "legally" assassinate the leaders of foreign nations who they consider to be terrorists. This reveals an updating of the rules and a changing of the methods of operation. However, it also reveals the weaknesses of dullness in thinking and singleness in method. It is said that the Americans have already decided to employ hacking methods to search for and seal up the bank accounts of bin Laden in various nations, so as to basically cut off his source of capital. This is no doubt a breakthrough in method of operation which goes beyond the military domain. However, we must also say that in this area, the new and old terrorists who consistently uphold the principle of resorting to every conceivable means are still the best teachers of each nation's government.

Cocktail in the Great Master's Cup

King Wu of the Zhou Dynasty three thousand years ago and Alexander the Great over two thousand years ago definitely would not have known what a cocktail was, and yet they were both masters of mixing "cocktails" on the battlefield. This is because, like mixing a cocktail, they were adept at ingeniously combining two or more battlefield factors together, throwing them into battle, and gaining victories. 1+1 is the most elementary and also the most ancient combination method. Long spears and round shields can prepare a soldier for both attack and defense and give a basis for advancing and retreating; two people comprise a unit, wherein "soldiers with long weapons are used for defense and those with short weapons are used for holding positions," a pair of soldiers coordinate with each other, and then form the smallest tactical unit. [11] The knight Don Quixote and his attendant Sancho signify that the separation of work of the general and the light soldier had already been formed, and thus the team could set off on a long journey to dispel evil for the imaginary princess. Such a simple combination embodies the profound theory of infinite changes on the battlefield. From cold weapons to hot weapons and then on to nuclear weapons and up to the combination of the so-called high technology weapons of today, the musical instrument in the victorious magical hand has always accompanied the entire history of warfare secretly influencing the outcome of each war. King Wu attacked Zhuo with 300 military vehicles, 3,000 brave warriors, and 45,000 armored soldiers, which was far less than the several hundred thousand foot soldiers of King Zhuo of the Shang Dynasty. However, this small army composed of both vehicles and soldiers became the cornerstone of the Zhou kingdom, because the proper combination greatly strengthened the combat strength in the wilderness war and became the evidence of the earliest combination war which we were able to find 3,120 years later. Given that this was the case in the East, the West was no exception. The reason why Alexander was able to defeat a large army during one decisive battle at Abeila was because he made adaptations just before going into battle, wherein a linear pushing square matrix changed so that the opponent was taken by surprise. His method was very simple. The position of the cavalry shifted back and obliquely along the two flanks of the square matrix forming a "hollow large square matrix," so that the flexibility of the cavalry and the stability of the foot soldiers achieved the ideal combination in a unique battle array wherein each developed their individual strengths most incisively. The result was naturally that Alexander, whose military force was at a comparative disadvantage, ultimately drank heartily the cup of victory. [12]

When perusing the military history of both East and West, we never find the expression "combination" in any of the descriptions related to methods of operation. However, all of the great masters of warfare throughout the ages seem to have instinctively known this principle well. The King of Sweden Gustav was the most highly praised military reformer at the beginning of the firearms period. All of the reforms that he carried out in terms of battle array and weapons deployment used the combination method. He very early realized that the falling behind of the lancers and arranging them together in battle array with the firearm soldiers allowed the former to be able to provide cover for the later between shootings. This developed the strengths of each to the greatest limits. He also often had mixed groupings of light cavalry, heavy cavalry and firearm soldiers who took turns initiating charges against the enemy's skirmish line under the heavy smoke of artillery fire. This king was later called the "first great field artillery expert," and he understood even better the functions and effects of artillery as the basis for engaging in battles. He took the light artillery as a combination of "regimental artillery" and infantry allowing the heavy artillery to independently form an army, and the seemingly separately deployed light and heavy artillery actually formed a perfectly integrated combination within the entire range of the battlefield. It can truly be said that the effects of the artillery were developed to the ultimate during that period. [13]

However, all of this occurred prior to the appearance of the expert of artillery technique, Napoleon. When compared with the short Corsican who pushed over 20,000 cannons on to the battlefield, the guns in the hands of Gustav can only be seen as "a small sorcerer in the presence of a great one." During the period from 1793 to 1814, a total of 20 years, no one understood cannons as completely as did Napoleon. No one was able to understand those under his command more precisely than this commander, and naturally there was no one who could fully combine the lethal force of artillery and the maneuverability of cavalry, as well as the loyalty and bravery of Commander Davout and the fierceness of Commander Murat to forge an offensive force which would make all of their enemies flee at the very sight of them, and change the French army into a fighting machine with which none in all of Europe could compete. This machine was used from Austerlitz to Borodino to formulate the myth that Napoleon won nearly every battle. [14]

General Schwarzkopf who created the miracle of a major battle in which only over one hundred soldiers were lost cannot be considered to be on the great master level. However, his luck appears to have been as good as all of the masters of military techniques. Actually, what was really important was not luck, but rather that this commander led a large modern army which, like his predecessors, even moreso gave importance to the combination of the important elements of warfare. This is because during the 1990s the cards which he held in his hand were many more than those held by his predecessors. For him, the key to driving the Iraqi army out of Kuwait, restoring the lifeline of oil to the West, and regenerating America's influence in the Middle East, depended on how to ingenuously use the alliance, manipulate the media, use economic blockades, and other methods, along with developing and bringing together various armed services of the army, navy, air force, space, electronics, etc., comprised by the militaries of over 30 nations, and thus jointly becoming an iron fist to pound Saddam. He accomplished this and yet his opponent quite shockingly was not at all aware of this. A great army of several hundred thousand, several thousand tanks, and several hundred aircraft were like unmixed cement, sand and reinforcing steel dispersed on the battle line, penetrating several hundred kilometers and being basically unable to bear the bitter attacks of the American-style "fists" [as printed loaquan 5071 2164], which fully combined the rear solid structural components to become as hard as reinforced concrete. In addition, there was first detainment and then release of Western hostages, followed by one mistake after another, and there was poor response in the areas of breaking political isolation and economic blockades.

Regardless of whether the war was 3,000 years ago or at the end of the 20th century, it seems that all of the victories display one common phenomenon: the winner is the one who combined well.

While being able to ever increase the means used for warfare, as well as make continuous improvements today so that the denotation of warfare is quickly being amplified, the connotation of this has also begun to deepen. More factors which had never appeared in the warfare of the past have entered the world of warfare through the combination of various different methods. The addition of each new element possibly causes changes in the modality and type of warfare up until the outbreak of military revolution. Looking back upon the history of warfare, regardless of whether it is stirrups, rifles, breechloaders, smokeless gunpowder, field telephones, wireless telegrams, submarines, tanks, aircraft, missiles, atomic bombs, computers, non-lethal weapons, or division troop system, staff systems, "wolf pack tactics," [15] blitz, carpet bombing, electronic countermeasures, and air-land battles, the appearance of all of these elements all combine with earlier key battlefield elements to display hybrid advantages and enrich the present world of warfare to different degrees.

Over the last 20 years, information technology, computer viruses, Internet, financial derivation tools, and other sources, as well as the technology of non-military means even moreso reveal the difficulties of predicting the prospect for the outcome of tomorrow's wars. However, to date, for the vast majority of soldiers or high-ranking military officers utilizing the element combination method to carry out warfare is often a non-conscious action. Therefore, their combinations often remain on the level of weapons, deployment methods and the battlefield, and the drawn-up war prospects are also mostly only limited to the military domain and revel in it. Only those trailblazing military geniuses are able to stand alone in breaking convention, breaking through limitations and consciously combining all of the means available at the time to play the ageless masterpiece by changing the tonality of the war.

If it is said that combination was only a winning secret formula of a few geniuses, then consciously making combination the trend of a method of operations now is already becoming clearer day after day, and warfare is now being taken into an even broader and even more far-reaching domain; however, all of that provided by the age of technological integration leaves combination with more seemingly infinite possible space. It can be affirmed that whoever is able to mix a tasty and unique cocktail for the future banquet of war will ultimately be able to wear the laurels of success on his own head.

Using Addition to Win the Game

All of the cards have now been shown. We already know that war will not again be displayed in its original form. To a very great extent, war is no longer even war but rather coming to grips on the Internet, and matching the mass media, assault and defense in forward exchange transactions, along with other things which we had never viewed as war, now all possibly causing us to drop our eyeglasses. That is to say, the enemy will possibly not be the originally significant enemy, the weapons will possibly not be the original weapons, and the battlefield will also possibly not be the original battlefield. Nothing is definite. What can be ascertained is not definite. The game has already changed, and what we need to continue is ascertaining a new type of fighting method within various uncertainties. It should not be that type of single prescription for treating the symptoms and not the disease, but rather a hybrid type of learning widely from the strong points of others and gathering advantages so as to allow a pear tree to bear both peaches and apples. This then is combination. We had actually shown this card already above.

What we have still not spoken of is another term: addition.

Addition is the method of combination.

In a boxing arena, a person who from start to finish uses only one type of boxing method to fight with an opponent is naturally not one who can combine straight punches, jabs, swings and hooks to attack his opponent like a storm. The principle of this can be said to be extremely simple: one plus one is greater than one. The problem is that such a simple principle which even a preschooler can understand has been surprisingly unclear to many persons responsible for the success and failure of the security and warfare of nations. These people can excuse themselves saying they are using the method of combination boxing to attack opponents. They have never forgotten the addition of technology with technology, tactics with tactics, weapons with weapons, and measures with measures. Moreover, they can also contemptuously come to conclusions and combinations which cannot be considered to be anything new. This has been done from Alexander to Napoleon and even up to Schwarzkopf. They do not know that their ability to understand or not understand combinations is not the key to the problem. What is truly important is whether or not one understands what goes with what to implement combinations and how to combine. Lastly, but certainly not the least important point, is whether or not one has thought of combining the battlefield and non-battlefield, warfare and non-warfare, military and non-military which is more specifically combining stealth aircraft and cruise missiles with network killers, combining nuclear deterrence, financial wars and terrorist attacks, or simply combining Schwarzkopf + Soros + Xiaomolisi [transliteraton 1420 5459 6849 2448] + bin Laden.

This then is our real hand of cards.

Whether it is combination or addition, both are but empty frames. Only when blood or cruelty are added in is the situation able to become severe and begin to be shocking.

Being confronted with this completely new concept of warfare, there is no doubt that the impression of war to which people have already become accustomed will be shaken. Some of the traditional models of war, as well as the logic and laws attached to it, will also be challenged. The outcome of the contest is not the collapse of the traditional mansion but rather one portion of the new construction site being in disorder. From the perspective of law, most of us will see collapse.

Up to this point, we have already found the reason, beginning from the appearance of "high tech" on stage, that this military revolution has slowly been unable to be completed. From the perspectives of human history and the history of warfare, there has never been one military revolution which was declared to have been completed merely after technology or organizational revolutions. Only after signifying the appearance of this revolution of military thought with the highest achievement will the entire process of the military revolution be finalized. This time is no exception, so that whether or not the new military revolution brought about by high technology can bring it to a final conclusion depends on whether it can travel far upon the road of the revolution of military thought. It is only this one time that it needs to jump outside the ruts made by the war spirit that has persisted for several thousand years.

To accomplish this, it is only necessary to be able to seek help from addition. However, prior to utilizing addition, it must go beyond all of the fetters of politics, history, culture, and ethics and carry out thorough thought. Without thorough thought, there can be no thorough revolution. Before this, even Sun Zi and Clauswitz locked themselves in the barrier of the military domain, and only Machiavelli approached the realm of this thought. For a very long period of time, owing to the fact that the thought of the Prince and its author were both way ahead of their time, they were held in contempt by the knights or rulers. They would naturally not be able to understand that going beyond all limits and boundaries was an ideological revolution, which included the premise of a revolution of military thought. In the same way, to date, those who only understand an imposing array of troops on the battlefield and who think that war is just killing people and methods of operation are just methods to kill people and that there is nothing worth giving attention to other than this, have been unable to understand this point.

The Americans have actually not been so dull as to not have the slightest reaction to this problem. Steven Maizi [as printed 7796 5417] and Thomas Kaiweite [0481 4850 3676] of the Strategic Institute of the Army War College of the United States who brought forth the problem of "the frequency band width of the new military revolution" had actually become sensitive to this point. They discovered the gap between the American military in terms of military thought and the real threat facing national security. Having thought lag behind reality (much less to speak of surpassing it) is not only a shortcoming of American soldiers, but it is very typical of them. When "a military gives excessive focus on dealing with a certain specified type of enemy," this can possibly result in their being attacked and defeated by another enemy outside of their field of vision. Steven Maizi and Thomas Kaiweite correctly expressed their concerns about this. They further pointed out that "Even though official documents stress the army (we can understand it as meaning the entire American military— note by the authors [Steven Maizi and Thomas Kaiweite]), it is necessary to break through fixed modern Western thinking to broaden the conception of future conflicts. However, most of the descriptions of how the digitized troops of the 21st century will conduct war sound like an armored war using new technology to fight with the Warsaw Pact nations." It is because the American military is making war preparations guided by this type of military thinking that they naturally hope war is like running into their own muzzle which is what they expect. Such ridiculous wishful thinking can only bring on one type of future prospect, "The vast majority of development plans of the present American military, such as those of the army for the 21st century, are all focused upon dealing with an enemy with conventional heavy armor, and if the United States encounters an enemy with low level technology, an intermediate level enemy, or one with equivalent power at the beginning of the next century, then the problem of insufficient frequency band width will possibly occur." [16] Actually, with the next century having still not yet arrived, the American military has already encountered trouble from insufficient frequency band width brought on by the three above mentioned types of enemies. Whether it be the intrusions of hackers, a major explosion at the World Trade Center, or a bombing attack by bin Laden, all of these greatly exceed the frequency band widths understood by the American military. The American military is naturally inadequately prepared to deal with this type of enemy psychologically, in terms or measures, and especially as regards military thinking and the methods of operation derived from this. This is because they have never taken into consideration and have even refused to consider means that are contrary to tradition and to select measures of operation other than military means. This will naturally not allow them to add and combine the two into new measures and new methods of operation. In actuality, it only requires broadening one's outlook a little and being uninhibited in thought to be able to avail oneself of the lever of the great volumes of new technology and new factors springing up from the age of integrated technology, thus prying loose the wheel of the military revolution rusted as a result of lagging behind in terms of thinking. We can here appreciate the deep significance of the old saying, "a stone from other hills may serve to polish the jade of this one."

It would be well if we were somewhat bold and completely mixed up the cards in our hand, combined them again, and saw what the result would be.

Supposing a war broke out between two developed nations already possessing full information technology, and relying upon traditional methods of operation, the attacking side would generally employ the modes of great depth, wide front, high strength, and three-dimensionality to launch a campaign assault against the enemy. Their method does not go beyond satellite reconnaissance, electronic countermeasures, large-scale air attacks plus precision attacks, ground outflanking, amphibious landings, air drops behind enemy lines . . . the result is not that the enemy nation proclaims defeat, but rather one returns with one's own spears and feathers. However, by using the combination method, a completely different scenario and game can occur: if the attacking side secretly musters large amounts of capital without the enemy nation being aware of this at all and launches a sneak attack against its financial markets, then after causing a financial crisis, buries a computer virus and hacker detachment in the opponent's computer system in advance, while at the same time carrying out a network attack against the enemy so that the civilian electricity network, traffic dispatching network, financial transaction network, telephone communications network, and mass media network are completely paralyzed, this will cause the enemy nation to fall into social panic, street riots, and a political crisis. There is finally the forceful bearing down by the army, and military means are utilized in gradual stages until the enemy is forced to sign a dishonorable peace treaty. This admittedly does not attain to the domain spoken of by Sun Zi, wherein "the other army is subdued without fighting." However, it can be considered to be "subduing the other army through clever operations." It is very clear who was superior and who inferior when comparing these two methods of operation. This is, however, only a thought. However, it is certainly a feasible thought. Based on this thought, we need only shake the kaleidoscope of addition to be able to combine into an inexhaustible variety of methods of operation.

Military Trans-military Non-military

Atomic warfare Diplomatic warfare Financial warfare
Conventional warfare Network warfare Trade warfare
Bio-chemical warfare Intelligence warfare Resources warfare
Ecological warfare Psychological warfare Economic aid warfare
Space warfare Tactical warfare Regulatory warfare
Electronic warfare Smuggling warfare Sanction warfare
Guerrilla warfare Drug warfare Media warfare
Terrorist warfare Virtual warfare (deterrence) Ideological warfare

Any of the above types of methods of operation can be combined with another of the above methods of operation to form a completely new method of operation. [17] Regardless of whether it is intentional or unintentional, the carrying out of combined methods of operation using different methods of operation that go beyond domains and categories has already been applied by many nations in the practice of warfare. For example, the countermeasure used by the Americans against bin Laden is national terrorist warfare + intelligence warfare + financial warfare + network warfare + regulatory warfare; another example is what the NATO nations used to deal with the Southern Alliance Kosovo crisis: deterrence with the use of force + diplomatic warfare (alliance) + regulatory warfare; prior to this, the United Nations under pressure mainly from the United States adopted the methods of operation against Iraq: conventional warfare + diplomatic warfare + sanction warfare + media warfare + psychological warfare + intelligence warfare, etc. We also noticed that the means adopted by the Hong Kong government during the financial security warfare in August of 1998 to deal with financial speculators were: financial warfare + regulatory warfare + psychological warfare + media warfare, and even though they paid a heavy price, yet the results of the war were very good. In addition, the methods for matters, such as the large quantity printing of counterfeit Renminbi in Taiwan, very easily became a warfare measure of financial warfare + smuggling warfare. We can see from these examples the miraculous effects of applying addition-combination in methods of operation. If it is said that, owing to the limitations of technical measures and conditions, those engaged in warfare in the past were still unable to freely combine all factors for winning wars, then today the great explosion of technology led by information technology has already provided us with this type of possibility. Only if we are willing and do not allow subjective intentions to depart from objective laws, will we then be able to arrange the cards in our hand into various types of hands based on need until finally winning the entire game. However, there is no one who can write a guaranteed winning prescription for all future wars. Various types of methods of operation have appeared in the history of human warfare, and most have been forgotten with the passage of history. When examining the reasons, all of these methods of operation were all determined based upon a specific target, and when the target disappeared, then the method of operation also lost its existing value. Methods of operation which truly possess vitality must be an "empty basket." This empty basket only relies upon its thinking and principle of utilizing the non-changing to deal with the myriad changes. The combination of which we speak is just this type of empty basket, an empty basket of military thinking. It is not the same as any of the very strongly directed methods of operation of the past, for only when the basket is filled with specific targets and contents does it begin to have directionality and aim. The key to whether or not victory is won in a war is nowhere else but in what things you are able to pack into this basket.

Yue Fei, the military strategist during the Song Dynasty in China, stated when discussing how to employ methods of operation that "the subtle excellence of application lies in one-mindedness." Although this statement sounds very abstruse, yet it is actually the only accurate explanation of the correct application of combination. Only if we understand this point will we then be able to attain a method of operation which goes beyond the multitude of methods of operation. This is then having the myriad methods converge into one. It is even the final stage of methods of operation. Aside from combining the transcendence of being unfettered, you have no way of imagining what other method of operation can transcend the net of combination. The conclusion is thus so simple, and yet it will definitely not arise from a simple brain.

Notes

[1] War is the most typical game, and yet it is often not susceptible to the theories of classical games. War is intrinsically the irrational behavior of man, and based on the various conjectures of the "rational man," it naturally and easily fails. The fearful aftereffects of nuclear weapons have caused mankind to gradually find its way back to the long-lost rationality from the most irrational behavior. Moreover, the course of globalization has pushed mankind to accord with the thinking of the "rational man" while seeking national security, learning how to cast off the "predicament of the convict," and no longer falling into the hegemony-type "cockfight game" of the United States and the Soviet Union. The economic game with both cooperation and competition has begun to seep into the military sphere and influence warfare in the new era. (Reference can be made to the discussion in Zhang Weiying's [1728 4850 6601] *Game Theory and Information Economics*, Sanlian Bookstore of Shanghai, Shanghai People's Press, 1996.)

[2] Beginning on March 15, 1997, the United States' Army carried out 14 days of digitized brigade task force high level operations exercises at the Fort Irwin National Training Center in California. According to remarks by Army Chief of Staff General Rymer, the aim of this test was to determine whether or not troop technology of the 21st century would be able to instantly answer three crucial questions in actual warfare: Where am I? Where are my companions? Where is the enemy? In view of the test conditions, the troops that underwent rearrange-

ments and used new weapons with digital technology had much faster operating speed, greater killing power, and stronger survival capabilities than the present army. See the reports in *Defense News of the United States*, March 17–23 of 1997, for details regarding this exercise.

[3] It was again stressed in the "1997 National Army Strategy" of the United States that the task and military capability level of the United States Army was to simultaneously win two large-scale regional wars. This actually still continued the military strategy and army building policy of the "Cold War" era. James R. Blacker pointed out in his article entitled "Building a Military Revolution-Type United States Army—A Troop Reform Plan Different From the 'Four Year Military Examination Report'" that this policy "was a military plan designed 20 years ago and selected during a period which ended 10 years ago." (Summer edition 1997 of the American magazine *Strategic Review*)

[4] See the research report of the Strategic Research Institute of the United States Army War College, Strategy and the Military Revolution: From Theory to Policy, Section 8.

[5] Actually this was an Iraqi problem which Bush was also unable to thoroughly resolve. Saddam increasingly became a sore point which the Americans found difficult to remove.

[6] The "Desert Fox" action adopted recently by the United States and England is also an obvious serious offense of large nations in violation of the United Nations' Charter.

[7] The original meaning of "hacker" was neutral and did not carry any derogatory sense. Early hackers used their obsession with technology and good intentions for society to form a unique hacker standard of logic which was strictly adhered to by many people over several generations of hackers. However, in the network space of today where the moral degeneration is getting worse day by day, there is no longer this gentlemanly attitude.

[8] In 1996, the Information System Office of the United States Department of Defense was set up so as to strengthen the protection of military information systems. In the same year, the establishment of the President's Committee on the Protection of Key Infrastructure of the United States was also announced. This Committee is responsible for protecting the telecommunications, financial, electric power, water, pipeline, and transport systems. All of this was directed at real threats, and the FM100-6 Field Command Information Operations of the United States military clearly stated that "the threats facing the information infrastructure are real, their source is the entire globe, they are manifested in many areas of technology, and moreover these threats are growing. These threats originate from individuals and groups and what is driving them is the military, po-

litical, social, cultural, religious, or individual and trade benefits. These threats also come from information madmen." (Chinese translation [of FM100- 6], p. 7)

[9] What is most satirical is that the construction company of the bin Laden family had been the builder of the barracks of the American army in Saudi Arabia.

[10] The most unsettling aspect of finance terrorism is "hot money" which is able to launch destructive attacks upon a nation's economy within several days, and the target varies from national central banks to poor people.

[11] *The History of Warfare in China*, Military Translations Press, Vol. 1, p. 78, Wilderness Wars Section.

[12] *Military History of the Western World*, written by J.F.C. Fuller, translated by Niu Xianzhong [4781 0341 6988].

[13] *The Evolution of Weapons and Warfare*, T.N. Dupuit, pp. 169–176.

[14] *Biography of Napoleon* by Taerli [as printed 4781 0341 6988]. *Biography of Napoleon I* by John Roland Ross.

[15] A technique for attacking merchant vessels during World War I using submarines invented by Dengnici [as printed 6772 1441 5412], Commander of the Submarine Forces of the German Navy. The main method of operation was that after a submarine discovered a merchant vessel, it immediately notified other submarines, and after waiting for many submarines to arrive, the submarines then launched an attack like a pack of wolves against a prey.

[16] Research Report of the Strategic Institute of the United States Army War College, Strategy and the Military Revolution: From Theory to Policy.

[17] In our view, the three types of warfare here are all down-to-earth warfare and not allegorical or descriptive. Military-type wars are always traditional and classical wars which use weapons; the various types of wars among the non-military type are confrontational and nothing abnormal, yet they display warfare behavior and they are all novel; trans-military type wars are situated between the two wherein some have previous methods such as psychological warfare and intelligence warfare, and some are comprised of completely new methods such as network warfare and virtual warfare (this refers to the methods of electronic virtual and of Mozi [1075 1311] thwarting Gong Shu Ban [0361 6551 3803]. See the chapter entitled Gong Shu Ban Sets Up Machinery for the State of Chu to Attack the State of Song in Strategies of the Warring States, Protective Strategies of the Song).

Chapter 6

Seeking Rules of Victory: The Force Moves Away From the Point of the Enemy's Attack

"I usually make surprising moves; the enemy expects surprising moves; but I move in an unsurprising manner this time to attack the enemy. I usually make unsurprising moves; the enemy expects unsurprising moves; but I move in a surprising manner this time to attack the enemy."—Li Shimin

However much is said about combination, we still have to say that it is not enough to focus on combination. It is necessary to further sharpen the focus, to see whether there is any secret closer to the core. Without understanding the secret of how to conduct combination, it will be useless to conduct combination 100 times incompetently.

In the history of war, there has never been a victory achieved in a smooth manner. Thus, in all its versions, the book *Jun Yu* [*Military Talk*] contains such terms as direction of main attack, main targets of striking, feint attack, feint move, and outflank which entail distinguishing between the main and secondary actions. What is behind such terms is not only consideration of the need to deceive the enemy or the sound use of force. There must be some other reasons. In terms of instinct, all those famous generals who have won countless victories, or obscure people, have all realized the existence of something which perhaps should be called "rules of victory." Those people have also got close to such rules tens of thousands of times. Nevertheless, to this day, no commander or philosopher has ever dared to say: I have found the rules. Not even the job of naming such rules has been completed. But, actually, the rules are hidden in the waves of military practice of mankind. It is proper to say that every classical victory has testified to the rules. However, each time, people either do not want to admit or do not dare to affirm their encounters with rules of victory, but, instead, often attribute the effects of the rules to the favor of some mysterious fate. Many "belated pronouncement" works on military history offer arguments which are difficult for people to grasp because the arguments describe the rules' effects in an excessively mysterious manner. But rules of victory do exist. They are there. Like an invisible man, they accompany every war of mankind. The party to which their golden fingers point will go through the arch of triumph by stepping on the sorrow of the vanquished. However, even the victors in war have not truly seen their real faces.

Secretly Conforming to the Rule of the Golden Section

"Everything is a matter of numbers." Along this line of thought, the ancient sage Pythagoras [1] unexpectedly encountered a set of mysterious digits: 0.618. As a result, he found the rule of the golden section!

[A mathematical formula showing the derivation of the figure 0.618 omitted]

In the 2,500 years since then, this formula has been considered by formative artists as the golden rule of aesthetics. As convincingly testified to by the history of arts, almost all artistic works considered masterpieces, whether created in a casual manner or through intentional effort, have all been close to or in accord with this formula in their basic aesthetic features. People had long marveled at the beauty of the Parthenon Temple of ancient Greece, suspecting it to be the creation of a god. With measurement and calculation, it was found that the relationship between its vertical lines and horizontal lines were entirely in accord with the 1:0.618 ratio. In his book *Vers Une Architecture*, the great modern architect Le Corbusier also established his most important theory of "basic design scale" on the basis of the rule of the golden section, a theory which has had profound and extensive influence on architects and architecture in the world. [2] Regrettably, this formula which the Creator may have meant to use for revealing to mankind a rule for all spheres through a demonstration in one sphere has never moved beyond the realm of artistic creation. Except those Muses with extraordinary gifts, almost no one has realized that this golden rule of aesthetics may become, or is, a rule that should also be followed in other spheres. It was not until 1953 that J. Kieffer, an American, discovered that seeking experiment points according to the rule of the golden section would make it possible to reach the optimal state the most quickly.

His discovery was refined by the Chinese mathematician Hua Luogeng and turned into the "optimum seeking method," or the 0.618 method. The method was popularized in China for a time. As far as we know, such a popularization campaign based on the human-wave tactic produced little effect, but this episode demonstrated the prospect of applying the rule of the golden section in spheres other than the sphere of arts. [3] [The text does not indicate the location of footnotes 4–12, although they are included in the footnote section at the end of the chapter.] In fact, before the emergence of the notion of consciously grasping the rule of the golden section, people had repeatedly applied it to their own spheres of practice on the basis of their instincts. Of course, the military sphere had not been left out. We can easily see the ephemeral marks of the paws of this mysterious beast in the famous amazing campaigns and battles in the history of war. Without looking afar, you will see examples of conforming to this rule everywhere in the military realm. The shadow of 0.618 can be seen in such things ranging from the arc of the cavalry sword to the apex of the flying trajectory of a bullet, shell, or ballistic missile and from the optimum bomb-release altitude and distance for an aircraft in the dive bombing mode to the relationship between the length of the supply line and the turning point in a war.

By casually reading pages of the history of war, you will be certain to be silently amazed by the fact that 0.618, like a golden belt, can be faintly seen in ancient, modern, Chinese, and foreign wars. In the Yanlin battle between Jin and Chu during the Spring and Autumn Period, Duke Li of Jin led a military force in attacking Zheng. The Jin force had a decisive battle with the Chu force at Yanlin. Adopting advice made by Miao Penghuan, a defector from Chu, Duke Li used a portion of his middle army to attack the left army of the Chu force, used another portion to attack the middle army of the Chu force, and used the upper army, lower army, new army, and forces of the lords to attack the right army of the Chu force. The point of attack selected was exactly at the point of the golden section. We mentioned above the Battle of Arbela between Alexander and Darius. The Macedonians selected the juncture of the left flank and the center of the Persian force as the point of their attack; marvelously, the point was exactly the "golden point" for the entire front.

For hundreds of years, people have found it difficult to understand why the Mongol cavalry of Gengis Khan were, like a hurricane, able to

sweep across the Eurasian continent. Such factors as the barbarians' truc-
ulence, cruelty, and cunningness or the mobility of the cavalry did not provide convincing explanations. Perhaps there were other more important
reasons? As can be expected, the rule of the golden section showed its
miraculous power again: We can see that the battle formation of the Mongol cavalry was different from the Western traditional phalanx. In regard
to their five-row formation, the ratio of heavy cavalry to light cavalry was
2:3, with 2 for armored heavy cavalry and 3 for fast and mobile light cavalry, that is, another example of the golden section! You have to admire the
genius-level understanding achieved by that thinker on horseback. It was
natural for a force under the command of such a commander to have more
striking power than the European forces that it confronted.

It seems that, while highly gifted in applying the rule of the golden
section to religion and arts, Christian Europeans were late in coming to
understand the application of this rule to other spheres. The Dutch general Maurice, who had been the first to transform the traditional phalanx
by mixing similar numbers of musket-armed soldiers and pike-armed soldiers, failed to realize this point even in the black powder period when
muskets were gradually replacing pikes. It was King Gustavus of Sweden
who adjusted this formation of a strong front and weak flanks, thereby
turning the Swedish army into an army with the strongest combat power
in Europe of that time. What he did was to have an additional 96 musket-
armed soldiers in addition to the squadron composed of 216 pike-armed
soldiers and 198 musket-armed soldiers. This change gave immediate
prominence to the use of firearms, thereby becoming the watershed separating battle formations of the periods of cold weapons and hot weapons.
Needless to say, we again saw the shining light of the rule of the golden
section in the ratio of 198 plus 96 musket-armed soldiers to 216 pike-
armed soldiers.

There is still more. Let us see how it had stubbornly "manifested"
itself to give us clear suggestions before we recognized it as something
more than a rule of arts. Napoleon attacked Russia in June 1812. In September, after failing to eliminate effective Russian forces in the Borodino
battle, he entered Moscow. At that time, Napoleon did not realize that his
genius and luck were gradually leaving him bit by bit, and that the peak and
turning point of his lifelong career were approaching simultaneously. A
month later, the French forces withdrew from Moscow as it snowed heav-

ily. There were three months of victorious advance and two months of declining. It seems that, in terms of the time sequence, the French emperor was standing on the line of the golden section when looking down at the city of Moscow through the burning fire. In another June 130 years later, Nazi Germany started the Barbarossa Plan against the Soviet Union. For as long as two years, German forces maintained their offensive momentum. It was in August 1943 that German forces turned into defense at the conclusion of the Castle action and would no longer be able to launch an action that can be called a campaign against the Soviet forces. Perhaps we also have to call the following fact a coincidence: The battle of Stalingrad, which has been considered by all historians of war to be the turning point in the Soviet Patriotic War, happened exactly in the 17th month of the war, that is, November 1942. This was the "golden point" in the time axis encompassing 26 months during which the German forces turned from booming to declining.

Let us also take a look at the Gulf War. Before the war, military experts estimated that the equipment and personnel of the Republican Guard would basically lose their combat effectiveness when losses resulting from aerial attacks should total or exceed 30 percent. To make Iraqi forces' losses reach this critical point, U.S. forces extended the bombing time repeatedly. When the Desert Sword was taken out of its shield, Iraqi forces had lost 38 percent of their 4,280 tanks, 32 percent of their 2,280 armored vehicles, and 47 percent their 3,100 artillery pieces, and only around 60 percent of the strength of the Iraqi forces was left. Through such cruel data, the mysterious light of 0.618 began to flicker again in the early morning of 24 January 1991. The Desert Storm ground war ended 100 hours later.

Such instances scattered across history have truly been something marvelous. When viewed in isolation, they do look like accidents happening one after another. But the Creator never does anything without a reason. If too many accidents demonstrate the same phenomenon, can you still calmly view them as accidents? No, at this moment, you have to admit that there is a rule here.

Victory's Grammar—The Side-Principal Rule

In Chinese grammar, there is a basic sentence structure. This structure divides a sentence or phrase into two parts, the modifier and the center word.

The relationship between them is that of modifying and being modified, that is, that the former modifies the latter and determines the tendency and features of the latter. Put more clearly, the former constitutes appearance, and the latter constitutes the organism. We usually determine the difference between one person or object with another person or object not according to his (its) existence as an organism or mechanism but according to his (its) appearance and look. From this perspective, relative to the center word, the modifier should, to a greater extent, be considered the center of a sentence or phrase. For instance, red apple. Before being modified by "red," apple only refers to a kind of fruit in general and is thus general in nature. But "red" gives this apple a specificity that makes it possible to determine it to be "this one." Obviously, "red" plays a significant role in this phrase. Also, for instance, special economic zone. Without the word "economic," special zone is only a concept of geographical division. When modified by "economic," it acquires a special character and orientation, becoming the point of support for the economic lever used by Deng Xiaoping to reform China. This structure is a basic mode in Chinese grammar: the side-principal structure.

This structure of having the principal element modified by a side element exists extensively in the Chinese language to the extent that a Chinese speaker will not be able to speak without using it. For, if there are only subject words in a sentence, without directing modification, the sentence will lack clarity because of the absence of such elements as degree, location, and mode which can be grasped in a concrete manner. For example, if the modifiers in such phrases as "good person," "good thing," "tall building," "red flag," and "slow running" are all removed, then the center words will all become neutral words without specific references. As shown here, in the side-principal structure, the "side" element, as compared with the "principal" element, is in the position of qualitatively determining the sentence or phrase. In other words, in a certain sense we can use the understanding that in the side-principal structure the center word is the principal entity, with the modifier serving as the directing element, that is, that the "principal" element is the body for the "side" element, while the "side" element is the soul of the "principal" element. With the body established as the premise, the role of the soul is obviously of decisive significance. The relationship of the principal entity's being subordinate to the directing element is the foundation for the existence of the side-principal structure. At the same time, as one of the forms of structure of the system of symbols corresponding to the objective world, it seems to suggest to us something lawlike which goes beyond the scope of language.

Going along this path, we will soon see that the side-principal relationship exists in a big way not only in such phrases as "good person," "bad thing," "tall building," and "red flag" or such military terms as aircraft carrier, cruise missile, stealth aircraft, armored personnel carrier, self-propelled artillery, precision bombs, rapid response force, air-land war, and joint operation. This relationship also exists everywhere in the world outside the scope of language in a myriad manner. This is the significance of our borrowing—just borrowing but not copying—this rhetorical device, only seen in human language systems, in our theory. We do not intend to arbitrarily juxtapose war with rhetoric, but only intend to borrow the term "side-principal" to enunciate the deepest core element of our theory. For we believe this side-principal relationship exists in a big way in the movement and development of many things, and that in such a relationship the "side" element, instead of the "principal" element, often plays the role as the directing element. For the time being, we describe this role as "modification by the side element of the principal element" (note: this is not the original meaning of the side-principal structure as a rhetorical device, but an extended meaning as used by us). For instance, in a country, the people are the principal entity, while government is the directing element of the country; in an armed force, soldiers and middle- and lower-level officers constitute the principal entity, while the command headquarters constitute the directing element of the armed force; in a nuclear explosion, uranium or plutonium is the principal entity, while the means of bombarding them constitute the directing element for triggering chain reactions; in a Southeast Asian-style financial crisis, the victim countries are the principal entities, while financial speculators are the directing element generating the crisis. Without the direction provided by government, the people will be a heap of loose sand; without the direction provided by the command headquarters, soldiers will constitute a mob; without means of bombardment, uranium and plutonium will be a heap of minerals; without financial speculators' activity to create disturbance, the regulating mechanisms of victim countries should have enabled them to avoid financial catastrophes. In such a relationship, if the factor of two-way interactions is put aside, it is self-evident which is the side element, which is the principal element, and which modifies which.

As shown through discussions above, this side-principal structure is an asymmetrical structure. Thus, the relationship between the side element and the principal element is an unbalanced relationship. On this point, the situation is very similar to that regarding the rule of the golden section: 0.618 and 1 form an asymmetrical structure and an unbalanced relationship. We are fully justified in regarding it as another way of stating the side-principal formula. For, in this side-principal structure, what is important is the side element, but not the principal element. This is also true with the rule of the golden section. What is important is 0.618, but not 1. This is the common feature of the two. Laws tell us that two things with similar features must follow some similar rules. If there is any common rule governing the golden section and the side-principal structure, it should be the following:

$$0.618 = \text{deviation toward the side element}$$

The best case to illustrate this point is perhaps the story of Tian Ji's horse racing. In a situation of inferior overall strength, the great military strategist Sun Bin made his classical move which was an adequate example of Chinese gaming wisdom. He started by racing Tian Ji's worst horse with the best horse of the king of Qi. After inevitably losing that race, he used his side's middle and best horses to beat the opponent's worst and middle horses, thereby ensuring the two-win advantage necessary for achieving a victory. This method of using the strategy of losing one and winning two (directing element) to win the overall game (principal element) can be viewed as having a typical side-principal structure. The result of winning two of three games conformed entirely to the golden ratio of 2:3. Here, we are seeing the perfect confluence and unity of the two rules:

The golden rule = the side-principal rule.

Finding a rule is both the end and the beginning of studying an issue. As long as we believe that something called the side-principal rule can be seen in the functioning of all things, we should also believe that this rule, like the rule of the golden section, will not leave the military sphere untouched.

Facts are indeed so.

The Changshao battle between Qi and Lu: As the two forces confronted each other on the battlefield, the Qi force was very aggressive, but the Lu force remained motionless. The Qi force attacked three times with three rounds of drum beating but failed to unsettle the front of the Lu force, resulting in an obvious decline in momentum. The Lu force took the opportunity to launch a counterattack, achieving a complete victory. After the battle, the advisor Cao Gui revealed the reason for Qi's defeat and Lu's victory in this battle: The enemy force "had a great momentum at the first round of drum beating, had a weaker momentum at the second round, and was exhausted at the third round. As the enemy force was exhausted, while our force had full vigor, our force prevailed." The entire process of the battle can be divided into five phases: the Qi force's first round of drum beating—the Qi force's second round of drum beating—the Qi force's third round of drum beating—the Lu force's counterattack—the Lu force's chase. From the first to third phases, Cao Gui adopted the strategy of avoiding the enemy's attack, so that the Qi force quickly passed the golden point of its attack power without achieving any results. Meanwhile the Lu force precisely selected this point as the time of counterattack, thereby fully testifying to the rule of the golden section on the battlefield 2,700 years ago (3:5 approximately equals 0.618). It can be certain that at that time Cao Gui could not have known Pythagoras and his theory of the golden section of 200 years later. Furthermore, even if he had known the theory, it was not possible to accurately determine where the 0.618 point was amid an ongoing battle. But, by instinct, he found the point of section with flickering golden light. This is a gift common to all military geniuses.

Hannibal thought in the exactly same way as Cao Gui during the Cannae battle. As Cao Gui did, he understood the secret of declining attack power of enemy forces. Thus, unusually, he deployed the weakest force from Gaul and Spanish infantry at the center of the front where the best force should have been deployed, letting such weak forces bear attacks from Roman forces. As such forces were unable to withstand the attacks, there gradually emerged a crescent-shaped indentation. Whether this curve was created intentionally by Hannibal or accidentally, it became a huge buffer for absorbing the attack power of the Roman forces. As this strong power gradually weakened because of the lengthening of the front and came to the low point of its momentum at the time of approaching the bottom part of the Carthaginian front, the Carthaginians, who were inferior in overall strength but superior in cavalry force, quickly launched their flanking cavalry forces to complete the encirclement of the Roman forces, thus turning Cannae into a killing field for killing 70,000 people. The two battles were different but had a common way of working. In both, the dominant strategy was to evade enemy frontal attacks and to weaken the enemy momentum. An operational approach of obviously deviating from frontal fighting was adopted, and the point of decline of enemy attack power was properly selected as the optimal moment for the relevant forces' own counterattacks. The operational method used obviously conformed to the rule of the golden section and the side-principal rule.

If the two cases of warfare are not viewed as coincidental or isolated phenomena, then we will see the shining of the light of the rule of the golden section move widely in the history of war. This point has been perhaps even more prominent in modern warfare. During the Second World War, the entire German operation of attacking France was immersed in the pith of the two rules that we discussed. Such moves as changing tanks from being subordinate to infantry being the main battle weapons, using blitzkrieg as the main operational doctrine on the basis of discarding First World War practices, and selecting the Ardennes mountains as the main direction of attack of the German forces, an action which surprised not only the enemy but also conceptually obsolete old generals at the German high command, must have seemed to be unorthodox and had a prominent character of deviation toward the side element. It was this deviation character that led to the fundamental change in military thinking of the entire German military and also made Schlieffen's dream of "sweeping across the English Channel" a nightmare for the British at Dunkirk. Before that time, who would have thought that the blueprint of this miracle would come from the hands of two relatively low-level officers—Manstein and Guderian?

During the same world war, there was also the Japanese attack on Pearl Harbor, which was similar to the operation of attacking France, an operation with a prominent side-principal tendency. Isoroko Yamamoto used aircraft carriers in the same way Guderian used tanks. Conceptually, Yamamoto still viewed battleships as the main force for decisive naval battles in the future, but sensitively and correctly selected aircraft carriers and their carrier-borne aircraft as the principal weapons for operations against the U.S. Navy. More interestingly, he did not carry out frontal attacks on the long Pacific coast of the continental United States when launching attacks on the Americans. At the same time, he fully considered the attack radius of his joint fleet, that is, the optimal location that his fist was capable of hitting. Thus he selected, as the point of attack, Hawaii which, while being of critical importance to controlling the entire Pacific Ocean, the Americans refused to believe to be the point of attack even after receiving intelligence before the operation. As should be pointed out, this believer in decisive naval battles chose a sneak attack on Pearl Harbor, instead of a naval battle dreamed about by him all the time, in the first major battle bearing on the future course of the war. Consequently, he won a victory with surprising moves by hitting side targets

With the analysis above, we should understand that neither the rule of the golden section nor the side-principal rule should be understood literally in a narrow manner; instead it is necessary to grasp their essence. A rapidly changing battlefield will give any military leader or commander neither adequate time nor adequate information for carefully determining the point of the golden section or the degree of deviation toward the side element. Even the two core elements of the two rules, 0.618 and "deviation toward the side element," are not constants in a mathematical sense. Rather, they represent the thousands of manifestations of the god of victory in ever-changing courses of wars, battlefields, and war situations.

It is sometimes manifested in the selection of means. For instance, during the Gulf War, Schwarzkopf used aerial bombings as the dominant means, while using as supporting forces the army and the navy which had always been the main combat forces.

It is sometimes manifested in the selection of tactics. For instance, Donitz changed ship-to-ship naval warfare into submarines' attacks on merchant ships; this "Wolfpack" tactic posed a much greater threat to Britain than naval battles.

It is sometimes manifested in the selection of weapons. For instance, Napoleon's artillery, Guderian's tanks, Yamamoto's aircraft carriers, and the precision ammunition used in Operation Gold Coast were all main weapons which were able to shift the balance in war.

It is sometimes manifested in the selection of the point of attack. For instance, during the Trafalgar naval battle, Nelson wisely selected the rear portion, instead of the forward portion, of the French fleet as the main point of attack, thereby producing a naval war victory, which would lead to the birth of a maritime empire. [13]

It is sometimes manifested in the selection of opportunities of fighting. For instance, in the Fourth Middle East War, Sadat selected 6 October, in the month of Ramadan for Muslims, as the D-day for Egyptian forces' crossing of the Suez Canal, and launched the attack in the afternoon when sunlight, going from west to east, was directed at the pupils of the Israelis' eyes, thereby demolishing the myth of Israeli invincibility. [14]

It is sometimes manifested in the uneven deployment of forces. For instance, before the First World War, the German High Command formulated the Schlieffen Plan for invading France, planning the bold move of deploying 53 of the 72 German divisions on the right flank to be used as the main attacking force and deploying the remaining 19 divisions along the long frontlines of the left flank and the center. In this way, the sand-table exercise became the most famous war plan in history which was never implemented.

It is sometimes manifested in the use of stratagem. For instance, in 260 B.C., there was a rivalry between Qin and Zhao. The Zhaoxiang King of Qin was not in a hurry to have a decisive battle with the enemy, and adopted Fan Sui's advice, first attacking Shangdang in Han to deprive Zhao of its backing. Then he faked a willingness to negotiate a peace, and, as a result, the lords stopped giving assistance to Zhao. He used the stratagem of sowing discord, and, as a result, the king of Zhao dismissed General Lian Po and appointed armchair strategist Zhao Kuo as commander. As a consequence, the Zhao force was defeated at Changping. Qin's victory and Zhao's defeat in this battle should be, more properly, be attributed to Fan Sui's stratagem, rather than to the Qin force's powerfulness. [15]

We should also pay focused attention to and study another phenomenon, that is, that more and more countries are looking beyond the military sphere when handling important issues such as political, economic, and national security issues. They use other means to supplement, enrich, or even replace military means, so as to achieve objectives which cannot be achieved by military force alone. This has been the most important episode of the side element's modifying the principal element in relation to war on the basis of a conception of war. At the same time, this also indicates that in future wars there will be increasingly frequent occurrences of the side-principal structure formed by the military means and other means.

All the selections discussed above had the character of "deviation toward the side element." Like the rule of the golden section, the side-principal rule is opposed to all forms of parallel placement, balance, symmetry, being all-encompassing, and smoothness, but, instead, advocates using the sword to cut the side. Only by avoiding frontal collisions will it be possible for your sword to cut apart things without being damaged. This is the most basic grammar of victory for the ancient article of war.

If we call the rule of the golden section in the sphere of art the rule of aesthetics, then why do we not also call the side-principal rule—its mirror image in the military sphere—the rule of victory?

The Dominant Element and the Whole Thing: the Essence of the Side-Principal Structure

Among the many internal elements comprising a thing, there must be a certain element which assumes a prominent or dominant position among all the elements. If the relationship between this element and the other elements is harmonious and perfect, it will be in accord with the 0.618:1 formula in some places and, also, in accord with the side-principal rule. For, here, "all the elements" constitute the main body, that is, the principal element; the "certain element" serves as the directing element and is thus the side element. Once an object has acquired specific purposefulness, the side element and the principal element will form a dominant-subordinate relationship. When two bulls fight, the bulls constitute the principal element, while the horns constitute the side element. When two swords are pitted against each other, the swords constitute the principal element, while the edges constitute the side element. It is very clear which is dominant and which is subordinate. When the purpose is changed, a new dominant element will emerge and replace the old dominant element and form a new side-principal relationship with all the existing elements. Grasping the relationship between the dominant element and all the elements in an object is tantamount to grasping the essence of the rule of the golden section and the side-principal rule.

On the basis of such an understanding, we can quickly establish five most important relationships among all the complex relationships of war: the dominant weapons and all the weapons; the dominant means and all the means; the dominant force and all the forces; the dominant direction and all the directions; and the dominant sphere and all the spheres. The relationship between the five dominant elements and all the elements in the five areas basically represent the side-principal relationship which exists in wars in a widespread manner. Take again the example of the Gulf War. In Operation Desert Storm, the dominant weapons used by the Allied forces were stealth aircraft, cruise missiles, and precision bombs, with all other weapons playing a subordinate role. The dominant means was the 38 consecutive days of aerial bombardment, with other means playing a supplemental role. The dominant force was the air force, with all other forces playing a supporting role. The dominant direction was to hit the Republican Guard as the target of focused attacks, with all other battlefield targets serving as secondary targets. The dominant sphere was the military sphere, with all other spheres providing comprehensive support in the forms of economic sanctions, diplomatic isolation, and media offensives.

However, it is not our goal to just clarify such relationships. To people engaged in war, what is the most important is not to clarify things but to grasp and apply such relationships. As we know, all countries' war resources are limited. Even such a powerful country as the United States still has to continually think about cost-effectiveness (the principal of the "least consumption of energy") and how to fight wars in a more marvelous way and to produce more splendid war results. Therefore, it is very necessary for any country to use and allocate war resources in a sound and strategic manner. This will require finding a correct method, that is, the issue of how to consciously apply the side-principal rule. In fact, many countries have already subconsciously applied this rule before now.

After the dissolution of the former Soviet Union, Russia's military capability has declined continually. It has not only lost its superpower position of confronting the U.S. forces, but has even found it difficult to maintain national security now. Under such circumstances, the Russian high command has adjusted its future strategy in a timely fashion, despite being in a difficult position, making tactical, or even strategic, nuclear weapons the dominant weapons of first choice if a war is launched against Russia. On the basis of this decision, it has also adjusted the distribution of conventional weapons and nuclear weapons in an overall way. Contrary to Russia, being the only superpower in the world, the U.S. Armed Forces have established as their new strategic objectives for the three services a "comprehensively superior" (army), [16] a (navy) "moving from sea to land," and a "globally engaged" (air force)." [17] On that basis, digitized equipment, new types of amphibious attack vessels, and long-range stealth aircraft have been selected as a new generation of weapons, which appear to be replacing contemporary trump cards like tanks of the M-1 series, aircraft carriers, and F-16 fighters as the dominant weapons in the U.S. arsenal.

As can be seen in the strategic adjustments made by Russia and the United States in regard to their respective dominant weapons, it seems that the practice of selecting the dominant weapons on the basis of the magnitude of destructive power is obsolete. As far as the selection of the dominant weapons is concerned, the destructive power of weapons is but one of many items of technical performance of weapons. What is more important than technical performance is the basic consideration of the war aim, operational objectives, and security environment. Thus, the dominant weapons should be the most effective weapons for accomplishing the above-mentioned goals. Furthermore, it is necessary to have them organically combined with other weapons, so as to formulate the dominant element of a complete arms system. Under conditions of modern technology, dominant weapons are no longer individual weapons, but "systems of weapons," which are also components of larger systems. [18] The emergence of a lot of high and new technology and the continual adjustment of war aims have provided enough space for the selection of dominant weapons and the combination of dominant weapons with other weapons, and have, at the same time, also made the dominant-subordinate relationship between dominant weapons and the other weapons even more complicated. [19]

The same factors are also affecting the use of the means of war. It is becoming obsolete to automatically consider military action the dominant means and the other means supporting means in war. Perhaps, in the not too distant future, the military means will be only one of all the available means in wars such as one of fighting terrorist organizations of the bin Laden category. A more effective means that can strike at bin Laden in a destructive way is perhaps not the cruise missile, but a financial suffocation war carried out on the Internet.

As means have become more complicated, there has emerged a consequence that is unexpected to all soldiers: the civilianization of war. Therefore, here the issue of the relationship between the dominant force and all forces under discussion here also encompasses the issue of degree of participation of the entire population in war, in addition to the deployment, allocation, and use of military forces in combat operations. As professional soldiers' war or quasi-war activities have increasingly become an important factor affecting national security, the issue as to which constitute the dominant force in future wars, an issue which has never been a question, has become a question worldwide. For example, the incidents of attacks conducted by "web rascals" on the network centers of the U.S. Defense Department and the Indian Defense Ministry were evidence in this regard.

Whether an action is a pure war action, a nonwar military action, or a nonmilitary war action, any action of a combat nature will entail an issue of how to accurately select the main direction of operation and the main point of attack, that is, to determine your main orientation in view of all the factors of the war concerned, the battlefields, and the battle fronts. This is the most difficult issue even for all those commanders who are in control of good weapons, a multitude of means, and sufficient manpower. However, Alexander, Hannibal, Nelson, and Nimitz as well as Sun Wu and Sun Bin of ancient China were good at selecting main directions of attack which would surprise enemy forces completely. Liddle Hart also noted this point. He referred to the approach of selecting the line of least resistance and the direction of action least expected by the enemy as the "indirect strategy." As the arena of war has expanded, encompassing the political, economic, diplomatic, cultural, and psychological spheres, in addition to the land, sea, air, space, and electronics spheres, the interactions among all factors have made it difficult for the military sphere to serve as the automatic dominant sphere in every war. War will be conducted in nonwar spheres. This notion sounds strange and is difficult to accept, but more and more signs indicate that this is the trend. In fact, even in ancient times, war was not always confined to one single sphere. Lian Xiangru's diplomatic battle of "returning the jade in an undamaged condition to Zhao" and the virtual war conducted by Mo Zi and Gongshu Ban were classical examples of winning or precluding a war with nonmilitary actions. This method of resolving the problem of war through actions in multiple spheres should give insights to people today. The era of comprehensive use of highly developed technologies has provided us with much greater room for applying wisdom and means than ancient people, so that people's dream of winning military victories in nonmilitary spheres and winning wars with nonwar means can now become reality. If we want to have victory in future wars, we must be fully prepared intellectually for this scenario, that is, to be ready to carry out a war which, affecting all areas of life of the countries involved, may be conducted in a sphere not dominated by military actions. It is now still unknown what weapons, means, and personnel such wars will use and in what direction and sphere such wars will be conducted.

What is known is one point, that is, that whatever the mode of warfare, victory always belongs to the side which correctly uses the side-principal rule to grasp the relationship between the "dominant" and the "whole."

A Rule, Not a Set Formula

War is the most difficult to explain and understand. It needs support from technology, but technology cannot substitute for morale and stratagem; it needs artistic inspiration, but rejects romanticism and sentimentalism; it needs mathematical precision, but precision can sometimes render it mechanical and rigid; it needs philosophical abstraction, but pure thinking does not help to seize short-lived opportunities amid iron and fire.

This is no formula of war. No one dares to arrogantly claim to have the perfect method in the sphere of war. No one has ever been able to use one method to win all wars. But it does not mean that there are no rules regarding war. A few people have had their names listed in the roster of ever-victorious generals because they have discovered and grasped rules of victory. Those names testify to the existence of rules of victory, but no one has revealed the secret. For a long time—almost as long as the history of war—people have regarded them as flashes of electricity in the brains of gifted commanders, but have seldom realized that they are hidden in bloody fighting characterized by collisions of swords and the smoke of gunpowder. In fact, any rule is like a sheet of paper, and what is important is whether you are able to poke a hole in it.

The side-principal rule is just such a sheet of paper. It is both simple and complicated and both fluctuating and stable. As has often happened, a person with a lucky finger sometimes unintentionally pokes a hole in it, and the door of victory opens to him immediately. It is so simple that it can be expressed by a set of digits or a rule of grammar. It is so complicated that you are unable to find an answer even if you are proficient in mathematics and grammar. It is like smoke and is difficult to grasp. It is as constant as a shadow and accompanies every sunrise of victory.

Consequently, we regard the side-principal rule as a principle, but not a theorem. We have taken full account of the relativity of the principle. Relative things should not be applied mechanically and require no precise measurement. Relativity is not absolute whiteness, and thus does not fear black swans. [20]

However, through study of the history of war, we have determined that the side-principal rule is a rule of victory, but how it can be used correctly will be an issue for each individual operator to determine in view of the particular circumstances. For the phenomenon of antimony in war has always puzzled every person pursuing victory: those acting against the laws will undoubtedly fail, but those sticking to set practices are also unlike to win. "Six multiplied by 6 is 36. There are stratagems in numbers, and there are numbers in stratagems. The yin and the yang are coordinated. Opportunities are there. It is not possible to manufacture opportunities. Manufacturing will not work." The "36 stratagems" constitute the revealing of the way things work. That is, no matter how many examples of war we can find to demonstrate that the causes of victories involved were in accord with 0.618, the next person who plans a war, battle, or engagement strictly in accordance with the rule of the golden section will almost certainly eat the bitter fruit of defeat. Whether the rule of the golden section or the side-principal rule is involved, the key is to grasp the essence and apply the principle, instead of making mechanical applications, as the legendary Dong Shi emulated the beauty Xi Shi. In the famous Rossbach battle and the Luzern battle in European history, the attacking sides in both cases used the Alexander-style "diagonal attack formation," but the results were totally different. In the Rossbach battle, commanders of the French-Austrian force copied the history of war faithfully. They made troop movements and built battle formations right under the eyes of Frederick the Great. The French-Austrian force attempted to use the diagonal formation to attack the left wing of the Prussian force. As a result, it was thoroughly beaten by the Prussian force which made adjustments in deployment in a timely manner. A year later, at Luzern, Frederick again encountered an Austrian force which was three times as large as Frederick's force. But, this time, he performed brilliantly. He also used the diagonal attack formation, but managed to annihilate the Austrian force. It is thought-provoking that the same method of operation produced entirely different results. [21] This incident tells us that there is no method of war which is always right. There are only rules which are always correct. It also tells us that correct rules do not guarantee that there will always be victories; the secret to victory is to correctly apply rules. Similarly, with regard to the side-principal rule, the emphasis is on using the side element for modifying the principal element, but it is not the case that deviation toward the side element will always produce a victory. Deviation toward the side element means mainly deviation in terms of lines of thought and essence, instead of deviation in form. For instance, in actual warfare, it is not the case that every time the point of attack should be located at the point of deviation in a 0.618 style in order to be in accord with rules of victory. It is possible that this time, rules of victory call for frontal breakthroughs. Thus, this time, the "principal" element is the "side" element. This is the nature of war as art. This art element cannot be replaced by mathematics, philosophy or other areas of science and technology. [22] Thus, we are sure that in this sense the military technological revolution cannot replace the revolution in the art of military affairs.

As should also be indicated, the side-principal principle is unavoidably similar to the "surprise/non-surprise" principle advocated by ancient Chinese strategists; nevertheless they are not entirely the same, for ancient strategists advocated the use of surprise moves and non-surprise moves at different times. As Sun Zi said, "in fighting, it is necessary to use non-suprise moves to gather strength and to use surprise moves to achieve victory. Fighting entails just surprise and non-surprise moves. There is endless change to the use of surprise and non-surprise moves." [23] The side element and the principal element are not two methods which can each be used without the other, but are an expression of an objective law. The most important distinction is the following: It is certainly true that in the history of war the cases of winning with surprise moves have all been marvelous because of their excellent execution, but not all victories have been achieved through surprise moves. There have also been many examples of achieving victories through non-surprise moves. The side-principal principle is different. Through analysis, the trace of the rule of victory can be seen in every victory, whether the victory has been achieved through surprise or non-surprise moves: that is, that the victory is the effect of the side-principal principle demonstrated in either in a "surprise" or "non-surprise" way.

No matter how clear we state the side-principal rule or the rule of victory, we can only proceed with the application of the rule in a fuzzy way.

Sometimes, being fuzzy is the best way of reaching clarity. For only fuzziness is good for being grasped in an overall manner. This is the Eastern style of thinking. But, in a peculiar way, it has met Occidental wisdom at the golden point of 0.618. As a result, Occidental logic, reasoning, and precision and Eastern instinct, understanding, and murkiness have provided the basis for joining Eastern and Occidental military wisdom and have generated the rule of victory that we have discussed. It shines with glitter, has both Eastern mystery and Occidental rigor, as if eaves at the Taihe Palace are placed on a column at the Pathernon Temple, looking majestic and vibrant.

Notes

[1]   Pythagoras was a philosopher and mathematician of ancient Greece whose famous axiom was "Everything is a matter of numbers." That is, all existing things can be viewed, in the final analysis, as relationships of numbers. In Pythagoras' theory, things rational and things non- rational were mixed, but his theory still exerted profound influences on the development of ancient Greek philosophy and Medieval European thought. Copernicus recognized Pythagoras' astronomical concepts as precursors of his proposition. Galileo was also considered an advocate of Pythagoras' theory. Using the golden section to demonstrate harmonious relationships in the world was only one specific application of Pythagoras thinking; see *Concise Encyclopedia Britannica*, Vol. 1, p. 715.

[2]   See Summerson, *Classical Language of Architecture*, p. 90.

[3]   Divide a straight line of the length of L into two sections in such a way that the ratio of one section to the entire line equals the ratio of the other section to this section, that is, X:L=(L-X):X. Such a division is called the "golden section," and the ratio is approximately 0.618. From ancient Greece to the 19th century, people believed this ratio was of aesthetic value in formative art. In actual application, the simplest method is to use as approximate values such ratios as 2:3, 3:5, 5:8, and 8:13 produced on the basis of the series of numbers of 2, 3, 5, 8, 13, 21 . . . ; see *Ci Hai* [*A Grand Dictionary*] (Shanghai Dictionary Press), 1980, pp. 2057–2058.

[4]   Dive bombing is a main method used by attack aircraft to launch short-range missiles, rockets, and guided and unguided bombs. During an attack, an attack aircraft flies at a low altitude to reach the combat point (40–50 km from targets) and then rises to 2,000–4,000 meters, changing into the combat direction. At 5–10 km from the target, it begins to dive and drops ordinance at 1,300–1,600

meters and 600–1,000 meters from angles of 30–50 degrees. In diving attacks, weapons' destructive precision is the highest [graph omitted]; see the Russian periodical *Foreign Military Reviews*, No. 10 (1992).

[5] See *Zhongguo Lidai Zhanzheng Shi* [*The History of War of China*] (Military Translation Press), Vol. 1, pp. 257–273, illustrations 1–26 of the annex.

[6] See Fuller, *A Military History of the Western World*, Vol. 1, p. 117. This book contains a good analysis of the battle of Arbela and also illustrations graphically depicting the situations of the battlefield.

[7] Masaier Boduo (France), *Di Er Ci Shijie Dazhan Lishi Baikequanshu* [*Encyclopedia of the History of World War II*] (PLA Press, 1988). "The Soviet Union's War Against Germany," pp. 684–694.

[8] See "Biographies of Sun Zi and We Qi," in *Shi Ji* [*Records of History*].

[9] See "Cao Gui's Analysis of War," in *Zuo Zhuan*. Later, when participating in the Qi-Lu meeting at Ke, Cao Gui seized Duke Heng of Qi with a knife, thereby forcing Qi to return to Lu land seized from Lu. He was a good general, with both courage and wisdom; see "Biographies of Assassins," in *Shi Ji*.

[10] The battle of Cannae was the most famous battle in Western history and has been mentioned in almost all works on the history of war. The book *How Great Generals Win*, written by Bevin Alexander (U.S.), depicts the battle of Cannae vividly with the support of illustrations, and can help to understand the "side-principal rule" that we have discussed; see *Tongshuai Juesheng Zhi Dao* [*How Great Generals Win*] (Xinhua Press, 1996), pp. 11–13.

[11] In 1937–1938 Manstein was the first deputy chief of staff of the German Army. Because of internal conflicts in the German Army, Manstein was expelled from the Army Command and became commander of the 18th Division. In 1939, the German Army Command issued an operational plan for the western front, the "Yellow Operation Plan," indicating the intention to use frontal assaults carried out by strong right flank forces to defeat the British-French forces expected to be encountered in Belgium, while using weaker forces to cover the flanks. Obviously, this plan was a refurbished version of the 1914 Schliffen Plan. Manstein, then chief of staff of Group Army A, formulated his own operational plan in the name of Group Army A. He submitted the plan to the Army Command repeatedly in the form of a memorandum or a draft operational plan. But it was rejected by high-raking generals of the Army Command each time. Annoyed at Manstein, the Army Command transferred Manstein to the post of commander of the 38th Army. Manstein reported to Hitler his ideas by taking advantage of his meeting with Hitler, and persuaded Hitler who, entirely a layman in the area of military affairs, had a high level of capacity for understanding. The main point of one plan, called the Manstein Plan by Liddle Hart after the war, was to

conduct a surprise attack through the Ardennes mountains, conducting focused assaults on the left flank and using armored forces in a concentrated way; see Mansitanyin [Manstein], *Shiqu de Shenli* [*Lost Victory*] (The Academy of Military Science of the Chinese People's Liberation Army, 1980). Guderian was commander of the 19th Armored Army and the best implementing agent of the Manstein Plan; see Gudeli'an [Guderian], *Shanji Yingxiong* [*Blitzkrieg Heroes*] (Zhanshi Press, 1981).

[12]   After becoming commander of a joint fleet, Yamamoto rejected the Japanese Navy staff's idea of attacking the Philippines first and believed it necessary to launch a sneak attack on the U.S. Pacific Fleet first, so as to paralyze it. On 7 December 1941, under General Nagumo's command, 6 aircraft carriers with 423 aircraft attacked Pearl Harbor according to Yamamoto's plan, sinking the battleship Arizona and three other battleships of the U.S. Navy and destroying aircraft, greatly damaging the U.S. Pacific Fleet; see Liddle Hart, *History of the Second World War*, pp. 276–335.

[13]   Before the Trafalgar naval battle, Nelson told his subordinate captains a "secret method," that is, to change the traditional naval linear operational method by dividing the warships into two groups. One group would attack the middle of the enemy fleet at a 90-degree angle, separating the rear portion from the middle portion. Then concentrated force would attack ships of the rear portion of the enemy fleet. Another group would separate the middle portion from the forward portion and conduct a concentrated attack on the middle portion. It would be too late when ships of the forward portion of the enemy fleet should try to come back to provide help. The Trafalgar naval battle proceeded almost exactly as Nelson predicted. Although he was killed from a battle wound, the British Navy achieved a complete victory; see Ding Chaobi, *Shijie Jindai Haizhan Shi* [*The History of Modern Naval Wars of the World*] (Haiyang Press, 1994), pp. 143–155.

[14]   *Geha'erde Kangce'erman* [as printed 2706 0761 1422 1795 1660 4595 1422 2581] (Germany), *Di Si Ci Zhongdong Zhanzheng* [*The Fourth Middle East War*] (Shangwu Press, 1975); *Qiaoen Jinqi* [as printed 0829 1869 6855 1142] (U.S.) and others, *Zhongdong Zhanzheng* [*Middle East Wars*] (Shanghai Translation Press, 1979).

[15]   See *Zhongguo Lidai Zhanzheng Shi* [*The History of War in China*] (Military Translation Press), vol. 2, p. 197.

[16]   "Comprehensive superiority" was a strategic goal advocated by the U.S. Army in its document, "Conception of the Army in 2010."

[17]   "Global engagement" was a 21st-century air force development strategy put forward by the U.S. Air Force at the end of 1997 to replace the "global force for global reach" strategic doctrine used to deal with the situation after the Cold

War. In this respect, the six core areas of capability of the air force were emphasized: air and space superiority; global attack; global rapid mobility; precision
strike; information superiority; and flexible operational support; see "Global Engagement and the Conception of the U.S. Air Force in the 21st Century."

[18]   The concept of the "system of systems" was the result of joint research conducted
by Admiral Owens, the former vice chairman of the Joint Chiefs of Staff, and
his senior advisor, Black. According to Owens, the contemporary military technological revolution is no longer a matter of revolution with regard to warships,
aircraft, tanks, and other weapon platforms, but there has been the entry of such
factors as sensor systems, communication systems, and precision guided
weapons systems. The entry of such systems will generate a fundamental revolution in the force structure and modes of operation of the military. Perhaps, in
the future, there should no longer be the division into an army, a navy, and an air
force, but the division into a "sensor force," "mobile striking force," and "smart
support force"; see the interview of Owens by Chen Bojiang, Guofang Daxue
Xuebao, Xiandai Junshi, and Shijie Junshi.

[19]   We do not support the optimistic view of the technology faction with regard to
the military revolution. We do not believe that technology can penetrate the fog
of the "contingency" of war, for contingency in war does not come from physical or geographical obstacles, but from people's minds.

[20]   The side-principal rule is not the kind of theorem such as the statements that
"all men will die" and that "all swans are white." Rather it is a rule for guiding
people to victory in war.

[21]   See Fuller, *A Military History of the Western World*, Vol. 2, p. 201; A Concise
History of War, p. 86.

[22]   We do not reject or neglect mathematical analysis, especially in the era of widespread use of computers and in this country of ours where there is a tradition of
advocating fuzziness and a dislike of precision. In his *Guoji Zhengzhi Yu Junshi
Wenti Ruogan Shulianghua Fenxi Fangfa* [*Several Methods of Quantitative Analysis of International Political and Military Issues*], Li Hongzhi mentioned the use
by Nigula Shiweite [as printed 1441 0657 2139 2457 1218 3676] of the "Beiyete
[as printed 6296 0673 3676] method" to analyze the Vietnam War, the Sino-
Soviet conflict, and the Arab-Israeli wars. In 1993 Li Hongzhi and others made
accurate forecasts of the Bosnia-Herzegovina war by using the method; see
Guoji Zhengzhi Yu Junshi Wenti Ruogan Shulianghua Fenxi Fangfa (Military
Science Press).

[23]   The quotation is from "Momentum," in *Sun Zi Binfa* [*Art of War* by Sun Zi].
The "surprise-non- surprise" principle is an important concept used by ancient
military strategists in relation to methods of war. To unpredictably make moves

unexpected by the enemy is the "surprise" method; to confront the enemy on the battlefield in an open manner is the "non-surprise" method. Emperor Taizong of Tang had a good understanding of the "surprise-non-surprise principle." The Weiqing engagement was an example in this regard. "A Dialogue Between Emperor Taizong of Tang and Li Weigong" recorded the views of Li Shimin and Li Jing on the "surprise-non-surprise principle."

Chapter 7

Ten Thousand Methods Combined as One: Combinations That Transcend Boundaries

Today's wars will affect the price of gasoline in pipelines, the price of food in supermarkets, and the price of securities on the stock exchange. They will also disrupt the ecological balance, and push their way into every one of our homes by way of the television screen.—Alvin Toffler

Understanding the rules by which victory is achieved [the subject of the previous chapter] certainly does not equate to having a lock on victory, any more than knowing the techniques of long-distance racing equates to being able to win a marathon. Discovery of the rules of victory can deepen people's knowledge of the laws of warfare, and increase the standard by which military arts are practiced. But on the battlefield, the victor will certainly not have won because he has detected more of the rules of victory. The key will be which contender truly grasps the rules of victory in their essence.

In a possible future war, the rules of victory will make extremely harsh demands on the victor. Not only will they, as in the past, demand that one know thoroughly all the ingenious ways to contest for victory on the battlefield. Even more so, they will impose demands which will mean that most of the warriors will be inadequately prepared, or will feel as though they are in the dark: the war will be fought and won in a war beyond the battlefield; the struggle for victory will take place on a battlefield beyond the battlefield.

Using this specific meaning, even modern military men like Powell, Schwarzkopf, or even Sullivan [U.S. Army Chief of Staff, 1991–1995] or Shalikashvili cannot be considered "modern." Instead, they seem more like a group of traditional military men. This is because a chasm has already appeared between traditional soldiers and what we call modern soldiers. Although this gap is not unbridgeable, it does require a leap in terms of a complete military rethink. To many professional military people this is potentially something they could not hope to achieve if they spent the rest of their lives on it. In fact it is very simple. The [necessary new] method is to create a complete military Machiavelli.

Achieve objectives by fair means or foul, that is the most important spiritual legacy of this Italian political thinker of the Renaissance. [1] In the Middle Ages, this represented a breakthrough against romantic chivalry and the declining tradition of knighthood. It meant using means, some possibly comprehensive, without restraint to achieve an objective; this holds for warfare also. Even though Machiavelli was not the earliest source of "an ideology of going beyond limits" (China's Han Feizi preceded him [2]), he was its clearest exponent.

The existence of boundaries is a prerequisite for differentiating objects one from another. In a world where all things are interdependent, the significance of boundaries is merely relative. The expression "to exceed limits" means to go beyond things which are called or understood to be boundaries. It does not matter whether they fall into the category of physical, spiritual, or technical, or if they are called "limits," "defined limits," "constraints," "borders," "rules," "laws," "maximum limits," or even "taboos." Speaking in terms of war, this could mean the boundary between the battlefield and what is not the battlefield, between what is a weapon and what is not, between soldier and noncombatant, between state and non-state or supra-state. Possibly it might also include technical, scientific, theoretical, psychological, ethical, traditional, customary, and other sorts of boundaries. In summary, it means all boundaries which restrict warfare to within a specified range. The real meaning of the concept of exceeding limits which we propose is, first of all, to transcend ideology. Only secondarily does it mean, when taking action, to transcend limits and boundaries when necessary, when they can be transcended, and select the most appropriate means (including extreme means). It does not mean that extreme means must be selected always and everywhere. When speaking of military people in this technologically integrated era, there are actually more facets to consider now, an abundance of usable resources (meaning all material and non-material resources), so that no matter what limits military people face, there is always a means which can break through those limits, many more means than in the environment from whence Machiavelli came.

Thus, the requirements for modern military people with regard to transcending their way of thinking also involve being more thorough.

We said earlier [p. 115] that combinations were the cocktails in the glasses of the great masters of warfare. [That is, Alexander the Great and the martial kings of the Zhou Dynasty never heard of cocktails, but they knew the value of the combined use of things.] But in past wars, the combination of weapons, means, battle arrays, and stratagems was all done within the limits of the military sphere. This narrow sense of the concept of combinations is, of course, very inadequate for today. He who wants to win today's wars, or those of tomorrow, to have victory firmly in his grasp, must "combine" all of the resources of war which he has at his disposal and use them as means to prosecute the war. And even this will not be enough. He must combine them according to the demands of the rules of victory. Even this will still not be enough, because the rules of victory cannot guarantee that victory will drop like ripe fruit into a basket. It still needs a skilled hand to pluck it. That hand is the concept of "going beyond limits," surpassing all boundaries and conforming with the laws of victory when conducting warfare with combinations. Thus we obtain a complete concept, a completely new method of warfare called "modified combined war that goes beyond limits." ["pian zheng shi chao xian zuhe zhan" 0252 2973 1709 6389 7098 4809 0678 2069]

Supra-National Combinations [Chao Guojia Zuhe]

[Combining National, International, and Non-State Organizations]

It seems we now face another paradox: in terms of theory, "going beyond limits" should mean no restrictions of any kind, going beyond everything. But in fact, unlimited surpassing of limits is impossible to achieve. Any surpassing of limits can only be done within certain restrictions. That is, "going beyond limits" certainly does not equate to "no limits," only to the expansion of "limited." That is, to go beyond the intrinsic boundaries of a certain area or a certain direction, and to combine opportunities and means in more areas or in more directions, so as to achieve a set objective.

This is our definition of "combined war that goes beyond limits."

As a method of warfare with "beyond limits" as its major feature, its principle is to assemble and blend together more means to resolve a problem in a range wider than the problem itself. For example, when national security is threatened, the answer is not simply a matter of selecting the means to confront the other nation militarily, but rather a matter of dispelling the crisis through the employment of "supra-national combinations." We see from history that the nation-state is the highest form of the idea of security. For Chinese people, the nation-state even equates to the great concept of all-under-heaven [tianxia 1131 0007, classical name for China]. Nowadays, the significance of the word "country" in terms of nationality or geography is no more than a large or small link in the human society of the "world village." Modern countries are affected more and more by regional or world-wide organizations, such as the European Community [sic; now the European Union], ASEAN, OPEC, APEC, the International Monetary Fund, the World Bank, the WTO, and the biggest of them all, the United Nations. Besides these, a large number of multinational organizations and non-state organizations of all shapes and sizes, such as multinational corporations, trade associations, peace and environmental organizations, the Olympic Committee, religious organizations, terrorist organizations, small groups of hackers, etc., dart from left and right into a country's path. These multinational, non-state, and supra-national organizations together constitute an up and coming worldwide system of power. [3]

Perhaps not many people have noticed, but the factors described above are leading us into an era of transformation in which great power politics are yielding to supra-national politics. The main characteristic of this era is that it is transitional: many indications of it are appearing, and many processes are just now beginning. National power is a main part, and supra-national, multinational, and non-state power is another main part, and the final verdict on which of these will play the main role on the international stage has yet to be delivered. On the one hand, the big powers still play the dominant part. In particular, that all-round big power, the United States, and the big economic powers like Japan and Germany, and the rising power China, and the fading power Russia, are all trying to exert their own influence on the overall situation. On the other hand, there are far-sighted big powers which have clearly already begun to borrow the power of supra-national, multinational, and non-state players to redouble and expand their own influence. They realize they cannot achieve their objectives by relying only on their own power. The most recent and most typical example is the use of the euro to unify the European Community. This vigorous process has continued to today, but it has just now emerged from a period of floundering. The time when the process will conclude is still far off. The recent direction and the long-range prospect are not clear-cut. They are things which come about as a matter of course. Nevertheless, some signs of a trend are evident; that is, the curtain is now slowly falling on the era in which the final decision on victory and defeat is made by way of state vs. state tests of strength. Instead, the curtain is quietly opening on an era in which problems will be resolved and objectives achieved by using supra-national means on a stage larger than the size of a country.[4]

In view of this, we list "supra-national combinations" as being among the essential factors of warfare that exceed limits.

In this world of mutually penetrating political, economic, ideological, technical, and cultural influences, with networks, clones, Hollywood, hot girls [la mei 6584 1188—Internet pornography], and the World Cup easily bypassing territorial boundary markers, it is very hard to realize hopes of assuring security and pursuing interests in a purely national sense. Only a fool like Saddam Hussein would seek to fulfill his own wild ambition by outright territorial occupation. Facts make it clear that acting in this way in the closing years of the 20th century is clearly behind the times, and will certainly lead to defeat. Also pursuing its national security and national interests, as a mature great power the United States appeared much smarter than Iraq. Since the day they stepped onto the international stage, the Americans have been seizing things by force or by trickery, and the benefits they obtained from other countries were many times greater than anyone knows than what Iraq got from Kuwait. The reasons cannot be explained as merely "might makes right," and they are not just a problem of an evasion of international norms and vetoes. This is because, in all its foreign actions, the United States always tries to get as many followers as possible, in order to avoid becoming a leader with no support, out there all alone. Except for small countries like Grenada and Panama, against which it took direct and purely military action, in most situations the United States pursues and realizes its own interests by using supra-national means. In coping with the Iraq problem, the method the Americans used was a very typical supra-national combination. During the entire course of their actions, the Americans acted in collusion with others, maneuvering among various political groups, and getting the support of practically all the countries in the United Nations. The United States got this, the premier international organization in all the world, to issue a resolution to make trouble under a pretext provided by the United States, and dragged over 30 countries into the joint force sent against Iraq. After the war, the United States was again successful in organizing an economic embargo of Iraq which has continued for eight years, and it used arms inspections to maintain continuous political and military pressure on Iraq. This has left Iraq in long-term political isolation and dire economic straits.

Since the Gulf War, the trend toward supra-national combinations in warfare or other conflicts has been increasingly obvious. The more recent the event, the more prominent this characteristic is, and the more frequently it becomes a means used by more and more countries. In the past ten years this trend has become the backdrop for drastic international social turbulence. Worldwide economic integration, internationalization of domestic politics, the networking of information resources, the increased frequency of new technological eras, the concealment of cultural conflicts, and the strengthening of non-state organizations, all bring human society both convenience and troubles, in equal means. This is why the great powers, and even some medium and small sized countries, act in concert without need of prior coordination and set their sights on supra-national combinations as the way to solve their problems. [5]

It is for just this reason that threats to modern nations come more often from supra-national powers, and not from one or two specific countries. There can be no better means for countering such threats than the use of supra-national combinations. In fact, there's nothing new under the sun, and supra-national combinations are not newly discovered territory. As early as the Spring and Autumn period [770–476 B.C.], the Warring States period [475–221 B.C.], and the Peloponnesian War [431–404 B.C.], supra-national combinations were already the oldest and most classical of methods employed by ancient strategists in the east and in the west. [6] The idea has not lost its fascination to this day. Schwarzkopf's supra-national combination in the Gulf War can be called a modern version of the classical "alliance + combined forces." If we must point out the generation gap between ancient times and today and describe the difference between them, then it is that for the ancients the idea was combinations of state with state, and not vertical, horizontal, and interlocking supra-national, transnational, and non-state combinations. [7] These three ancient peoples could not have imagined that the principle would remain unchanged in the present. Nor could they imagine the revolutionary changes which have occurred, from technical means to actual employment. The brand-new model of "state + supra-national + trans-national + non-state" will bring about fundamental changes in the face and final outcome of warfare, even changing the essential military nature of warfare which has been an unquestionable truth since ancient times. This method, resolving conflicts or conducting warfare not just with national power, but also with combinations of supra-national, trans-national, and non-state power, is what we mean by the general term supra-national combinations. From an examination of some prior, successful examples it can be foreseen that from now on, supranational combinations will be a country's most powerful weapon in attempting to accomplish national security objectives and secure strategic interests within a scope larger than the country itself. [8] As the world's only world-class superpower, the United States is the best at using supranational combinations as a weapon. The United States never misses any opportunity to take a hand in international organizations involving U.S. interests. Another way to put it is that the United States consistently sees the actions of all international organizations as being closely related to U.S. interests. No matter whether the nature of the international organization is European, American, Asian, or some other region, or worldwide, the United States always strives to get involved in it, and manipulate it. The 1996 U.S. Department of Defense Report put it straightforwardly: "To protect and achieve U.S. interests, the U.S. Government must have the capability to influence the policies and actions of other countries. This requires the United States to maintain its overseas involvement, especially in those areas in which the most important interests of the United States are endangered." [9] For example, regarding the establishment of the Asia-Pacific Economic Cooperation organization, the initial idea of its conceptualizer, Australian Prime Minister Hawke, was that it would only include Asian countries, Australia, and New Zealand. However, this idea immediately encountered strong opposition from President Bush, and it was then expanded to include the United States and Canada. At the same time, so as to check the momentum of Asia-Pacific economic cooperation, the United States spared no effort in instigating some Asian countries to sign independent agreements with the North American Free Trade Area. Not only did the United States make its way in, it also dragged others out. It might well be said that the United States used a double-combination tactic.

What people sense as a closely guarded secret is the attitude and methods of the Americans in dealing with the Asian financial crisis. When the storm erupted, the United States immediately opposed a Japanese proposal to set up an Asian monetary fund. Instead, the United States advocated the implementation of a rescue plan, with strings attached, by way of the International Monetary Fund, of which it is a major shareholder. The implication was that Asian countries should be forced to accept the economic liberalization policy promoted by the United States. For example, when the IMF extended a $57 billion loan to South Korea, it was with the condition that Korea must open up its markets completely and allow American capital the opportunity to buy up Korean enterprises at unreasonably low prices. A demand such as this is armed robbery. It gives the developed countries, with the United States as their leader, the opportunity to gain unrestricted access to another country's markets, or to get in and clear out some space there. It is little different from a disguised form of economic occupation. [10] If we completely tie together these sorts of American methods—the sniper attacks against the finances of Asian countries by the likes of Soros; the increase over ten years in the Americans' general fund total from $810 billion to $5 trillion, still growing at the rate of $30 billion per month [11]; Moody's, Standard & Poor's, and Morgan Stanley lowering the credit ratings of Japan, Hong Kong, and Malaysia at the most critical or most delicate times; Greenspan's concern over whether or not the Hong Kong government's counterattack against "fund raiders" will change the rules of the game; the Federal Reserve Bank's exception to the rules to aid the Long-Term Capital Management (LTCM) Corporation, which lost money on speculation; and hearing the sound of "no" during all the bustle and excitement in Asia and hearing the words "Asian Century" less frequently with each passing day—consider all this and discover how cleverly it is all seamlessly linked together. [12] Supposing these things were all combined and used to attack a long-coveted target, would not that be a successful combined action with supra-national organizations + trans-national organizations + non-state organizations? Although there is no direct evidence to prove that the United States government and the Federal Reserve have painstakingly designed and used this extremely powerful, concealed weapon, judging from the signs, at a minimum it can be said that certain actions had their prior encouragement and tacit consent. The key to the issues which we want to discuss here certainly does not lie in whether or not the Americans have intentionally used such a weapon. But as a super-weapon, is it practical? The answer is affirmative.

Supra-Domain Combinations
[Chao Lingyu Zuhe 6389 7325 1008 4809 0678]

[Combinations Beyond the Domain of the Battlefield]

"Domain" is a concept derived from the concept of territory and used to delineate the scope of human activities. Seen in this sense, a domain of warfare is a demarcation of the scope of what is encompassed by warfare. As with the concept of "supra-national combinations," the idea of "supra-domain combinations" which we propose is also a shortened form. To be precise, these terms should be followed with the words "of actions in warfare" if we are to convey in full the intent of these concepts which we are constructing and employing. This is to make clear the point that views about "supra . . . combinations" driven by beyond-limits thinking are confined to the scope of warfare and its related actions.

The concept of supra-domain combinations lies between the previously discussed concept of supra-national combinations and the concept of supra-means combinations [chao shouduan zuhe 6389 2087 3008 4809 0678], which will be explained below. As with its placement in our discussion, the concept of supra-domain combinations is an indispensable link in the groundbreaking line of thought about going beyond limits. Just as aircraft had to break the sound barrier before they could fly at supersonic speeds, those who are engaged in warfare must break out of the confines of domains if they are to be able to enter a state of freedom in thinking about warfare. Breaking the boundaries of ideology is a prerequisite for breaking the boundaries of action. Without breaking ideological boundaries, even in the event of a breakthrough in action being made by relying on intuition, it will still be difficult in the end to achieve complete peace of mind. For example, the U.S. Army's doctrine of "full-dimensional operations" [see TRADOC Pamphlet 525-5] and our "supra-domain combinations" are different in approach but equally good in their effect (the term "full dimensional" means in all domains), but the U.S. Army's "full-dimensional operations" seems more like a burst of unusual thinking by a group of smart military people, and not something built on the foundation of a line of thought which is by its nature a complete breakthrough. And so, because ideas which are not completely thought out will certainly face all sorts of obstacles, this ideological spark which could have set off a revolution in military affairs very quickly, and regrettably, died out.[13]

The expansion of the domain of warfare is a necessary consequence of the ever-expanding scope of human activity, and the two are intertwined. Mankind's understanding of this phenomenon has always lagged behind the phenomenon itself. Although as long ago as Cao Gui [hero of the Spring and Autumn period] and as recently as Collins [John M. Collins, author of *Grand Strategy: Principles and Practices*] there have been farsighted possessors of superior insight who to varying degrees pointed out the mutually restricting relationships among the various domains of warfare, up to now most people involved in warfare considered all the non-military domains where they were as being accessories to serve military needs. The narrowness of their field of vision and their way of thinking restricted the development of the battlefield and changes in strategy and tactics to within one domain. From Kutuzov torching Moscow [before abandoning it in 1812], without pity destroying over half the country in the strategy of strengthening defense works and laying waste to the fields as his way of dealing with Napoleon; to the massive bombing of Dresden and the nuclear destruction of Hiroshima and Nagasaki, inflicting countless civilian casualties in the pursuit of absolute military victory; to the strategic propositions of "massive retaliation" and "mutually assured destruction," none of these broke this mold. It is now time to correct this mistaken trend. The great fusion of technologies is impelling the domains of politics, economics, the military, culture, diplomacy, and religion to overlap each other. The connection points are ready, and the trend towards the merging of the various domains is very clear. Add to this the influence of the high tide of human rights consciousness on the morality of warfare. All of these things are rendering more and more obsolete the idea of confining warfare to the military domain and of using the number of casualties as a means of the intensity of a war. Warfare is now escaping from the boundaries of bloody massacre, and exhibiting a trend towards low casualties, or even none at all, and yet high intensity. This is information warfare, financial warfare, trade warfare, and other entirely new forms of war, new areas opened up in the domain of warfare. In this sense, there is now no domain which warfare cannot use, and there is almost no domain which does not have warfare's offensive pattern. On October 19, 1987, U.S. Navy ships attacked an Iranian oil drilling platform in the Persian Gulf. News of this reached the New York Stock Exchange and immediately set off the worst stock market crash in the history of Wall Street. This event, which came to be known as "Black Monday," caused the loss of $560 billion in book value to the American stock market. This is an amount equal to the complete loss of one France. In the years since then, time after time military actions have touched off stock disasters which then led to economic panic. In 1995–96, mainland China announced that it would conduct test launches of missiles in the Taiwan Strait and that it would conduct military exercises. As the missile tracks etched the sky, the Taiwan stock market immediately slid downward like an avalanche touched off by a bang. Although these two events are not examples of the supra-domain combinations of which we are speaking, these two especially do fall in the category of stupid acts like lifting a rock only to smash one's own foot with it. Their unexpected outcomes nevertheless suffice to set our train of thought into motion: if one intentionally takes two or more mutually unconcerned domains and combines them into a kind of tactic one can use, isn't the result better?

From the point of view of beyond-limits thinking, "supra-domain combinations" means the combining of battlefields. Each domain may, like the military domain, constitute the principal domain of future warfare. But one of the objectives of "supra-domain combinations" is to consider and select which domain will be the main battlefield, the one most favorable for the accomplishment of the objectives of the war. From the practical experience of the conflict between the United States and Iraq we can see that the 42-day military action of Desert Storm was followed by eight continuous years of military pressure + economic blockade + weapons inspections, which was [an example of] the United States using supra-national combinations to attack Iraq on new battlefields. And without mentioning the huge non-military damage caused in Iraq by the economic blockade, the attack on Iraq's military potential in the form of the United Nations Special Committee for Weapons Inspections led by Butler, checking and melting down large numbers of casualty-producing weapons for several years, has already far exceeded the results of the bombing during the Gulf War.

These things make it clear that warfare is no longer an activity confined only to the military sphere, and that the course of any war could be changed, or its outcome decided, by political factors, economic factors, diplomatic factors, cultural factors, technological factors, or other non-military factors. Faced with the far-reaching influence of military and non-military conflicts in every corner of the world, only if we break through the various kinds of boundaries in the models of our line of thought, take the various domains which are so completely affected by warfare and turn them into playing cards deftly shuffled in our skilled hands, and thus use beyond-limits strategy and tactics to combine all the resources of war, can there be the possibility that we will be confident of victory.

Supra-Means Combinations
[Chao Shouduan Zuhe 6389 2087 3008 4809 0678]

[Combination of All Available Means (Military and Non-Military) to Carry Out Operations]

During a war between two countries, during the fighting and killing by two armies, is it necessary to use special means to wage psychological war aimed at soldiers' families far back in the rear area? [14] When protecting a country's financial security, can assassination be used to deal with financial speculators? [15] Can "surgical" strikes be made without a declaration of war against areas which are sources of drugs or other smuggled goods? Can special funds be set up to exert greater influence on another country's government and legislature through lobbying? [16] And could buying or gaining control of stocks be used to turn another country's newspapers and television stations into the tools of media warfare? [17]

Apart from the justifiability of the use of the means, that is, whether or not they conform to generally recognized rules of morality, another point in common among the above questions is that they all touch on the use of means in a supra-national, supra-domain way. They are also issues in what we are talking about when we say "supra-means combinations." And if we are to make clear what supra-means combinations are, and why there should be such things, then we must first make clear the following: What are means? This question is practically not a question at all. Everybody knows that a means is a method or tool by which to accomplish an objective. But if things as big as a country or an army and as small as a stratagem are all imprecisely called means, then the question is far from simple. The relativity of means is an issue on which people have expended considerable effort. We can see this sort of relativity in the fact that on one level, something may be a means, while on another level it may be an objective. When speaking of supra-national actions, a country is a means, but when speaking of national actions, an armed force or another country's force is a means, and the country becomes an objective. Pushing further with this reasoning, means of unequal size are like a set of Chinese boxes one inside the other. A means at one level serves a higher objective, while at the same time being the objective for the means at the next lower level. Dropping this discussion of objectives, the complexity of what a means is still remains. We can take any object and examine it from any angle or on any level and understand what a means is. From the angle of domains, the domains of the military, politics, diplomacy, economics, culture, religion, psychology, and the media can often be seen as means. And domains can be subdivided. For example, in the military domain, strategy and tactics, military deterrence, military alliances, military exercises, arms control, weapons embargoes, armed blockades, right down to the use of force, these are all without doubt military means.

And although economic assistance, trade sanctions, diplomatic mediation, cultural infiltration, media propaganda, formulating and applying international rules, using United Nations resolutions, etc., belong to different domains such as politics, economics, or diplomacy, statesmen use them more and more now as standard military means. From the angle of methods, philosophical methods, technical methods, mathematical methods, scientific methods, and artistic methods are all used by humanity to bring benefit to itself. However, they can also be used as means in war. Take for example technology. The emergence and development of information technology, materials technology, space technology, bioengineering technology, and all other new technologies are part of the expanding array of means. Another example is mathematics. There is nowhere in which the influence of mathematical methods is not seen in military terminology such as disposition of forces, base figures [used to plan consumption] of ammunition, calculation of trajectories, probabilities of deaths and woundings, combat radii, and explosive yields. Moreover, philosophical, scientific, and artistic methods are also effective in supporting military wisdom and military action. This is why people often refer to military ideology, military theory, and military practice as military philosophy, military science, and military art. Liddell Hart [British officer and military theorist] defined the word strategy as "the art of using military means to achieve political objectives." From this we can see that the concept of means covers a lot of territory, on numerous levels, with overlapping functions, and thus it is not an easy concept to grasp. Only by expanding our field of vision and our understanding of means, and grasping the principle that there is nothing which cannot be considered a means, can we avoid the predicament of being confronted with too many difficulties to tackle all at once and being at wit's end when we employ means. During the crisis in 1978 when Iran occupied the U.S. Embassy and took hostages, at first all the United States thought of was the rash use of military means. Only after these failed did it change its tactics, first freezing Iran's foreign assets, then imposing an arms embargo, and supporting Iraq in the war with Iran. Then it added diplomatic negotiations. When all these channels were used together, the crisis finally came to an end.[18] This shows clearly that in a world of unprecedented complexity, the form and the scope of application of means is also in a state of continuous change, and a better means used alone will have no advantage over several means used in combination. Thus, supra-means combinations are becoming extremely necessary. It's a pity that not many countries are aware of this. On the contrary, it is those non-state organizations in pursuit of various interests which are sparing no effort in search of the use of means in combination. For example, the Russian mafia combines assassination, kidnapping for ransom, and hacker attacks against the electronic systems of banks in order to get rich. Some terrorist organizations pursue political objectives by combining means such as throwing bombs, taking hostages, and making raids on networks. To stir up the waters and grope for fish, the likes of Soros combine speculation in currency markets, stock markets, and futures markets. Also they exploit public opinion and create widespread momentum to lure and assemble the "jumbos" such as Merrill Lynch, Fidelity, and Morgan Stanley and their partners [19] to join forces in the marketplace on a huge scale and wage hair-raising financial wars one after the other. Most of these means are not by their nature military (although they often have a tendency to be violent), but the methods by which they are combined and used certainly do not fail to inspire us as to how to use military or non-military means effectively in war. This is because nowadays, judging the effectiveness of a particular means is not mainly a matter of looking at what category it is in, or at whether or not it conforms to some moral standard. Instead, it mainly involves looking at whether or not it conforms to a certain principle; namely, is it the best way to achieve the desired objective? So long as it conforms to this principle, then it is the best means. Although other factors cannot be totally disregarded, they must fulfill the prerequisite that they be advantageous to achieving the objective. That is, what supra-means combinations must surpass is not other [means], but rather the moral standards or normal principles intrinsic to the means themselves. This is much more difficult and complex than combining certain means with certain other means. We can only shake off taboos and enter an area of free choice of means—the beyond-limits realm—if we complete our picture of the concept of beyond-limits. This is because for us, we cannot achieve objectives merely by way of ready-made means. We still need to find the optimum way to achieve objectives, a correct and effective way to employ means. In other words, to find out how to combine different means and create new means to achieve objectives. For example, in this era of economic integration, if some economically powerful country wants to attack another country's economy while simultaneously attacking its defenses, it cannot rely completely on the use of ready-made means such as economic blockades and trade sanctions, or military threats and arms embargoes. Instead, it must adjust its own financial strategy, use currency revaluation or devaluation as primary, and combine means such as getting the upper hand in public opinion and changing the rules sufficiently to make financial turbulence and economic crisis appear in the targeted country or area, weakening its overall power, including its military strength. In the Southeast Asian financial crisis we see a case in which the crisis led to a lowering of the temperature of the arms race in that region. Thus we can see the possibility that this will happen, although in this case it was not caused by some big country intentionally changing the value of its own currency. Even a quasi-world power like China already has the power to jolt the world economy just by changing its own economic policies. If China were a selfish country, and had gone back on its word in 1998 and let the Renminbi lose value, no doubt this would have added to the misfortunes of the economies of Asia. It would also have induced a cataclysm in the world's capital markets, with the result that even the world's number one debtor nation, a country which relies on the inflow of foreign capital to support its economic prosperity, the United States, would definitely have suffered heavy economic losses. Such an outcome would certainly be better than a military strike.

The reality of information exchanges and intertwining interests is continually broadening the meaning of warfare. Also, any country which plays a decisive role has various capabilities to threaten other countries, and not just with military means. The use of means singly will produce less and less effect. The advantages of the combined use of various kinds of means will become more and more evident. This has opened the door wide for supra-means combinations, and for the employment of these sorts of combinations in warfare or quasi-war actions.

Supra-Tier Combinations
[Chao Taijie Zuhe 6389 0669 7132 4809 0678]

[Combine All Levels of Conflict Into Each Campaign]

When a war becomes a phase of history, the course of the war emerges little by little, like the gradual cooling of molten steel. From the earliest small-scale local fights, to campaigns consisting of interrelated battles on all sides, to wars consisting of a few or even several campaigns, and finally to the possibility that a war could spread and become a great intercontinental or worldwide war; in this way a war proceeds tier by tier up invisible steps. Possibly it might also go back down. On each level are strewn moaning casualties and the bodies of the dead, the muzzles of the victor's guns raised high and the rifles of the defeated lying abandoned, as well as many plans and stratagems, either wise or stupid. If we start with the last page of a war's history and go backwards chapter by chapter, we will discover that the entire process is an accumulation, and all of the outcomes resulted from this accumulation. Victory's an accumulation, and so is defeat. In terms of the two combatant sides, they followed a single road to their outcomes. The only difference is to be seen in whether one ascended the stairs and went higher or ascended the stairs and fell on them. Leaps and sudden changes all occur when you set foot on the final step.

This is practically a rule.

But rules must be respected. To evade or break the rules requires prudence.

The issue is that what we are thinking about is precisely how to evade or break such rules. We do not believe that all wars must gradually progress in level-by-level sequence, accumulating until a fateful moment of destiny is reached. We believe that moment is something which can be created. Finding a way by which we can continuously create that moment and not wait for the accumulation, and then fixing that method as a kind of strategy, that is the thing which we should do.

Of course, we know that one battle does not constitute a war, any more than one soldier constitutes an army. But this is not the issue we want to talk about. Our issue is how to use some method to break down all the stages, and link up and assemble these stages at will. For example, take a fight or an action on the tactical level, and combine it directly with an action on the level of wars, or on the strategic level. We could change warfare into something like a dragon with interchangeable limbs, torsos, and heads, which we could put together as we like, and which could swing freely in any direction.

This is what is meant by the method "supra-tier combinations." A level is also a kind of restriction, similar to national boundaries, territorial boundaries, and the boundaries around means. All are boundaries which must be surpassed in the actual practice of supra-combinations warfare.

Herman Kahn divided the threshold to nuclear war into a number of stages. Stages like them exist in other forms of warfare as well. But if we truly follow Kahn's line of thought, we discover that the delineation of his levels is excessively fine, and is not easy to work with. [20] Also, because he focused more on dividing warfare into stages based on intensity, he lacked penetrating insight into the essential nature of the levels of war. In our view, if the cuts dividing the levels of war are made based on the two aspects of the scale of war and the corresponding methods of war, then the levels of war are greatly simplified, and division into four levels is sufficient. On this point, our views and those of some American military analysts are basically the same, and differ only in their wording. Our specific delineation is as follows:

Grand War - War Policy [dazhan - zhance 1129 2069 - 2069 4595]
War - Strategy [zhanzheng - zhanlue 2069 3630 - 2069 3970]
Campaigns - Operational Art [zhanyi - zhanyi 2069 1763 - 2069 5669]
Battles - Tactics [zhandou - zhanshu 2069 2435 - 2069 2611]

The first level is "grand war - war policy." In terms of scale, this is military and non-military actions of warfare with supra-national as the upper limit and the nation as the lower limit. The function corresponding to it is "war policy," which is what Collins calls "grand strategy." We call it "war

policy" because strategy at this level mainly involves the political stratagems for warfare. The second level is "war - strategy." National level military actions include non-military actions of warfare on this level. The function corresponding to it is "strategy," that is, a country's military stratagems
or stratagems of war.

The third level is "campaigns - operational art." In terms of scale, this
refers to combat actions lower than a war but higher than battles. The
function corresponding to this level has no title, and often the concept
of "campaigning" is used indiscriminately. Obviously this obscures the
implications of the scope and methods of combat operations, and so we
have chosen the term "operational art [zhanyi; or war arts or art of warfare].
The selection of the positioning of this level, lower than strategy and
higher than tactics, would require elaboration on the meaning of the art of
warfare.

The fourth level is "battles - tactics." This is combat actions on the
most basic scale. The function corresponding to them is "tactics."

It can be seen at a glance that each of these levels has a corresponding
combat function

Speaking of traditional military men, perhaps throughout their lives
their lessons were on how to be skilled in employing these functions and
fighting well at whatever level they were on. But for soldiers who are about
to be in the next century, it is far from sufficient for them just to practice
these functions on these four fixed levels. They must study how to disrupt
these levels, to win wars by combining all the factors from supra-national
actions to specific battles. This is certainly not a mission which cannot be
accomplished. To put it quite simply, as an attempt to match up war policy, strategy, operational art, and tactics with methods, the principle of
supra-tier combinations is nothing more than a matter of interchangeable
and easily transposed roles. Examples are using a strategic method which
is some sort of non-military action to go along with the accomplishment
of a tactical mission, or using a tactical method to accomplish an objective
on the war policy level. This is because the trend of warfare shows more
and more clearly this sort of indication: it is definitely not the case that the
problems at one level can only be solved by the means at one level. No matter whether it is allocating only a fraction of the resources, or using a big
machete to kill a chicken, it is a feasible method so long as it works well.

Bin Laden used a tactical level method of only two truckloads of explosives and threatened U.S. national interests on the strategic level, whereas the Americans can only achieve the strategic objective of protecting their own safety by carrying out tactical level retaliation against him. Another example is that in past wars, the smallest combat element was the combination of a man and a machine, and its usefulness would normally not go beyond the scale of battles. In beyond-limits war, by contrast, the man-machine combination performs multiple offensive functions which span the levels from battles to war policy. One hacker + one modem causes an enemy damage and losses almost equal to those of a war. Because it has the breadth and secrecy of trans-level combat, this method of individual combat very easily achieves results on the strategic and even war policy levels.

This is the gist and significance of supra-level combinations.

In warfare and non-military warfare which is primarily national and supra-national, there is no territory which cannot be surpassed; there is no means which cannot be used in the war; and there is no territory and method which cannot be used in combination. The applicability of the actions of war to the trend of globalization is manifested in the word "beyond." This word is sufficient to mean using one to apply to ten thousand, but what we mean by ten thousand methods combined as one is precisely covered by the word "beyond." It must be pointed out once again that combined war that goes beyond limits is first of all a way of thinking, and only afterwards is it a method.

Notes

[1] B. Russell said of Machiavelli, "People are always shocked by him, and sometimes he was indeed shocking. But if people could shake off their hypocrisy, as he did, then quite a few of them would think as he did . . . (as Machiavelli saw it,) if an objective is considered to be good, then we definitely must select some means which are sufficient to accomplish it. As for the issue of the means, this can be handled with a purely scientific approach, without regard for whether the objective is good or bad." (*Junwang Lun* (*On Monarchs*), Hunan People's Publishing House, 1987, pp. 115–123.)

[2] Born during the Warring States period [475–221 B.C.], Han Feizi was the great product of the Legalist school of thought. In speech and actions, he emphasized the actual effect, as in "the target at which words and deeds are aimed is results."

There were no other objectives or constraints. (See *Zhongguo Sixiang Tongshi* (*A Comprehensive History of Chinese Thought*), Hou Wailu et al., eds., People's Publishing House, 1957, p. 616.)

[3]   In his book *Powershift : Knowledge, Wealth, and Violence at the Edge of the 21st Century*, Alvin Toffler devotes a small section to a discussion of "new types of worldwide organizations:" "We are now seeing an extremely significant shift of power, namely, from single countries or blocs of countries to worldwide 'wrestlers'." By worldwide wrestlers he means non-state bodies, large and small, from the European Community to multinational corporations. According to statistics from the United Nations' 1997 Investment Report, the world then had 44,000 multinational parent corporations and 280,000 foreign subsidiary companies and subordinate enterprises. These multinationals controlled one third of the world's production, and had within their grasp 70% of the world's direct foreign investment, two thirds of the world's trade, and over 70% of all patents and other technology transfers. (Source: *Guangming Daily*, Dec. 27, 1998, p. 3, essay by Li Dalun titled "The Duality of Economic Globalization.")

[4]   In Brzezinski's view, a number of groups of countries will appear in the 21st century, such as a North American group, a European group, an East Asian group, a South Asian group, a Moslem group, and an Eastern European group. The struggle among these groups will dominate conflict in the future. (*Da Shikong yu Da Hunluan*, a Chinese translation of *Out of Control : Global Turmoil on the Eve of the Twenty-first Century*, China Social Sciences Publishing House, p. 221.) The usefulness of the United Nations will increase continually, a trend which is already evident. (See *Zouxiang 21 Shiji de Lianheguo* (*The United Nations, Toward the 21st Century*), World Knowledge Publishing House.

[5]   For example, ASEAN, the OAU, and other organizations have become or are now becoming supra-national, regional problem solving groups which cannot be ignored.

[6]   The "north-south" (six states united in opposition to the Qin) and "east-west" (Qin united as one, or an alliance of a number of states to attack another) of the Warring States period are examples of alliances between countries. (*Zhanguo Ce Zhushi* (*Warring States Strategy Explained*), China Press, 1990, p. 4)

[7]   Today, supra-national combinations are not just among countries. They also include combinations between countries and trans-national or even non-state organizations. In the Southeast Asian financial crisis we can see some countries working in combination with the International Monetary Fund, and good cooperation against fund raiders.

[8]   In his new [1997] work, *The Grand Chessboard: American Primacy and its Geostrategic Imperatives*, Brzezinski writes out a new prescription for world security, the establishment of a "trans-Eurasian security arrangement." The center

of this system is the United States, Europe, China, Japan, Russia, India, and other countries. No matter whether Brzezinski's prescription is effective or not, at least it clearly points out a line of thought identical to our own, that of resolving national security problems in a larger sphere. Carl Doe has said, "International organizations are frequently seen as the optimum path by which to lead mankind out of the ethnic national era," and that the primary mission of integration is "to maintain peace." (See *Guoji Guanxi Fenxi* (*Analysis of International Relations*), World Knowledge Publishing House, p. 332.) [author's name approximated from the Chinese version]

[9]   Annual Report of the Secretary of Defense, Fiscal Year 1996 [translated into Chinese], Military Sciences Publishing House [Beijing], p. 5.

[10] In an essay titled "A Discussion of the New Asian Resistance to Foreigners," in the August 1998 edition of the Japanese magazine *Bungei Shunju*, Shintaro Ishihara expresses the view that these various moves by the United States make clear its strategic plot to attack Asia. Although the opinions of this "Mr. No" [he was a co-author of the nationalistic book *The Japan That Can Say No*] are somewhat extreme, but not unique to him. (See *Cankao Xiaoxi* (*Reference News*), 202 August 15–16, 1998.) [*Reference News* is a newsletter with internal distribution only among China's Party and government officials.]

[11] See *Reference News*, September 29, 1998, p. 11, reprinting an article from the American magazine Fortune.

[12] The number of observers who hold views similar to those of Shintaro Ishihara is certainly not small. Economic observer Konstanin Sorochin expressed a similar opinion in an article titled "What Role does the CIS Play in the Asian Financial Crisis?" published on July 16 in the Russian publication Forum. (See *Reference News*, August 15, 1998.)

[13] In today's U.S. Army, "full-dimensional" is a concept limited to the military sphere. For example, the principle of "full-dimensional protection" in Joint Vision 2010 mainly means strengthening the U.S. military's information protection. In the opinion of General [Johnnie] E. Wilson of the U.S. Army Materiel Command, the "Army of the future" capable of moving throughout the entire world is a "full-dimensional force." So it can be seen that the U.S. Army's thinking on the concept of "full-dimensional" discards its essence and just keeps the name. (See *Joint Forces Quarterly*, Summer 1996.) [*Joint Forces Quarterly* is a publication of the U.S. National Defense University. That issue carried an article titled "Joint Vision 2010: America's Military-Preparing for Tomorrow."]

[14] The U.S. Department of Defense has tightened control over military web sites on the Internet to prevent hostile powers from using family addresses, Social Security Numbers, and credit card numbers to attack service members.

[15] Since the British government allows its secret agents to assassinate the leaders

of what are designated as terrorist countries, if some countries saw financial speculators who launch destructive attacks against their economies as war criminals or terrorists, would it be considered proper if those countries dealt with the speculators in the same manner?

[16] The legislatures of countries with representative forms of government cannot evade encirclement by lobbying groups. For example, America's Jewish organizations and its Rifle Association have well-known lobbying groups. Actually, this practice was to be seen long ago in ancient China. In the war between the Chu and the Han at the end of the Qin Dynasty [209–202 B.C.], Liu Bang gave Chen Ping a great deal of money in order to defeat Xiang Yu off the battlefield. [Rebel general Liu Bang ousted Xiang Yu, who had won the fight to succeed the Qin Dynasty.]

[17] An article revealed that Soros controls Albania's political scene through control of the country's newspapers.

[18] See Carl Doe, *Guoji Guanxi Fenxi* (*Analysis of International Relations*), World Knowledge Publishing House, pp. 272–273. [author's name approximated from the Chinese version]

[19] Morgan Stanley Holding Company's worldwide strategic analyst Barton Biggs is considered the world's most influential investment strategist because he is the president of that $30 billion company and he holds 15% of its stock. Before the financial storms in Thailand and Hong Kong, he and his company both took certain actions which pointed out the direction for speculators. (See the article "A Preliminary Exploration of the Patterns of Action of Today's International Capitalism," by Song Yuhua and Xu Yilin, in *Zhongguo Shehui Kexue* (*China Social Sciences*), No. 6, 1998.)

[20] Regarding Herman Kahn's Rungs of Escalation: A Conceptual (or Abstract) Explanation, see Carl Doe, *Guoji Guanxi Fenxi* (*Analysis of International Relations*), World Knowledge Publishing House, p. 234. [author's name approximated from the Chinese version] The U.S. military normally divides combat activities into three levels, strategic, campaign, and tactical. (See U.S. Air Force Manual AFM 1-1, Meiguo Kongjun Hangkong Hangtian Jiben Lilun (Basic Aerospace Doctrine of the United States Air Force), 1992 edition, Military Sciences Publishing House, pp. 106–111.)

Chapter 8

Essential Principles

"Principles are a code of conduct, but not an absolute one."—George Kennan

In the history of warfare, the first person credited with using principles to regularize methods of fighting should be Sun Tzu. Principles which he advocated, such as "know the enemy and yourself and in a hundred battles you will never be defeated," "strike where the enemy is not prepared, take him by surprise," and "avoid the solid and strike the weak," are still articles of faith for modern strategists. But in the West, 2,400 years later, Napoleon would reveal his real desire to the world famous Saint-Cyr Military Academy, which would one day emblazon his name above its main doorway: "To write a book, describing the principles of war precisely, and provide it to all soldiers." Unfortunately, when he fought and won wars he had no time to write, and after he was defeated he was no longer in the mood. To a marshal who created nearly 100 victories in his lifetime, this should be neither too big nor too little a regret. But having been born a great man, it was enough for him to leave behind a brilliant record of victories for posterity to scour in search of his path to victory. A hundred years afterwards, from the wars directed by this old enemy who elicited dread from British people both during life and after death, a British general by the name of J.F.C. Fuller induced five principles for directing modern wars. [1] All of the West's principles of modern warfare are descended from these. Although later military regulations of quite a few countries and several military theorists proposed this or that as a principle of war, all of those things differ only in minor ways with those originated by Fuller. [2] This is because, from the beginning of the Napoleonic wars to the time prior to the Gulf War, apart from the continual increase in lethality and destructiveness, there was no reason for an essential change in the nature of war itself.

175

Now the situation has changed, because of all that happened during and after the Gulf War. The introduction of precision guided weapons, non-lethal weapons, and non-military weapons has derailed warfare from its mad dash down the track toward increased lethality and destructiveness. Events have set in motion the first change of course since the dawn of history. This has laid a new track for war in the next century, and given rise to principles with which professional military people are unfamiliar.

No principle can rest on a flimsy platform waiting to collapse. This is even more true of principles of war. Regardless of which military thinker produced them, or whatever military headquarters regulations they come from, the principles are all undoubtedly the product of repeated tempering in the furnace and on the anvil of war. If there had been no wars in the Spring and Autumn period there would be no principles of Sun Tzu. If there had been no Napoleonic wars, there would be no principles of Fuller. In the same way, if there had been no large and small military, quasi-military, and even non-military wars throughout the world before and after the Gulf War, then there would not be proposals for new concepts such as the Americans' "full-dimensional operations" and our "beyond-limits combined war." And of course, the principles of war which emerge with these concepts would be out of the question.

While we are truly sorry that "full-dimensional operations" theory died on the vine, we are resolved that "beyond-limits combined war" will not be confined to the level of theoretical speculation. Instead, we want to see it incorporated into combat methods with practical application. Even though the intent of the "beyond limits" ideology which we advocate is to break through all restrictions, nevertheless there is one constraint which must be strictly observed, and that is to abide by essential principles when carrying out combat actions. Only in some exceptional situations should a principle itself be broken.

When deep thought about the rules of warfare congeals to become some type of combat method, a principle is born along with it. Whether or not these combat methods and principles, as yet untested in a new round of wars, can become road signs pointing the way to the next victory is still very hard to say. But the proposal of essential principles is no doubt an indispensable theoretical process for perfecting a combat method. Here's a gyroscope, let it dance here for us. Let's have a look at the principles below and see what they can bring to "beyond-limits combined war."

Omnidirectionality
Synchrony
Limited objectives
Unlimited measures
Asymmetry
Minimal consumption
Multidimensional coordination
Adjustment and control of the entire process

Omnidirectionality—360° Observation and Design, Combined Use of All Related Factors

"Omnidirectionality" is the starting point of "unrestricted war" ideology and is a cover [fugai mian 6010 5556 7240] for this ideology. As a general principle of war, the basic demands it makes on the prosecutor of a war are to give all-round consideration to all factors related to "this particular" war, and when observing the battlefield or a potential battlefield, designing plans, employing measures, and combining the use of all war resources which can be mobilized, to have a field of vision with no blind spots, a concept unhindered by obstacles, and an orientation with no blind angles.

In terms of beyond-limits warfare, there is no longer any distinction between what is or is not the battlefield. Spaces in nature including the ground, the seas, the air, and outer space are battlefields, but social spaces such as the military, politics, economics, culture, and the psyche are also battlefields. And the technological space linking these two great spaces is even more so the battlefield over which all antagonists spare no effort in contending. [3] Warfare can be military, or it can be quasi-military, or it can be non-military. It can use violence, or it can be nonviolent. It can be a confrontation between professional soldiers, or one between newly emerging forces consisting primarily of ordinary people or experts. These characteristics of beyond-limits war are the watershed between it and traditional warfare, as well as the starting line for new types of warfare.

As a very strong principle applicable to actual warfare, omnidirectionality applies to each level of beyond-limits combined war [described in Chapter 7]. At the war policy level, it applies to the combined use of a nation's entire combat power, up to supra-national combat power, in an intercontinental or worldwide confrontation. At the strategic level, it applies to the combined use in warfare of national resources which relate to military objectives. At the operational level, it applies to the combined use on a designated battlefield of various kinds of measures, and mainly an army or force of that scale, to achieve campaign objectives. And at the tactical level, it applies to the combined use of various kinds of weapons, equipment, and combat methods, and mainly one unit or a force of that scale, to execute a designated mission in a battle. It must be kept in mind that all of the above combinations must also include intersecting combinations among the respective levels.

Finally, it must be made clear that the scope of combat operations in each specific war will not always expand over all spaces and domains, but the first principle of beyond-limits combined war is to ponder omnidirectionality and grasp the combat situation.

Synchrony—Conducting Actions in Different Spaces within the Same Period of Time

The technical measures employed in modern warfare, and in particular the spread of information technology; the emergence of long-range warfare technology; the increased ability to transform the battlefield; the linking together of battlefields which stretch forever, are scattered, or are different by their nature; and the introduction of various military and non-military forces on an equal footing into the war—all these things greatly shrink the course of warfare. So many objectives which in the past had to be accomplished in stages through an accumulation of battles and campaigns, may now be accomplished quickly under conditions of simultaneous occurence, simultaneous action, and simultaneous completion. Thus, stress on "synchrony" in combat operations now exceeds the stress on "phasing." [4]

Taking as a given the requirement for thorough planning, beyond-limits war brings key factors of warfare which are dispersed in different spaces and different domains to bear in the same, designated space of time. These factors revolve around the objectives of the war, executing a well-arranged team-effort and combined attack to achieve surprise, secrecy, and effectiveness. A single full-depth, synchronized action may be just one short beyond-limits combat operation, but it may be enough to decide the outcome of an entire war. What we mean by "synchrony" here is not "simultaneity," differing by not even a second, but rather "within the same time period." In this sense, beyond-limits war is worthy of the name "designated time warfare."

Using this as a standard, the armed force whose military capabilities most nearly reach this level is that of the Americans. Given its current equipment and technology, one of the U.S. military's information campaign systems [xinxi zhanyi xitong] can within one minute provide data on 4,000 targets to 1,200 aircraft. In addition to this is the extensive use of long-range attack weapons systems. This has led to a proposal for a "full-depth simultaneous attack" operations ideology. In terms of space, the U.S. military is starting to abandon the pattern of actions with a gradual push from the periphery towards the depth, and in terms of time, it is abandoning the obsolete combat model of sequential actions. However, judging from some documents openly published by the military, the Americans' line of thought in this regard so far is still confined to the scope of military action, and they have been unable to expand it to battlefields beyond the military sphere. [5]

Limited Objectives—Set a Compass to Guide Action within an Acceptable Range for the Measures [Available]

Limited objectives means limited in relation to measures used. Thus, the principle of setting limited objectives means that objectives must always be smaller than measures.

When setting objectives, give full consideration to the feasibility of accomplishing them. Do not pursue objectives which are unrestricted in time and space. Only with limits can they be explicit and practical, and only with limits can there be functionality. In addition, after accomplishing an objective, one will then have the resilience to go on and pursue the next. [6] When setting objectives, one must overcome the mentality of craving great successes, and instead consciously pursue limited objectives and eliminate objectives which are beyond one's abilities, even though they may be proper. This is because every objective which is achievable is limited. No matter what the reason, setting objectives which exceed allowable limits of the measures available will only lead to disastrous consequences.

The most typical illustration of expanding objectives is the mistake which MacArthur made in the Korean War. Subsequent to that are similar mistakes committed by the Americans in Vietnam and the Soviets in

Afghanistan, which prove that no matter what sort of action it is and no matter who is executing it, when objectives are greater than measures, then defeat is certain. Not all of today's statesmen and strategists are clear on this point. The 1996 U.S. Department of Defense Report contains this premise from President Clinton: "As the world's most powerful nation, we have a leadership obligation, and when our interests and sense of values are subject to great danger we will take action." When he spoke those words, obviously even Clinton was unaware that national interests and sense of values are strategic objectives of two completely different scales. If we say that the former is an objective which American power can protect through action, the latter is neither an objective that its power can achieve nor is an objective which the United States should pursue outside its own territory. "World's number one," an ideology corresponding to "isolationism," always makes the Americans tend to pursue unlimited objectives as they expand their national power. But this is a tendency which in the end will lead to tragedy. A company which has limited resources but which is nevertheless keen to take on unlimited responsibilities is headed for only one possible outcome, and that is bankruptcy.

Unlimited Measures—The Trend is Toward Unrestricted Employment of Measures, but Restricted to the Accomplishment of Limited Objectives

We speak of unlimited measures as related to limited objectives. [7] The trend toward no limits is a trend toward continual enlargement of the range of selection and the methods of use of measures. It is not intemperate use of measures, and even less is it absolutist use of measures, or the use of absolute measures. Unlimited measures to accomplish limited objectives is the ultimate boundary.

Measures are inseparable from objectives. For a measure to be unlimited means that to accomplish some designated objective, one can break through restrictions and select among various measures. This is not to say that a measure can be separated from objectives and used however one likes. Atomic weapons, which can annihilate mankind, have been viewed as absolute measures precisely because they violated the principle that a measure must serve to accomplish an objective. Finally people laid them aside. The employment of unrestricted measures can only be, as Confucius put it, "as one pleases, but not beyond the rules." Here, "rules" means objectives. Beyond-limits ideology expands "as one pleases" the range of selection and the methods of use of measures, but this certainly does not mean expansion of objectives "as one pleases." It only means to employ measures beyond restrictions, beyond boundaries, to accomplish limited objectives. Conversely, a smart general does not make his measures limited because his objectives are limited. This would very likely lead to failure on the verge of success. Thus, the limited must be pursued by way of the unlimited.

Sherman's advance toward Savanna in the American war between the north and south was not in search of combat, it was to burn and plunder all along the way. It was a measure used to destroy the economy in the southern army's rear area, to make the southern populace and the southern army lose the ability to resist, thus accomplishing the north's war objective. This is an example of the successful use of unlimited measures to achieve a limited objective. In contrast to this example, in the fourth Mideast War [the Yom Kippur War, 1973], to accomplish the combat objective designated by its front-line generals, which was the occupation of the Sinai Peninsula, the battle plan of the Egyptian Army's Supreme Command was just to break through the Bar Lev Line and consolidate control of the Sinai. Egypt attempted to use limited measures to achieve a limited objective. The results are well known. Egypt lost its hold on victory when victory was in its very grasp. [8]

Asymmetry—Seek Nodes of Action in the Opposite Direction from the Contours of the Balance of Symmetry

"Asymmetry" [fei junheng 7236 0971 5899] as a principle is an important fulcrum for tipping the normal rules in beyond-limits ideology. Its essential point is to follow the train of thought opposite to the balance of symmetry [junheng duicheng 0971 5899 1417 4468], and develop combat action on that line. From force disposition and employment, selection of the main combat axis and the center of gravity for the attack, all the way to the allocation of weapons, in all these things give two-way consideration to the effect of asymmetrical factors, and use asymmetry as a measure to accomplish the objective.

No matter whether it serves as a line of thought or as a principle guiding combat operations, asymmetry manifests itself to some extent in every aspect of warfare. Understanding and employing the principle of asymmetry correctly allows us always to find and exploit an enemy's soft spots. The main fighting elements of some poor countries, weak countries, and non-state entities have all used "mouse toying with the cat"-type asymmetrical combat methods against much more powerful adversaries. In cases such as Chechnya vs. Russia, Somalia vs. the United States, Northern Ireland guerrillas vs. Britain, and Islamic Jihad vs. the entire West, without exception we see the consistent, wise refusal to confront the armed forces of the strong country head-to-head. Instead, the weaker side has contended with its adversary by using guerrilla war (mainly urban guerrilla war) [9], terrorist war, holy war, protracted war, network war, and other forms of combat. Mostly the weaker side selects as its main axis of battle those areas or battlelines where its adversary does not expect to be hit. The center of mass of the assault is always a place which will result in a huge psychological shock to the adversary. This use of asymmetrical measures which create power for oneself and make the situation develop as you want it to, is often hugely effective. It often makes an adversary which uses conventional forces and conventional measures as its main combat strength look like a big elephant charging into a china shop. It is at a loss as to what to do, and unable to make use of the power it has. Apart from the effectiveness it displays when used, asymmetry in itself is a rule of action suggested by the golden rule. Of all rules, this is the only one which encourages people to break rules so as to use rules. Also it is an effective prescription for methodical and well-balanced medical treatment for a chronic illness of thought.

Minimal Consumption—Use the Least Amount of Combat Resources Sufficient to Accomplish the Objective

The principle of minimal consumption is, first of all, that rationality is more important than thrift [10]; second, the size of combat consumption is decided by the form of combat [11]; and third, use "more" (more measures) to pursue "less" (lower consumption).

Rationality involves two aspects, the rational designation of objectives and the rational use of resources. Rational designation of objectives, besides specifying objectives that fall within the circle of the measures to be used, also refers to the need to compress the objectives' load, and as much as possible make them simple and concise. Rational use of resources obviously means using the most appropriate method to accomplish an objective, and not just imposing a single-minded requirement to economize. Economizing, that is, using the minimum amount of resources, has meaning only if the prerequisites for accomplishing an objective are met. More important than perfect familiarity with principles is how the principles are applied. Whether or not the minimum amount of combat resources is used to accomplish an objective depends on what form of combat operation is selected. The Verdun campaign is called by war historians a meat grinder, because both sides waged a senseless war of attrition. By contrast, the reason Germany was able to sweep away the joint British-French force after crossing the Maginot Line was because it combined the shortest length of time, the optimum route, and the most powerful weapons in a blitzkrieg. So it can be seen that the key to truly achieving "minimal consumption" is to find a combat method which makes rational use of combat resources. Today, with objectives and the measures to accomplish them assuming many complex forms as never before, confronting a complex objective in just one sphere and with just one measure will definitely fall short of the mark. The result of a mismatch between measures and objectives is inevitably high consumption and low effectiveness. The line of thought leading out of these difficulties is to use "more" to attain "less." That is, to combine the superiorities of several kinds of combat resources in several kinds of areas to form up a completely new form of combat, accomplishing the objective while at the same time minimizing consumption.

Multidimensional Coordination—Coordinating and Allocating All the Forces which can be Mobilized in the Military and Non-Military Spheres Covering an Objective

"Multidimensional" here is another way of saying multiple spheres and multiple forces. It has nothing to do with the definition of dimensionality in the sense of mathematics or physics. "Multidimensional coordination" refers to coordination and cooperation among different forces in different spheres in order to accomplish an objective. On the face of it, this definition is not at all novel. Similar explanations are to be found in many combat regulations, both obsolete and newly published. The only difference between it and similar explanations is, and this is a great difference, the introduction of non-military and non-war factors into the sphere of war directly rather than indirectly. In other words, since any sphere can become a battlefield, and any force can be used under combat conditions, we should be more inclined to understand multidimensional coordination as the coordination of the military dimension with various other dimensions in the pursuit of a specific objective. It is not the case that in all wars military action must be considered as the primary form of action. With warfare facing the equalization of the various dimensions, this concept will become a formula for addressing the questions of future wars. [12]

The concept of multidimensional coordination can only be established within the context of a specific objective. Without an objective, we cannot speak of multidimensional coordination. But the size of an objective determines the breadth and depth of the coordination of each dimension. If the set objective is to win a war at the war policy level, the spheres and forces needing coordination may involve the entire country, or may even be supra-national. From this we can generalize that in any military or non-military action, no matter what the depth of the spheres and the quantity of forces it involves, coordination among the various dimensions is absolutely necessary. This certainly does not imply that in each action the more measures mobilized the better. Instead, the limit is what is necessary. The employment of an excessive or an insufficient amount in each dimension will only cause the action to sway between edema and shriveling, and finally the objective itself will be in jeopardy. The bit of Eastern wisdom, "going beyond the limit is as bad as falling short," is helpful to our understanding and our application of this principle.

In addition, we urgently need to expand our field of vision regarding forces which can be mobilized, in particular non-military forces. Besides, as in the past, paying attention to conventional, material forces, we should also pay particular attention to the employment of intangible "strategic resources" such as geographical factors, the role of history, cultural traditions, sense of ethnic identity, dominating and exploiting the influence of international organizations, etc. [13] But this is still not enough. In applying this principle we must also come up with beyond-limits action, and to the greatest extent possible make multidimensional coordination a commonplace move in ordinary operations, and bring about interlocking, gradational combinations at every level from war policy to tactics.

Adjustment and Control of the Entire Process—During the Entire Course of a War, from its Start, through its Progress, to its Conclusion, Continually Acquire Information, Adjust Action, and Control the Situation

Warfare is a dynamic process full of randomness and creativity. Any attempt to tie a war to a set of ideas within a predetermined plan is little short of absurdity or naïveté. Therefore, it is necessary to have feedback and revisions throughout the entire course of a war while it is actually happening, in order to keep the initiative within one's grasp. This is what is meant by "adjustment and control of the entire process."

Because of the addition of the principle of synchrony, we cannot understand the adjusted and controlled "entire course" to be a prolonged one. With modern, high-tech measures, this process may take the blink of an eye. As we said before, the time it takes to fight one battle can be sufficient to wind up a whole war. This may make the entire course of a war extremely short, and incidentally make adjusting and controlling it much more difficult.

Today, with information technology welding the entire world together into a network, the number of factors involved in a war is much, much greater than in past wars. The ability of these factors to cloud the issues of war, and their intense influence on war, means that loss of control over any one link can be like the proverbial loss of a horseshoe nail which led to the loss of an entire war. [14] So, faced with modern warfare and its bursts of new technology, new measures, and new arenas, adjustment and control of the entire process is becoming more and more of a skill. It is not a kind of technology. What is needed to grasp the ever-changing battlefield situation is greater use of intuition, rather than mathematical deduction. More important than constant changes in force dispositions and continual updating of weapons is the whole set of combat rules which are the result of the shift of the battlefield to non-military spheres. The outcome of all this is that one will be sent to an unexplored battlefield to wage an unfamiliar war against an unknown enemy. Nevertheless, one must adjust and control this entire unfamiliar process if he is to win.

"Beyond-limits combined war" is this use of strange, completely new methods of combat to wage war.

All of the above principles are applicable to any beyond-limits combined war.

Victory is certainly not in the bag just because a side adheres to the above principles, but violating them no doubt leads to defeat. Principles are always essential conditions for victory in war, but they are not the only conditions.

In the absence of a principle that victory is certain, there are only essential principles. We should always remember this point.

Notes

[1]   The five principles which Fuller summarized from the Napoleonic wars are attack, maneuver, surprise, concentration, and support. Besides this, following the views of Clausewitz, Fuller also induced seven principles similar to those of the Napoleonic wars: maintain the objective, security of action, mobile action, exhaust the enemy's offensive capability, conserve forces, concentrate forces, and surprise. These principles became the foundation of modern military principles. (See "The Writings of Fuller" in *Zhanzheng Zhidao* (*Combat Command*), Liberation Army Publishing House, pp. 38–60.)

[2]   An example is the U.S. Army's nine main military principles: objective, offensive, concentration, economy of force, mobility, security, surprise, simplicity, and unity [of command]. These are very similar to the principles of war of the Napoleonic era.

[3]   The battlefield of beyond-limits war differs from those of the past in that it encompasses all natural spaces, such as the social realm, and the continually developing sphere of technology where space is now measured in nanometers. Today, these spaces are interlocked with each other. For example, outer space can be seen as a natural space, and also as a technological space, because each step in the militarization of outer space requires a technological breakthrough. In the same way, the interdynamics between society and technology are to be seen constantly. There is no more typical example of this than the effect of information technology on society. From these things we can see that the battlefield is ubiquitous, and we can only look upon it with "omnidirectionality."

[4]   Wars in the past involved, in terms of space, forces charging from boundary areas into depths, and in terms of time, division into phases. By contrast, in terms of space, beyond-limits war instead goes straight to the core, and in terms of time it is "synchronous" and will often no longer be characterized by phases.

[5]   [Footnote not marked in original text, but assumed to belong here] There is no

more typical example of this than four principles in the U.S. military's Joint Vision 2010, which are, "dominant maneuver, precision engagement, focused logistics, full-dimensional protection." All of these proposed new principles are for military warfare.

[6]   Setting limited objectives is not a matter of whether or not one is constrained subjectively, but rather whether or not restricted measures are exceeded. Measures are "restrictions" which cannot be exceeded when setting objectives.

[7]   For details, see *How Great Generals Win* by Bevin Alexander, pp. 101–125.

[8]   Before the Fourth Mideast War, the Egyptian "Baierde Plan" [inaccurate Chinese phonetic for "Badr"? (the war began on the anniversary of the Battle of Badr, 626 A.D.)] was divided into two steps. The first step consisted of forced crossings of the Suez Canal, breaking through the Bar Lev Line, and taking control of a 15–20 km [deep] area of the east bank of the canal. The second step was to attack and capture a line running from the Mitla Pass to the Giddi Pass to the Khatima Pass, guarantee the security of the east bank of the canal, and then expand into the enemy's depth as the situation warranted. But in actual combat, as soon as the Egyptian Army crossed the canal it went on the defensive. It was five days before it resumed its offensive, and this gave the Israeli Army an opportunity to catch its breath.

[9]   The famous researcher of the development of capitalist society, Buluodaier [Fernand Braudel? 1580 5012 0108 1422], placed particular emphasis on the "organizational usefulness" of large cities in the capitalist world. Despite its big size, this world nevertheless has a number of fulcrums, central cities such as New York, London, Tokyo, Brussels, and maybe Hong Kong. If these were attacked simultaneously or if guerrilla war broke out there simultaneously, it would leave the world in chaos. (*The Motive Force of Capitalism*, Buluodaier [Fernand Braudel?], Oxford Press)

[10]   Military principles have always included [the concept] "economize," mainly referring to the need to pay attention to controlling the consumption of manpower and materiel during wartime. In beyond-limits warfare, "rational usage" is the only correct [way to] economize.

[11]   Beyond-limits war allows for a great deal of leeway in the selection of the forms of combat. Naturally there is a big difference between the cost of conventional military warfare and warfare in which finance plays the leading role. Therefore, the cost of a future war depends mainly on what form of warfare is selected.

[12]   The most important [step toward] equality among various dimensions is to overcome the concept that "the military is supreme." In future wars, military measures will only be [considered] one of the conventional options.

[13]   In this regard, China is richly endowed by nature. A long cultural tradition,

peaceful ideology, no history of aggression, the strong economic power of the Chinese people, a seat on the United Nations Security Council, etc., all these things are important "strategic resources."

[14]   In modern warfare, fortuitous factors influence the outcome of wars just as they did in antiquity. If a fuse in a command center's computer were to get too hot and burn out at a critical moment, this could lead to a disaster. (This is entirely possible. It was a factor in a mistaken attack by an F-16 over the Gulf. It happened because the electrical circuit in the "friend or foe device" aboard a Blackhawk helicopter frequently overheated, and the aviators would occasionally switch it off to lower the temperature.) This is perhaps the modern version of the loss-of-a-horseshoe story. For this reason, then, "adjustment and control" must continue "through the entire course."

Conclusion

*"Computerization and globalization . . . have produced several thousand
global enterprises and tens of thousands of international
and inter-government organizations."—E. Laszlo*

*"Mankind is making progress, and no longer believes
that war is a potential court of appeals."—Bloch*

At a time when man's age-old ideal of "the family of man" is used by
IBM in an advertisement, "globalization" is no longer the prediction of futurists. An era in which we are impelled by the great trend of technological integration that is plastered all over with information labels, agitated by
the alternately cold and warm ocean currents from the clash and fusion of
civilizations, troubled by local wars rising first here then there and by
domino-like financial crises and the ozone hole over the South Pole, and
which causes everyone, including the futurists and visionaries, to feel
strange and out of place—[such an era] is in the process of slowly unfold-
ing between the dusk of the 20th century and the dawn of the 21st century.
Global integration is comprehensive and profound. Through its ruthless
enlightenment, those things which must inevitably be altered or even dis-
pelled are the positions of authority and interest boundaries in which nations are the principal entities. The modern concept of "nation states"
which emerged from the Peace of Westphalia [1] in 1648 is no longer the
sole representative occupying the top position in social, political, economic
and cultural organizations. The emergence of large numbers of metanational, trans-national, and non-national organizations, along with the
inherent contradictions between one nation and another, are presenting an
unprecedented challenge to national authority, national interests, and
national will. [2]

At the time of the emergence of the early nation states, the births of
most of them were assisted by blood-and-iron warfare. In the same way,
during the transition of nation states to globalization, there is no way to
avoid collisions between enormous interest blocs. What is different is that

189

the means that we have today to untie the "Gordian Knot" [3] are not merely swords, and because of this we no longer have to be like our ancestors who invariably saw resolution by armed force as the last court of appeals. Any of the political, economic, or diplomatic means now has sufficient strength to supplant military means. However, mankind has no reason at all to be gratified by this, because what we have done is nothing more than substitute bloodless warfare for bloody warfare as much as possible. [4] As a result, while constricting the battlespace in the narrow sense, at the same time we have turned the entire world into a battlefield in the broad sense. On this battlefield, people still fight, plunder, and kill each other as before, but the weapons are more advanced and the means more sophisticated, so while it is somewhat less bloody, it is still just as brutal. Given this reality, mankind's dream of peace is still as elusive as ever. Even speaking optimistically, war will not be wiped out rapidly within the foreseeable future, whether it is bloody or not. Since things which should happen will ultimately come to pass, what we can and must focus on at present is how to achieve victory. Faced with warfare in the broad sense that will unfold on a borderless battlefield, it is no longer possible to rely on military forces and weapons alone to achieve national security in the larger strategic sense, nor is it possible to protect these stratified national interests. Obviously, warfare is in the process of transcending the domains of soldiers, military units, and military affairs, and is increasingly becoming a matter for politicians, scientists, and even bankers. How to conduct war is obviously no longer a question for the consideration of military people alone. As early as the beginning of this century, Clemenceau stated that "war is much too serious a matter to be entrusted to the military." However, the history of the past 100 years tells us that turning over warfare to the politicians is not the ideal way to resolve this important issue, either. [5] People are turning to technical civilization, hoping to find in technological developments a valve which will control war. But what makes people despair is that the entire century is just about gone, and while technology has made great strides, war still remains an unbroken mustang. People still expect wonders from the revolution in military affairs, hoping that high-tech weapons and non-lethal weapons can reduce civilian and even military casualties in order to diminish the brutality of war. However, the occurrence of the revolution in military affairs, along with other revolutions, has altered the last decade of the 20th century. The world is no longer what it was originally, but war is still as brutal as it has always been. The only thing that is different is that this brutality has been expanded through differences in the modes in which two armies fight one other. Think about the Lockerbie air disaster. Think about the two bombs in Nairobi and Dar es Salaam. Then think about the financial crisis in East Asia. It should not be difficult to understand what is meant by this different kind of brutality.

This, then, is globalization. This is warfare in the age of globalization. Although it is but one aspect, it is a startling one. When the soldiers standing at the crossroads of the centuries are faced with this aspect, perhaps each of them should ask himself, what can we still do? If those such as Morris, bin Laden, and Soros can be considered soldiers in the wars of tomorrow, then who isn't a soldier? If the likes of Powell, Schwarzkopf, Dayan, and Sharon can be considered politicians in uniform, then who isn't a politician? This is the conundrum that globalization and warfare in the age of globalization has left for the soldiers.

Although the boundaries between soldiers and non-soldiers have now been broken down, and the chasm between warfare and non-warfare nearly filled up, globalization has made all the tough problems interconnected and interlocking, and we must find a key for that. The key should be able to open all the locks, if these locks are on the front door of war. And this key must be suited to all the levels and dimensions, from war policy, strategy, and operational techniques to tactics; and it must also fit the hands of individuals, from politicians and generals to the common soldiers.

We can think of no other more appropriate key than "unrestricted warfare."

Notes

[1] The general term for the European agreement of 1648. This brought an end to the 80-year war between Spain and Holland, and the Thirty Years' War in Germany, and it is also seen as laying the foundation for all the treaties concluded up to the breakup of the Holy Roman Empire in 1806.

[2] The state's position as the ultimate entity is being challenged from various quarters, and the thing that is most representative as well as being most worrisome, is that the state's monopoly on weapons is being seriously challenged. According to the views of Earnest Jierna [as published 0679 1422 4780] in *Nationality and Nationalism*, a state is defined as the only entity that can use force legally. According to a 1997 public opinion survey by *Newsweek* magazine in the United States re-

garding "where the threat to security will come from in the 21st century," 32 percent believed it would come from terrorism, 26 percent believed that it would be international crime and drug trafficking groups, 15 percent believed it would be racial hatred, with nation states only coming in fourth. In a small pamphlet that the U.S. Army has put on the Web, but which has not been published (TRADOC PAMPHLET 525–5: FORCE XXI OPERATIONS), the non-nation forces are clearly listed as "future enemies," saying that "non-nation security threats, using modern technologies that give them capabilities similar to those of nation states, have become increasingly visible, challenging the traditional nation state environment. Based on the scope involved, these can be divided into three categories.

(1) Subnational. Subnational threats include political, racial, religious, cultural, and ethnic conflicts, and these conflicts challenge the defining features and authority of the nation state from within.

(2) Anational. Anational threats are unrelated to the countries they belong to. These entities are not part of a nation state, nor do they desire to establish such a status. Regional organized crime, piracy, and terrorist activities comprise these threats.

(3) Metanational. Metanational threats transcend the nation state borders, operating on an interregional or even global scale. They include religious movements, international criminal organizations, and informal economic organizations that facilitate weapons proliferation. See *The World Map in the Information Age*, Wang Xiaodong, Chinese People's University Press, 1997, pp. 44–46. The U.S. military does not treat transnational companies which seize monopolistic profits as security threats, and in addition to their deeply-rooted awareness of economic freedom, this is also related to the fact that they still limit threats to the military arena. Transnational companies such as Microsoft and Standard Oil-Exxon, whose wealth rivals that of nations, may also constitute real threats to national authority, and can even have a serious impact on international affairs.

[3] Legend has it that after Alexander the Great led his army into the interior of Asia Minor, he went to worship in the temple of Zeus in the city of Gordium. In the temple there was a wagon which had formerly belonged to Midas, king of Phrygia. It was secured very tightly by a jumbled cord, and it was said that no one had been able to untie it. Faced with this, Alexander pondered for a moment, then suddenly pulled out his sword and severed it at one stroke. From this, "Gordian knot" has come to be another term for intractable and complex problems.

[4] In future wars, there will be more hostilities like financial warfare, in which a country is subjugated without spilling a drop of blood. Think about it for a moment. What would the disastrous impacts have been on the economies of Hong Kong and even China if the August 1998 battle to protect Hong Kong's finances

had failed? Furthermore, such situations are by no means impossible, and if it had not been for the collapse of the Russian financial market, which caused the financial speculators to be under attack from the front and the rear, it is still hard to predict how things would have turned out.

[5] Regardless of whether we are talking about Hitler, Mussolini, Truman, Johnson, or Saddam, none of them have successfully mastered war. This also includes Clemenceau himself.

Afterword

The motives for writing this book originated from military maneuvers which caught the attention of the world. Three years ago, due to participation in the maneuvers, Xiangsui and I encountered each other in a small city in Fujian called Zhao An. At the time, the situation was becoming daily more tense on the Southeast coast, both sides of the straits were all set for a showdown, and even the task force of two American aircraft carriers rushed a long way to add to the trouble. At that time, the storm was brewing in the mountains and the military situation was pressing so that people were suddenly moved to "think up strategies when facing a situation." We therefore decided to write this book, a book which would be able to concentrate together the concerns and thoughts each of us had over the past several decades and especially during the last ten years concerning military issues.

There is no way of relating in detail how many telephone calls we made, how much mail was sent, and how many nights we stayed awake over the next three years, and the only thing which can serve as evidence for all of this is this small and thin book.

We must first apologize to readers for the fact that, even though we were very conscientious and toiled painstakingly in the writing of this book, yet after the written word reflecting ideas were set down much like shooting stars traveling across the sky and cooling into meteorites, all of you (including ourselves) will still be able to find many mistakes and places which are inappropriate. We shall not employ the apologetic words of "We request your kind solicitude" to seek forgiveness but shall rather only make corrections in the second edition (if there is one).

Upon the occasion of the publication of this book, we would like to here sincerely thank the Chief-of-Staff Cheng Butao and Assistant Chief-of-Staff Huang Guorong, of the PLA Literature and Arts Publishing House for their unswerving support whereupon this book was able to be so quickly published within such a short period of time. We would also like to thank Xiang Xiaomi, Director of the First Book Editing Department. She has carefully and rigorously proofread the entire book as she had done with the other four books which we have edited, and provided many very valuable recommendations. We do not know any better way of expressing our thanks aside from the deep gratitude which we feel.

Lastly, we would also like to thank our families for the sacrifices they made towards the completion of this book, and this is again something which cannot be expressed in words. The entire book was completed in manuscript form between March 2 and December 8 of 1998 in Gongzhufen - Baizhifang in Beijing.

[Written on February 1, 1999]

Authors' Backgrounds

Qiao Liang [0829 5328], whose ancestors came from Hunan Province, was born in Xin [1823] County, Shanxi Province, to a military family in 1955. He is a member of the Chinese Writers' Union. Presently, he is assistant director of the production office of the air force's political department and holds the rank of senior colonel in the air force, along with being a grade one [yi ji 0001 4787] writer.

His most important works include *Gate to the Final Epoch* [*Mori Zhi Men* 2608 2480 0037 7024]; *Spiritual Banner* [*Ling Qi* 7227 4388]; and *Great Glacial River* [*Da Bing He* 1129 0393 3109]. He has repeatedly won national and military awards. In addition to his literary creations, he has applied himself over a long period of time to the research of military theory and joined with other writers to pen *A Discussion of Military Officer Quality* [*Junguan Suzhi Lun* 6511 1351 4790 6347 6158]; *Viewing the Global Military Big Powers* [*Shijie Junshi Lieqiang Bolan* 0013 3954 6511 0057 0441 1730 0590 6031]; and *A Listing of the Rankings of Global Military Powers* [*Quanqiu Junli Paihang Bang* 0356 3808 6511 0500 2226 5887 2831].

Wang Xiangsui [3769 3276 4482] was born in Guangzhou to a military family in 1954. He joined the army at the end of 1970. He successively assumed the positions of political instructor, group political commissar, section deputy head, regiment political commissar, and division deputy political commissar. Presently, he works in the Guangzhou Military Region Air Force Political Unit and holds the rank of senior colonel.

He has cooperated with other authors to write the books *A Discussion of Military Officer Quality*; *Viewing the Global Military Powers*; and *A Record of Previous Major Global Wars* [*Shijie Lici Dazhan Lu* 0013 3954 2980 2945 1129 2069 6922].

EP
BM We hope you enjoyed this title
from Echo Point Books & Media

Before Closing this Book, Two Good Things to Know

Buy Direct & Save

Go to www.echopointbooks.com (click "Our Titles" at top or click "For Echo Point Publishing" in the middle) to see our complete list of titles. We publish books on a wide variety of topics—from spirituality to auto repair.

Buy direct and save 10% at www.echopointbooks.com

DISCOUNT CODE: EPBUYER

Make Literary History and Earn $100 Plus Other Goodies Simply for Your Book Recommendation!

At Echo Point Books & Media we specialize in republishing out-of-print books that are united by one essential ingredient: high quality. Do you know of any great books that are no longer actively published? If so, please let us know. If we end up publishing your recommendation, you'll be adding a wee bit to literary culture and a bunch to our publishing efforts.

Here is how we will thank you:

- A free copy of the new version of your beloved book that includes acknowledgement of your skill as a sharp book scout.
- A free copy of another Echo Point title you like from echopointbooks.com.
- And, oh yes, we'll also send you a check for $100.

Since we publish an eclectic list of titles, we're interested in a wide range of books. So please don't be shy if you have obscure tastes or like books with a practical focus. To get a sense of what kind of books we publish, visit us at www.echopointbooks.com.

If you have a book that you think will work for us,
send us an email at editorial@echopointbooks.com

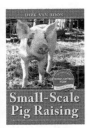
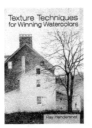
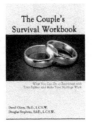